Out of the Fog:
Moving from Confusion to Clarity
After Narcissistic Abuse

Dana Morningstar

Printed in the United States of America

First Printing, 2017

Morningstar Media
PO Box 464
Mason, MI 48854

Dedication

A big thank you to those who help run the support groups and the book club. Without you, much of what I'm trying to do wouldn't be possible. Your time, help, and support means the world to me and to many others in the group, and you are beyond appreciated.

And to all those who have been impacted by narcissistic abuse, please know that you are not alone; you are not crazy, and you can move forward and heal from this.

Contents

Preface 1

Chapter 1: What is the FOG, and
How Did I get Here? 3

Chapter 2: Understanding Thought Holes:
What is a Thought Hole? 5

Chapter 3: A Light in the Fog: Questioning
What's Normal 7

Chapter 4: An Expanded View of Normal Behavior . 17

Chapter 5: Thought Holes vs. A More
Empowered Understanding 23

Chapter 6: Conclusion: Moving into Healing 357

About the Author 361

Preface

In my first book, *Start Here: A Crash Course in Understanding, Navigating, and Healing from Narcissistic Abuse* I listed what I believe to be the fundamentals of understanding narcissistic abuse. The goal of that book was to provide a crash course or a reference manual of sorts with the hopes of getting people as up-to-speed as possible so that they might be able to win a game they never intended to play— and that's what relationships of any kind are to an emotional manipulator: a game. And much like any other game, a person doesn't need advanced strategies to win— they often just need a solid grip on the fundamentals.

While the most important words and concepts surrounding narcissistic abuse can instantly help a person see many things clearly and help them to be able to respond in a more empowering way, what I've also found is that many people get tripped up with blurring many common concepts such as the difference between intensity and sincerity, love bombing and love, codependence and commitment, and forgetting and forgiving, to name a few. This book is my attempt to dive into the differences between these concepts (as well as many others) that tend

1

to keep a person stuck in the fog of manipulation. In short, the first book is more of a map of the terrain, and this second book has more to do with explaining the emotional climate (the FOG) and warning you about dangerous roads and resulting "thought holes" that can make for a difficult journey if you don't know what to watch out for.

So if you are already familiar with a lot of the common terms and concepts surrounding narcissistic abuse but are struggling with how to apply them or are finding yourself struggling with trusting your judgment and perception of people and situations, then this book is for you.

Chapter 1
What is the FOG, and How Did I get Here?

The "FOG" is an acronym for fear, obligation, and guilt, and was coined by Susan Forward & Donna Frazier in their book *Emotional Blackmail* to describe the emotions most commonly used by emotional manipulators to gain and keep control over others and over certain situations. When these emotions are being exploited, a "fog" of confusion sets in and the person in the fog has a hard time sorting out what's really going on and who has the issue—and, most importantly, what they need to do to get out (and stay out) of this fog.

For many targets of emotional manipulators, the emotions of fear, obligation, and guilt are only part of the fog of confusion. And emotional manipulators are only some of the people that are FOG inducing. The FOG can also come in the form of well-intended bad advice about commitment, family and friendship from pretty much everyone: friends, family, therapists, culture, religious leaders and texts, and society as a whole.

This type of bad advice is not only prevalent, but it's often passed off as good advice and is just as insidious and destructive as abuse itself. So what exactly is well-intended bad advice? I came across an analogy the other day that sums it up well, "Well-intended bad advice is like a monkey seeing a fish in a lake, and thinking the fish is drowning, rushes over to pull it out of the water so it can place it safely in a tree."

Because this well-intended bad advice is so unintentionally damaging, I think it can be helpful to think of it as more of a "thought hole."

Chapter 2

Understanding Thought Holes:
What is a Thought Hole?

For the purposes of this book, I'm using the term "thought hole" to describe the well-intended bad advice that we might come across. A thought hole is to our thinking what a pot hole is to our vehicle, Meaning, if we hit one, it can cause a lot of damage, leaving us stranded along the road to health and healing and stuck in an emotional fog.

What makes a thought hole so hard to see is that they are everywhere, and the worst ones tend to be hidden in the thickest emotional fog out there. Because they are so hard to see, we often don't realize we've hit one until we are much further down the road—and worse, we don't know how to stop hitting them if we don't realize they are what's causing us so much damage.

We all go through life hitting these "thought holes" until we experience enough pain from the damage that we realize what we're doing isn't working and that we need to do something different.

Where do Thought Holes Come From?

Thought holes come from all of our difference spheres of influence, which are around us from birth. These spheres of influence grow and change throughout our life as we ourselves grow and change and include: parents/primary caregivers, siblings, extended family, friends, peers, teachers, religion, culture, neighborhood, society (along with gender roles, expectations, etc.), media/music, educational system, and those we turn to for guidance, such as spiritual leaders, counselors, therapists, etc.

Our spheres of influence shape our thinking, feelings, and actions. They shape our morals and values, feelings and actions about ourselves and about others, and the way we interact with the world. Because we all are our own baseline for what's normal, and because it's human nature to befriend and be around other people who are similar to us, it often takes a tremendous amount of pain for us to have a wake-up call that perhaps our thinking and actions, or the advice that we've been taking from those closest to us is all a big part of the problem. It's like the saying goes, "the last thing the fish notices is the water" and it often takes a person decades to realize they've been swimming in a sea of dysfunction and dysfunctional thinking.

Chapter 3
A Light in the Fog: Questioning What's Normal

The first step in getting out of the FOG is to start by seeing thought holes for what they are and then learning to avoid them. In order to live a happy, healthy life, we have to first examine the dysfunction that has been pulling us down. And a great place to start is by questioning some of the more common advice that is floating around out there about what's "normal" especially in terms of our friendships, family dynamics, and other relationships.

When we start to question what we consider to be normal, reasonable, or rational, and realize that there have been some really problematic messages we've bought into, we can feel like Alice at the Mad Hatter's Tea Party, *especially* if we are the only ones in our inner circle who seem to be aware that there's an issue, let alone anything deeply wrong.

Like I mentioned before, the first step to getting out of the fog includes figuring out where those holes in our thinking are and then learning to avoid them. And perhaps the easiest place to start is to open up the discussion on what is normal and what is problematic. However, the challenge is that for the vast majority of people what's problematic *is normal.* It's like being in a cult, feeling like something is "off" and then turning to an advisor or trusted authority member *within that same cult* for guidance on what to do. Odds are other members of that cult are going to encourage them to try harder, or worse, deny that anything is wrong. And what tends to happen is that after the conversation the cult member then feels somewhat better that things can change if they double up their effort in things (or they try to brush off their doubts that something is wrong), telling themselves that a relationship takes work from both people, and that everything can be solved if they just try harder. And the cult advisor feels really good about themselves for helping the cult member work towards improving their communication and being a better partner and member of the community. And this cycle of well-intended bad advice continues until the cult member can't handle feeling all of this doubt and confusion any longer and leaves.

The hardest part about navigating around thought holes is that we generally don't know immediately if we've hit one. The results from the damage often take a while to appear, and so it can be difficult to link up the correct cause and effect so we can avoid these thought holes later. Not to mention that unlike a pot hole which makes a loud sound, thought holes don't sound like a "ka-chunk!" when we hit them. They sound more like:

"You need to invite Uncle Larry over for Christmas. I know he molested you when you were younger, but that was a long time ago and besides, he's family. What happened to your Christmas spirit? You are so unforgiving. I expected more from you."

"You need to have a relationship with your mother, even though she is verbally and emotionally abusive to you and your children. After all, she had a terrible childhood, and she is your mother. She's not getting any younger you know."

"You need to stay working at this job where you are being sexually harassed and bullied. No job is perfect, and things could always be worse."

"You need to stay in touch with your brother. I know he's stolen money and opened up credit cards in your name, but he's had a rough life, and you should be more compassionate."

"You should have your sister and her troubled children move in with you and your family. Sure, she's verbally abusive and is an addict, and her kids are all in and out of juvenile hall, but they are homeless and they are family."

"You should stay married because sure your spouse lies, manipulates, cheats, siphons funds, yells, puts you down, and has no sincere accountability for their actions, but you are married, and commitment is forever."

What makes these kind of statements problematic is that all of them pressure a person to put them or their children in harm's way in order to keep a relationship afloat. It doesn't matter if a person is family, if their behavior is going to sink you or your relationships, jumping in to help isn't a healthy or reasonable solution. And even me saying that might sound really outrageous and self-centered, like, how dare I even propose that we put our safety and sanity first! That's so selfish! And my response would be, my goal for this book isn't for you to think like me, it's for you to *think about what's healthy for you*, and to take action from a place of what's healthy for you and not from a place of feeling you need to sacrifice your safety and sanity out of fear, obligation, or guilt.

Learning to question everything is the first step in living an authentic life, and it isn't easy, *especially* if you've been driving down a road full of thought holes for decades and didn't realize it. Perhaps all you realized was that your life wasn't working, or that you kept attracting all the same toxic people, but didn't know why. To actually be authentically you, means that you aren't going to be like everyone else. It often means going against the grain of what your significant other, friends, family, culture, or religion are thinking and doing—and learning to be okay with this. And it will take practice and emotional strength and courage to carve out your own path, especially if you are surrounded by people who don't agree with the decisions you make or the boundaries you set. But having healthy boundaries is a big part of what living an authentic life is all about, and if we can't tell the difference between healthy actions (which come from a place of keeping ourselves safe and sane) and dysfunctional actions (which come from a place of fear, obligation, and guilt) then we aren't being rational, *we are rationalizing.*

There is no shortcut to thinking for yourself and making up your own mind about things, because:

- Emotional health and wellness, especially healthy boundaries and self-awareness isn't taught.
- Just because a person is a life coach, therapist, or psychiatrist doesn't mean that they don't have some majorly dysfunctional thinking.
- Just because something is normal doesn't mean it is "right." And just because something is "right," doesn't mean that it's normal.
- What is passed down through generations about what love and commitment are is often skewed (at best) or deeply dysfunctional at worse.

I'm not saying that I have it all figured out. I by no means do, but I can say that I have a lot of my own life more figured out. My thinking has come a long way over the years to being a lot healthier than it once was. Simply put, I no longer have friendships or relationships with people with squirrelly, confusing, condescending, critical, controlling, or crazy-making behavior. I'm also getting a lot better with not taking action from a place of fear, obligation, or guilt, and instead taking action from a place of what brings peace and enjoyment into my life. And again, this book isn't intended for you to think like me, the goal is for me to bring up a lot of the thought holes I was hitting that I see a lot of other people continually hit too. And I hope that you can benefit from me sharing my aha moments and the aha moments of others.

The first step in avoiding the overwhelming amount of well-intended bad advice that's floating around out there is to realize that you don't need to tolerate being mistreated. Simply being aware that you can distance yourself from problematic people, and that you don't need to be dragged through hell is often enough for most people to start getting more balance and peace in their lives. You might be thinking, "Well that's easier said than done" and it is…at first. The more you get comfortable with cutting out toxic people and situations out of your life, the faster you will get at this, and the more you practice setting and holding healthy boundaries that keep you safe and sane, the more you'll wonder how (and why) on earth you ever put up with so much before.

If you can examine and "fill in" your thought holes, your journey through life will be much smoother. …and you don't need to have 100% change or be 100% healed in order to live a radically different life. Sometimes a 10% (or even a 1% change) in direction—especially over time, is enough. Change, awareness, and healing are all related, and they all compound on themselves, and once you see what's really going on out there, it's very hard to not see it.

To begin doing this, you'll have to forget aiming for figuring out what's normal, because odds are that will lead you straight back into the fog of dysfunction. *Instead, start figuring out what's healthy and empowering and move away from anything that is oppressive or disempowering.* Once you start heading towards what's healthy for *you*, that's when your life will *radically* start to change for the better.

The last challenge with navigating thought holes is that once a person starts to see the thought holes out there, the vast majority of people around them *don't*, and will think they are crazy, or that they are making a big deal out of nothing. It doesn't matter how much evidence and proof you give to someone as to the existence of this thought hole—if they aren't ready to see it, they won't see it. They will continue to justify, rationalize, or flat out deny what's going on, and they'll try to push you back into acting out of fear, obligation, and guilt.

And once you are awake to the disempowering beliefs around you, you will most likely realize that there are some pretty major changes needed—especially within your inner circle. This can leave a person feeling either excited or depressed (or a little of both). If you do decide that you need to get some more like-minded people around you, then please realize there is a "lag time" that happens. This lag time is the time between when you clear out the old and start to gather up the new. It can be profoundly hard and lonely, and it can last for a while—sometimes several years, but please don't let that discourage you. The results are worth the struggle. Keep moving in the direction of what's empowering, and you'll soon start to meet people that are more in alignment with your new beliefs.

Like I mentioned before, this book is written from my experiences with narcissistic abuse, codependency, and navigating my way towards healing from both. My journey towards healing was a long one, and the road was, frankly, unnecessarily difficult. I don't know why this stuff isn't taught, and I don't know why there are so many therapists out there who give such dysfunctional, damaging, and, frankly, negligent advice. Don't get me wrong. I'm not saying all therapists are bad. What I am saying is that the quality of therapists, like any other professionals out there are on a spectrum. And just like in any other profession, about ten percent of them are awful, ten percent are worth their weight in gold, and eighty percent fall somewhere in between. The challenge is in sorting out the good from the bad. However, in therapy, the added challenge is a person is often in therapy because they are having trouble sorting out the good from the bad!

For what it's worth, in my experience, I really felt so profoundly alone after I got out of yet another narcissistically abusive relationship. I didn't know where I was going wrong, or what red flags I was missing, and worse, I didn't know how to prevent it from happening again. So I did what most people would probably do if they were in my situation and got into therapy. I'd go for 10-12 visits and not feel like I was getting anywhere. I didn't know if I just wasn't making the connections I needed to make, or if I had the wrong therapist, or if it was a little of both, or what. All I did know was that at the pace I was going, I was going to be 100 years old before I got the clarity I needed in order to get my life on track.

After several years, and several therapists later, I still didn't feel like I was any further along in my healing or understanding. In fact, during my last therapy visit, I had the distinct thought of "I feel like I'm following Moses through the desert here. How long is this going to take? Does she even know where she's going, and how can I be sure?" I had the very distinct impression that she was relying on me to lead the way, but I obviously didn't know where I was going or how to get there, or else I'd already be there! I began to get really discouraged and resigned myself to thinking that perhaps I needed to be patient, and that having insights and personal growth in general just took time. And so I spent years reading all kinds of self-help books and going to workshops and seminars, but my life still wasn't working, but I didn't know what pieces to the puzzle I was missing.

Chapter 4
An Expanded View of Normal Behavior

The biggest turning point in my healing was when I somehow stumbled into a support group for narcissistic abuse. Within a matter of hours, I found myself having aha moment after aha moment. I was completely overwhelmed with relief that I wasn't crazy or alone because I felt like I'd found the missing pieces to the puzzle that was my life. Within a few weeks I began to notice massive shifts in my thinking and what was perhaps the most interesting to me was that while I felt relatively healed from what had happened to me (at least to the point where it wasn't negatively consuming my life) I realized that I had only just started.

In many ways, the more aha moments I had, the crazier I began to feel, as any time I shared these insights with people outside of the group, I felt like they thought I was nuts. I'm not gonna lie; I had quite a few months there where I really did second guess myself and wonder if I was seeing problematic behavior (in others as well as within myself) correctly, or if I was making something out of nothing.

When I began looking up the term "narcissist" and "sociopath," that's when that first beam of light broke through the fog. So much began to make sense. I knew what I'd gone through in my own life was way outside the realm of normal problematic behavior, and so at that point I began to divide the world up into narcissists/sociopaths and "normal" people. I also became somewhat obsessed with understanding the line between normal behavior and pathological behavior. Dividing the world up into these two main categories gave me a lot of clarity (at first), because until that point I'd been walking around thinking that people were inherently good, and given enough love, understanding, rehab, religion, or therapy, they could be "fixed." And so after realizing that some people could get all these things and it could even make them worse (they learn to manipulate better), it also led to a lot more questions—and to more confusion. After all, didn't many "normal" people also lie, cheat, steal, yell, belittle, or even abuse?

Then I realized three more important things:

1. **All behavior is on a spectrum.** There are only degrees of dysfunctional and functional behavior. So while a person might not have majorly disordered or pathological behavior, this doesn't mean that their behavior isn't problematic or toxic to you in some way. And a person's behavior doesn't need to be 100% toxic, either;

1% can be enough to make you feel emotionally or physically "drained" or flat out sick. There's a saying that if you are on medication for depression or anxiety, make sure you aren't actually surrounded by toxic people. ... There's a TON of truth in this, as most people are used to living in a den of dysfunction, and they are out of tune with their emotions because they've been continually pushed into suppressing them. But all this generally does is reroute that emotional pain into something that they are more comfortable in handling which tends to be physical pain. Their body will begin to signal to them that something is off, and these feelings get louder and louder until we can't ignore them anymore. So ideally spend as much time as you can around the healthiest people you can find, and soon you'll get used to feeling peaceful, empowered, and good.

2. **There is a third category of "healthy."** Healthy people don't have highly problematic behavior, and they don't have highly problematic people as part of their inner circle. I kept landing in a ditch because I was taking well-intended bad advice from "normal" people. If I wanted my life to be healthy, then I needed to start looking at what healthy people did. But in order to do so, I needed to be able to sort out the difference between well-intended bad advice from well-

intended good advice. I realized that good advice is, at its core, advice that encourages and empowers a person to do what they need to do in order to stay safe and sane. Well-intended bad advice is advice that encourages people to put themselves (or continue to put themselves) in situations or relationships that are a threat to their safety and/or sanity. What is safe and sane for one person is not the same for another—not only that, but it will continue to change as we grow and change. The healthier you get, the less drama and dysfunction you will tolerate, because you will be a lot more in tune with how drama and dysfunction feels—and it feels like swimming in toxic sludge. Once you get more in tune with yourself and your body, and you realize just how toxic you feel being around toxic behavior, and you realize that you feel "poisoned" within a few minutes, you'll realize that it's no wonder you were anxious, depressed, exhausted, addicted, angry, had chronic pain, etc. You were having a very healthy and normal reaction to a very unhealthy and abnormal situation!

3. **Anyone can have toxic or problematic behavior.** Again, this may sound super obvious to you, but it wasn't for me. People are people, and anyone can have problematic behavior. So while we all like to think that we can spot

problematic behavior coming, that isn't often the case, as we all filter our experiences through our biases (as well as many other filters). Some examples of biases would be thinking that people who are police officers, military members, or who work in some sort of social enforcement (attorneys, judges, etc.) are all law-abiding citizens and have the greater good of society at the forefront of their mind. Or that religious leaders are moral. Or that therapists are emotionally healthy or have the skill set to guide others to become emotionally healthy.

Because they are people who are like the rest of us—all trying to figure things out, and most likely trying to deal with their own unresolved issues—it's important that we learn to think critically about what's going on, and to think for ourselves so we don't turn our power and control over simply because someone with a certain job title tells us that person is an expert.

So while it's really nice to have validation from others that what you are experiencing is indeed problematic, it's critical that you learn to trust your own judgment. *It's also important to realize that when we start feeling confused by what we are experiencing, it's generally because we realize on some level that what we are experiencing is indeed a problem—we just wish that it wasn't.*

Chapter 5

Thought Holes vs. A More Empowered Understanding

A Narcissist, Sociopath, or Psychopath vs. Being Narcissistic, Sociopathic, or Psychopathic

A Narcissist, Sociopath, or Psychopath

The word "narcissist" is one that is commonly used in the concept of narcissistic abuse; however, not all those who are abusive would qualify for a diagnosis of Narcissistic Personality Disorder or Antisocial Personality Disorder. In fact, I think you'd find that most of the time abusive behavior isn't even factored into making a diagnosis, which is a huge problem. From my experience, many mental health clinicians only look at severely exploitative behavior that lands a person in jail as a marker for a personality disorder and don't seem to give a lot of weight to them being interpersonally exploitative. Using, abusing, exploiting, or neglecting family tends to be minimized and treated as "family dynamics" which to anyone who has lived through this knows it's a lot more than that. Please realize that a person doesn't need to have a clinical diagnosis of a personality disorder in order for their behavior to be damaging or even deadly.

According to the Diagnostic and Statistical Manual of Mental Health, Fifth Edition, more commonly referred to as the "DSM V," in order for a person to qualify as having a personality disorder, they must have impairments in personality (self and interpersonal) functioning and the presence of pathological personality traits. In other words, their behavior must be pervasive (apparent in a wide range of situations), persistent (ongoing and not due to situational factors or substance use), and problematic to a pathological degree which negatively impacts themselves and/or others, regardless of whether or not they realize the impact.

According to the DSM-5, some behavior traits a person with Narcissistic Personality Disorder (NPD) would have would include: having an exaggerated sense of self-importance, having a sense of entitlement, expecting unquestioning compliance with their expectations, taking advantage of others to get what they want, behaving in an arrogant or haughty manner, and having an inability or unwillingness to recognize the needs and feelings of others.

And for a person to be diagnosed with Antisocial Personality Disorder (ASPD), some behavior traits would include: being driven by their need to gain self-esteem through personal gain, power, or pleasure, often at the expense of others; having a lack of concern for the feelings, needs, or suffering of others, a lack of remorse after mistreating another person, being incapable of having mutually intimate relationships, and mainly interacting with others through exploitation, deceit, and coercion. People with ASPD use dominance or intimidation to control others, and are often manipulative, deceitful, cold and callous to the impact of their behavior on others (but often come across as sincere and charming), and are hostile, as well as often irresponsible and impulsive. A person needs to be over the age of eighteen in order to be diagnosed with Antisocial Personality Disorder, and these behavior issues must exist outside of substance use, or what would be considered within the range of normal for their culture or developmental stage.

It's important to point out that all of these traits are human traits, and we all have them, or the capacity for them, to some degree at different points in our lives. *It's not necessarily the traits themselves that are the problem, it's the degree, frequency, and a person's unwillingness to change these traits that is the problem.* Narcissists not only have selfish and destructive behavior, they tend to feel superior to others because of it. So while they may realize on a certain intellectual level that their behavior is problematic, after all, they can see that it's a problem in others, they don't have the emotionally intelligence or insight to see these same problems within themselves. So what we would consider good behavior, such as being team-oriented, they would consider this to be a weakness.

In order for a person to be officially diagnosed as having either Narcissistic or Antisocial Personality Disorder (or any personality disorder) they need to be formally assessed by a mental health clinician. However, getting an accurate diagnosis can be very difficult as most people with those kinds of behavior traits won't go to therapy, or if they do, they can be very charming, and can do a great job at manipulating a mental health clinician—not to mention, even if the mental health clinician does see through their manipulations, there's a very good chance that they won't tell you or them that they have a personality disorder, because they most likely know that telling a narcissist they are a narcissist will only enrage them. Telling a sociopath or psychopath that they are one will only be something that they will further use for attention and feeling superior, as well as something to be used to justify their bad behavior and keep their targets roped in because they "can't help it."

So while I know that lots of people feel they really need something concrete to point to and say this person has a personality disorder, they may never get that validation. Frankly, I think even trying to go down that trail is a big waste of time and money and misses the larger point completely. The larger point is for us to think critically about what we are experiencing and to respond accordingly, and not turn our power and control over to other people or a diagnosis to tell us what's workable or a deal breaker.

I know that so many people get hung up on wanting to know for certain if this person in their life has a personality disorder, and I get it—I really do. I was stuck on that fence for a while too. My guess is that people want to know "for sure" because they are thinking about this problematic behavior in terms of "if it's a personality disorder then it's a legitimate problem and I need to walk away, but if it's not a personality disorder then they can be fixed." That's really problematic in itself because behavior and "cures" for behavior aren't a clear line in the sand, nor is changing them a simple or fast process; not to mention, if a person's behavior is problematic for *you* then that's worthy of being a deal breaker. It doesn't matter if everyone else is telling you it's not a personality disorder, or is somehow workable or even normal—if it's a problem for you then it's a problem. It's sort of like trying to determine what kind and how much poison is in the water you are drinking, when the reality is poison is poison, and any amount that you are ingesting is going to be harmful to you.

Being Narcissistic, Sociopathic, or Psychopathic

The term narcissistic tends to refer to selfish, self-centered, or self-absorbed behavior. The difference between the two terms is that "narcissist," "sociopath" or "psychopath" describes a person, and "narcissistic" or "sociopath" describes their behavior. A lot of people (myself included) tend to focus on wanting to know whether or not a person was a narcissist or a sociopath or if they "just" had problematic narcissistic or sociopathic behavior. And it really doesn't matter. It's not like a narcissist or a sociopath is a vampire, demon, or somehow not a human (even though it might seem like that!) They are still people, and there is no grand unmasking to be had. Some might argue that their brain chemistry is different, and while this may be true, brain scans aren't normally done on people, and even if one was to be done, there are lots of people who have altered brain chemistry who aren't destructive or dangerous. And let's take this a step further. Let's say you were to actually get a brain scan on someone who was dangerous and destructive, and their scan came back as normal. Would that mean that all their chronic lying, cheating, stealing, manipulating, and so on is somehow workable? A person is a person; *it's their behavior that sets them apart,* so focus on the behavior because the behavior is what matters.

"After seeing a therapist and being on anti-depressants for close to a year, my therapist finally mentioned to me that my husband sounded like a narcissist, and told me they don't change and that therapy doesn't help. I began looking into what that meant. I realized that described my ex and what I was experiencing. But then my husband went to a PhD level psychologist who told him that he wasn't a narcissist. I was very confused, and spent a lot of time trying to figure out who was right and if he really was a narcissist, or if he just had a lot of problematic narcissistic traits. I then realized that he wasn't sincerely motivated to change anyway, so it really didn't matter. I felt bad divorcing him because he wasn't abusive, but my therapist pointed out that him giving the silent treatment, as well as being controlling,

condescending, continually critical, and crazy-making was abusive. That was the validation and clarity I needed in order to leave, and I don't regret it one bit. I have no idea how I stayed married to him for so long. That relationship was sucking the life out of me, and I didn't even realize how bad things were until I left."

— *Janet*

"Before doing a lot of work on my boundaries and standards, I used my abusive ex as the measuring stick for what I wouldn't put up with in my life, as well as what a narcissist was. I now realize that I don't need to stick around for a person to prove that they are indeed a full-out narcissist or sociopath in order to leave. If a person is a problematically narcissistic or even has remotely sociopathic behavior, I'm out the door. I only want people who treat me with dignity, respect, kindness, and consideration in my life. That sounds so obvious right? It wasn't to me. It took me many years to realize that I kept finding myself in abusive or exploitative friendships or relationships because I thought that being used or abused to some degree was normal, and thankfully now I realize that it's not. This might sound strange, but the hardest part at first was walking away from people who started treating me poorly. I think this was because I was so lonely, I was very quick to make these people who tended to come on so fast a large part of my life, and so when they started showing their true colors, I didn't want to leave because then I was left with a big void in my life. And so, ironically, all that loneliness I was trying to avoid, and all that love I was seeking was what kept me drawn to emotional manipulators, who left me feeling even lonelier and unloved when those relationships went sour."

— *Rachel*

"Narcissist, narcissistic, sociopath, sociopathic, potato, potatoe. I don't care what people call it, a person who acts like a selfish, manipulative jerk is a deal breaker for me."

— *Scott*

A Partner vs. A Target

A Partner

A partner is someone who is ready, willing, and able to work together as a team towards some sort of shared goal. Some examples of shared goals might be: to be happily married, to raise children into healthy, responsible adults, or to have a certain degree of financial stability. When two people with a true team mentality come together as far as dating, marriage, friendship, or in a work environment, they create a partnership.

A Target

To be a target means to be someone who has been selected to be on the receiving end of some sort of attack, whether that attack is to be abused, used, exploited, or neglected in some way. Narcissists often form dynamics with people whom they have targeted as a source of "supply." Supply is what a narcissistic person is trying to gain from their target. Some common forms of supply are sex, money, housing, transportation, social status, public image, or to feed their own ego by grinding their target down so that they can feel better about themselves.

So for example, if that narcissist is a bully, then he'll target a person he thinks he can intimidate and harass, because it makes him feel stronger (or less weak). If that emotional manipulator is an online dating scammer, he will target people who look like they have money. If that emotional manipulator is a significant other, he may initially target a person because he thinks that person has money, or because he finds that person attractive or wants sex from them, or because dating that person helps with his public image; or that person might be targeted because he wants to break up their marriage because doing so makes him feel smug and superior. In terms of a really sadistic narcissistic person, he may target a person with the intention of taking them to the highest high emotionally and then dropping them to the lowest low; and the more pain that person experiences the more that narcissistic person enjoys it because it makes him feel strong and powerful.

The cycle that so many people with a narcissistic partner get stuck in is thinking that this person is actually a partner; meaning, that they are on the same team. *Narcissists are only ever on their team.* They might do a great job of trying to convince you that you are soul mates and that you are indeed on the same team, but their actions will consistently show otherwise. …If a person is working on the same team as you, they don't actively work against you (lie, cheat, steal) when you aren't looking. They don't grind you down with subtle put downs, insults, or a barrage of verbal and emotional abuse. They don't hit, demean, belittle, or induce fear. None of this is love, and none of this is how a partner treats the other. It can take a person many years, if not decades, to fully wrap their head around the fact that their significant other isn't a partner. It's hard for a person to understand how someone could be so emotionally detached and care so little about them or their children. If a narcissist stays married to someone, but continues to lie, cheat, siphon funds, etc., it's not because they view this person as a partner, it's because this person is their target, and they are using them. Maybe they don't want to move out, or maybe they don't want to pay child support, or because they like the social status or public image of being married— bottom line, they don't want to be inconvenienced in any way, shape or form.

Because this is all one giant manipulation, or game, where they want to win, they will often keep their partner on the hook by either increasing their abusive behavior or by telling them everything they need to hear and getting better at hiding what they are really up to. When the truth comes out, it really is just shocking to see their lack of conscience in motion because they will go to such great lengths to keep their current partner roped in, such as having another baby, buying a house, adopting a pet, you name it—and the whole time none of it means anything to them. If they are living a double life, they may be doing the exact same things with another person.

This is because there is no real depth to a narcissistic person's emotions, because it's all about them and what they want. This blinding degree of selfishness can cause a person to, at a minimum, neglect others around them, and at a maximum be driven to exploiting and abusing others in order to meet their own selfish needs.

To consider a narcissist a partner is like considering an online dating scammer, terrorist, or cult leader a partner.

It's important that we look at the other person's actions, and not keep someone in our life based simply on how we feel about them, but more so based on how they are treating us. You may love them, but if they are actively working against you, or are in any way dangerous or destructive, you'd be wise to distance yourself from them. If a person is pulling on the other side of the rope when you aren't looking, then you two are not on the same team. If they are pulling on the other side of the rope when you aren't looking, and then when they get caught start pulling on the same side of the rope...until you catch them again...then you are being manipulated. This person is not a partner, and you are a target.

"For years, I stayed married to a man because I thought we were partners in a committed relationship. I put up with his abuse, his lies, and his cheating all because I kept thinking we were partners, and that eventually he'd come around and start treating me and the children with respect. I guess I thought we'd eventually earn his love,

and that he would eventually change. Once I heard the word "target" my whole relationship (if you can even call it that) began to make a lot more sense. He didn't love me, he used me because I took care of him, and he used his children to feed his ego. I can't believe I mistook his abuse for something normal, let alone love."

— Tamara

It's a Problem vs. It Could Be Worse

It's a Problem

What's usually considered a major problem in a relationship generally includes any form of abuse, addiction, adultery, or treating the other partner with a lack of dignity or respect.

Abusive behavior tends to start off as a series of small boundary pushes, or comes across as insensitive, rude, or questionable behavior cloaked in a "you're the one with the problem" kind of way. If the target stays, then odds are the abusive (aka "problematic") behavior starts becoming more and more frequent, but since the abusive person continually denies, minimizes, or justifies their behavior, the target is left to wonder if perhaps they really are too sensitive, too emotional, can't take a joke, or are otherwise to blame. In this way, problematic behavior becomes their new normal.

It's very common for people who are in these dynamics to realize that things are a problem but not identify what they are experiencing is as big of a problem as it really is—even if there is abuse involved. This is because abusive behavior is *confusing* behavior. When a person starts to experience the cruel "Mr. Hyde" side of their partner, they often try to understand why they are acting like this. And if their partner is blaming their lashing out on them or on stress, work, the kids, you name it, then in an attempt to get the "Dr. Jekyll" back, they start walking on eggshells, thinking that if they can just resolve the stress or be a better partner then this will keep their partner faithful or friendly. For those who have been in abusive relationships, they know that there aren't enough eggshells in the world to walk on in order to change their partner into being someone who respects them or their relationship. So while they might view their relationship as having "problems," it often takes years (or someone else pointing it out) before they view it as abusive.

Another reason people have a hard time sorting out the difference between a problematic relationship and an abusive relationship is because everyone has their own preconceived idea of what an abusive relationship is, as well as has their baseline for what is normal, acceptable, or workable—which is in large part defined by what they've seen in the movies, experienced growing up, and what they've experienced from partners in the past. For example, if a person grew up in a home where they were beaten, they might not view their current partner's behavior as problematic since they aren't being hit, and have experienced much worse physical abuse in the past—even though they are being yelled at, ground down, or continually cheated on.

It Could Be Worse

It's very common for people to try to minimize their partner's problematic behavior, *especially* if they want to stay in the relationship. One way that people tend to rationalize what they are experiencing is by telling themselves that "things could always be worse." While it might be true that things could always be worse, it doesn't mean that things aren't a problem, or that they aren't worthy of being a deal breaker. And if our gauge for what's a problem is that things could always be worse, well then things could (and will) get worse until they can no longer handle how bad things have become.

The "it could be worse" justification is used by people in all kinds of problematic situations. Some examples are:

- "He made some weird comments about how attractive the waitress was, and how he was so glad he could check out other women without me getting jealous—because he's a guy, and that's just what guys do. I mean, I guess it could be worse; at least he's not flirting with the waitress, or cheating on me."

- "She racked up about $1,000 of credit card debt without me knowing, but it could be worse—I mean, it could have been $5,000."
- "Well, yeah, he yells a lot, but it could be worse—I mean, he's never yelled at me in front of the kids."
- "She called me some names, but she only yells at me like that. But it could be worse—I mean, at least she doesn't give me the silent treatment like my mom used to do."
- "He yells at me and the kids, but it could be worse—I mean, at least he doesn't hit us."
- "Yes, she hits us, but it's not that often, and it could be worse—I mean she could hit us every day."
- "He's hit me a few times, but it was never in my face. It could be worse—at least it didn't leave a bruise or anything."
- "She hit me in the face, and it left a bruise, but it's not that big…it could be worse—at least I can cover it with makeup…it's just how we fight."
- "He beat me up, but he didn't break any bones or anything." It could be worse—my ex (or, my father/mother) beat me and my sister up worse.
- "She broke one of my ribs, and fractured my arm, but it's not that bad. I was only in the hospital for a few hours."

Just because something could be worse and the person can still tolerate what they are being put through doesn't mean that it's not a problem.

Any form of abusive behavior is a problem, and *all* forms of abuse are traumatic and can be equally damaging. It's damaging to the person going through it, and it's damaging to the children who are watching it happen, or who are experiencing it themselves.

"My ex-boyfriend was incredibly abusive, and, although I didn't realize it until recently, that relationship was the one that I compared all my other relationships to. If I was treated abusively, I'd think to myself, "well, it could be worse…it's nothing compared to how "John" treated me. I realize now that abuse is abuse, and that using how John treated me as a measuring stick for what was okay or not okay was a mistake. I had to work a lot on my self-esteem to realize that I was worthy of being treated with dignity and respect, and that settling for anything less would never be okay."

— *Cheryl*

An Attitude of Scarcity vs An Attitude of Abundance

An Attitude of Scarcity

It's very common for former targets of narcissistic abuse to have their world flipped upside down after being used, abused, or exploited. Perhaps one of the largest struggles that a survivor has is with trust. They often have a hard time trusting others as well as their perception of events and their own instincts about people and situations. This leaves a person feeling very disoriented, fearful, anxious, and wanting to isolate. These feelings of distrust are often due to gaslighting, which is form of psychological abuse where one person (the gaslighter) denies or distorts their target's reality into what they want either because they don't want the truth to be acknowledged or because they are sadistic and enjoy eroding another person's sanity. Most people who experience gaslighting often don't realize what is going on, and start to feel like they are losing their mind. Once they come across this term, they are often relieved that they are not "crazy" and often become outraged at how another person could do this to them. The aftereffects of gaslighting tend to be long-lasting, as when a person's sense of reality has been altered it takes a while to get back. In addition, because other people who have never experienced gaslighting are often full of well-intended bad advice and are quick to dismiss their concerns or want to push them back out into interacting with people, telling them that they just need to get back out there again and not let what happened to them rule their life. A large part of what's really going on is that a person who has gone through gaslighting and abuse of any kind is usually *a lot* more aware of what abusive behavior is—and they are picking up on things that a person who has never gone through something like this has. Usually this picking up of subtle cues and mannerisms of abuse happens on a subconscious level, and can (and often does) start to register with a person through feelings that something is "off," feelings of confusion, anxiety, nightmares, or a tightness in their chest when they are experiencing it.

What I see often (and personally experienced) is that this person who is feeling lonely and damaged is seeking to heal those wounds through dating/finding love, instead of spending time with friends, cultivating their support system and developing hobbies. So they start dating again, get caught up with someone who starts giving them a lot of attention, and are quick to start talking or texting with this person for hours every day. When red flags start to surface, they often feel confusion, which, if that feeling grows, leads to mental anguish. During this time, they are often told by friends, family, and maybe even their therapist that they are pushing away love because they are afraid of being hurt or that they are being too picky.

Because they are lonely, have a fear of being alone, or are looking for a friend in a person they are dating, they have a subconscious attitude of scarcity when it comes to other people which is driving them to make problematic relationships work. They may also be concerned with a fear of missing out on a great person because they have issues with trust, and so they stuff their concerns down deep and keep moving forward in this relationship, and they usually stay in it until their original concerns are proven right. And many times a person goes from abusive relationship to abusive relationship because they get caught up in the intensity and the resulting whirlwind that these relationships form. When the relationship ends they don't know why this keeps happening to them or how to break this cycle, and they often start feeling cursed, or like all men (or women) are abusive, and so they swear off dating.

An Attitude of Abundance

A person with an attitude of abundance realizes that there are lots of people in the world, and they aren't worried about missing out on a good one. They realize that if a person has problematic or "squirrelly" behavior, then they aren't missing out on anything if they let them go, because there is nothing solid there to begin with. It's a lot easier to have an attitude of abundance and to leave problematic situations if we have something else to fall back on. This is why having a solid support system in place is so important. For example, it's a lot easier to leave an awful job if we have another job offer waiting for us, or if we have some savings set aside. It's a lot easier to leave a problematic relationship during the first few weeks if we make sure to continue spending time with friends and with our hobbies. It's a lot harder if we have nothing fun or exciting going on in our life, and talking to that new person is the only way we know how to make ourselves feel loved or important.

"When I met Bob, I started having nightmares about my abusive ex. I thought it was because I was dating again, and had a bunch of unresolved issues. He seemed so into me right off the bat, and was in hot pursuit. We were talking for hours every day, and even though my gut instinct was telling me that things were moving too fast, I didn't

want to slow things down and risk losing him because I had concerns. After all, he seemed like such an amazing guy and he was so different from my ex. Whenever I brought up my concerns to my friends and therapist, they'd offer up excuses for all his behavior, and kept telling me that I needed to let my guard down or I was going to miss out on a good guy. I dated Bob for close to a year, and he was an amazing boyfriend...until I found out he was married, and had been married for ten years. I'm not mad at my friends or therapist for pushing me into dating him, I'm more mad at myself for not trusting my gut instinct about him. I will never go against my gut instincts again. If something feels off, it's because it's off. The right people and situations don't make me feel like an anxious, confused mess, and if the person is right, I know now that I will slow things down, and if they aren't comfortable at the pace I want to move then they aren't right for me."
— *Jill*

Who Society Tends to Think Can Be Abusive vs. The Types of People Who Are Abusive

Who Society Tends to Think Can Be Abusive

Society tends to think that women—especially mothers—are not or cannot be abusive, and that men are the abusive ones. In order to back this up, they will point to the statistics collected, which show that 85% of domestic violence cases are with a male abuser and a female target. So it makes sense that people would think that, based on this information, men are abusive, when these are the statistics floating around out there. The truth is that *abuse is not about gender; it's about behavior.* Women can be (and many are) just as abusive.

Now don't get me wrong; violence against women is a very real problem, and there does need to be education out there. However, the unintended consequence of only focusing on female victims of abuse is that this only addresses half of the issue. In addition, by not discussing what men and boys go through, they are much less likely to identify that they are being abused, and so they are much less likely to seek help. When the issue of abuse is addressed as mainly a female issue, many men often struggle with shame, embarrassment, and feeling emasculated because they are being abused by a woman.

Any type of person can have abusive behavior—they can be male or female, young or old. They can be a parent, a child, a sibling, a significant other, a friend. They can be any nationality, any religion, any sexual orientation, any education level, any profession, any income level; you name it.

"I was in a friendship for many years with a woman who was jealous, controlling, paranoid, possessive, and hypocritical. She would demand to know who I was out with, where I was, and so on. When she got her way, and when she was in a good mood, she was fun to be around, but when she wasn't getting enough attention or things weren't going her way, she was awful. It was like dealing with a bratty child in an adult body. I used to joke with people that I felt like I was in an abusive relationship. I had always thought of an abusive

relationship as something between two people that were dating or married. It took me many years to realize that I was, and that "friends" could be abusive too."

— *Lisa*

"My mother was and still is incredibly abusive, but my father and everyone else blamed her childhood and blamed us for not being more understanding and sympathetic towards her. She used to yell at and beat us kids like you couldn't imagine. She was horrible. But out in public, she volunteered for all kinds of things and seemed like a caring mother. I don't think anyone realized we were being abused in part because she was so different in front of other people and in part because no one thinks a woman or a mother would act like how she did."

— *George*

Who Society Thinks Can Be a Target of Abuse vs. Who Is a Target of Abuse

By and large, society as a whole tends to think of abuse as a women's issue, and that men (specifically husbands or boyfriends) are the ones who abuse them. However, according to the National Coalition of Domestic Violence, one in three women have experienced physical violence by an intimate partner in their lifetime, and for men that number is one in four...and that's only what's reported. Frankly, my guess is that number is much higher for men, but because there is very little information out there that speaks directly to what men go through, not nearly as many are able to identify what they went through as abuse.

When I first started my YouTube channel, I only spoke about the female experience as far as abuse goes—from what I had experienced, as well as what I had been trained in when I was working at a domestic violence shelter. A few months into making videos, I began to receive messages from both men (straight and gay) and gay women who were seeking clarity as to their experiences. It was at that point that I realized with a great deal of sadness that there really was a huge gap in education and awareness when it came to identifying what abusive behavior looked like if it was outside the traditionally understood (and stereotypical) male/female dynamic, and that I'd been unintentionally contributing to minimizing them and their experiences. Like with anything else in life, once we know better, then we can start to do better. It's so critical that as a society we understand what ALL forms of abusive behavior look like, as well as understand that anyone can have abusive behavior, if we ever want to raise true awareness and develop successful prevention and treatment.

Because the full picture is that *anyone* can be a target of abuse. Abuse can and does happen to people regardless of gender, age, size, strength, nationality, socio-economic status, sexual orientation, religion, profession, you name it. *Abuse isn't about gender; it's about power and control.*

"I was doing an externship abroad for my PhD program. The professor I was working with was very esteemed in his field and brought in a lot of

grant money for the university. At first, he was friendly, and I enjoyed working with him. Then one day, it was like a switch flipped, and he became sexually inappropriate and verbally abusive with me. I was terrified and felt like if I didn't give into his sexual demands that I wouldn't be able to complete my PhD program. I was stuck overseas and couldn't easily leave. I endured his abuse for six weeks until I left. The whole experience has left me traumatized, and when I returned and told the university, they basically told me that he'd had many complaints before, but that he was an esteemed professor. They shrugged it off. I was in therapy for awhile after this, and that's where I learned that I had PTSD, and that what I had experienced was abusive."

— *Susan*

What People Tend to Think is at the Core of Abusive Behavior vs. What is Actually at the Core of Abusive Behavior

Most people tend to think that anger issues, poor coping methods, ineffective communication, addiction, or stress are at the core of abusive behavior.

While many of these behaviors and issues go hand-in-hand with abusive behavior, they are not the root cause of it. The core of abusive behavior is the desire to get and keep power and control over others and over situations—and this need for power and control comes out in seven main ways: verbal, emotional, psychological, financial, sexual, spiritual, and/or physical. When abuse is present, it is very rare that it's only one type of abuse.

Narcissistic people are driven by a staggering degree of both selfishness and entitlement. It's all about them and what they want—all of the time—and they go about getting what they want by using power and control (the use of control being perhaps more easily identifiable). They get control over others in ways that are physical, such as isolating their target by moving them away from friends and family, or by limiting their access to a vehicle. They may isolate them in emotional ways such as through love bombing, in which they are spending hours and hours every day communicating with their target (this is most commonly associated with online dating scammers and cults—but it happens within other dynamics with a narcissistic person).

They may attempt to control their target emotionally through creating (or recreating) a "soul mate" type of connection where they are charming, attentive, affectionate (oftentimes the perfect partner in bed), and exploit their partner's optimism and hope by offering up promises of change.

They may attempt to control their target spiritually by using guilt, obligation, and their faith to control their behavior.

They may control their target financially by driving them into debt, forcing them to work several jobs (and then turning over all their money), or forcing them to not work at all.

They may control them sexually by using guilt, obligation, shame, and embarrassment to use, abuse, molest, or rape them.

They may control them psychologically by use of gaslighting, lying, and manipulation to control their target's perceptions of reality and what they are up to.

They may control their target verbally and emotionally by a series of subtle put-downs, mean sarcasm, cruel teasing, bullying, and overall grinding down a person's self-esteem to where they think the narcissistic person is the best they can do—and the abuse is either not happening (usually telling the target, "You are making a big deal out of nothing"), or it's the target's fault such as "You are too sensitive, too emotional, can't take a joke, don't clearly communicate, that's what happens when you talk about our business to other people, or your friends or family are the problem."

All of these excuses and manipulations can really simultaneously grind a person down as well as "groom" them to start walking on eggshells—doubling up their efforts at being a better partner in order to earn their partner's love or loyalty (or both.)

When one person is driven by power and control, this is an individual issue. This is not a relationship issue—because they bring that mindset with them everywhere they go. And because it's an individual issue, this is one of the main reasons therapy often makes narcissistic people worse and not better—especially couples' counseling, because you have one person (the partner) who is making themselves even more vulnerable by having open, honest, sincere, solutions-oriented communication and the controlling partner who is gaining information about all of their concerns, fears, and insecurities which will be used against their partner later on—even if they are saying everything they need to say in therapy to charm both their therapist and their partner. Make no mistake: narcissistic people don't play fair; they play to win, at whatever cost. The cost of their marriage, their relationship with their children, their job; you name it. And they will destroy everything if that's what it means to them to "win."

"I thought his abuse and cheating was due to anger, or alcohol, or my appearance, and so I went to great lengths to not make him angry— but nothing I did was ever enough. He needed to control every little thing, and lied and manipulated to do so. Trying to make our relationship work and keep him happy was like trying to hit a moving target. Just when I thought I was able to keep the peace, I'd either find out about more cheating or drinking or debt he'd racked up, or he'd start yelling or putting me down about something else."
— *Linda*

A "Normal" Relationship vs. an Abusive Relationship

A normal relationship is one that is built on the foundation of mutual trust and support, in which both people treat each other with dignity and respect. Their communication is open, honest, sincere, and solutions-oriented . A normal relationship has issues, but not to the point where it becomes a one-sided relationship, to where one person's behavior is dragging the other through hell.

It's very common for people who are either in an abusive relationship or who have been in a series of abusive relationships (oftentimes starting with abuse or neglect as a child) to struggle with defining what a normal relationship is, what healthy boundaries are, what workable behavior is, and that there need to be deal breakers. This is because when a person has been around dysfunction for so long, it becomes their "normal." So if we want our lives to change, we have to get a healthier idea of what "normal" is—and everyone's idea of what is healthy or normal (as well as what deal breakers are for them) is different. The best way for you to get that clarity is to turn inward and do some soul searching for what you want your life to look like, and what you want your life to feel like, and then to base your decisions on bridging the gap between where you are and where you want to be. What's helped me the most has been to get clear (and honest) with myself about what drains my energy and what gives me energy, and to do more of the things (and be around the people) that empower and excite me, and to do less of the things (or be around people) who drain my energy.

The most important difference between a normal relationship and an abusive relationship is that an abusive relationship is a one-sided relationship where one person has all (or the majority) of the power and control, and is focused on what they want—especially when the other partner isn't looking—and feels entitled and justified in treating others, their partner, and their relationship however they want. And generally the other one is either scared to leave, focused on keeping the relationship together at all costs, or is forever trying to figure out how to "fix" their partner's behavior.

An abusive person goes about gaining that power and control through a series of boundary pushes, manipulation, emotional highs and lows, physical and/or emotional isolation, financial dependency, and lies. When done steadily over time, this subtle mistreatment becomes seen as "normal" the person in this dynamic most likely does not even realize that they are in an abusive relationship. They tend to realize that something is "off," which often registers as perpetual confusion about their partner's behavior, their relationship, and if they are the problem.

It is critical that for those who are trying to help someone who is in an abusive relationship dynamic to realize that they aren't simply in a "bad" relationship, and that there are not two equally valid sides to the story. They are in a hostage situation and most likely don't even realize it— just like many cult members tend to not realize that they are in a cult until things get so dangerous and destructive that they realize they need to get out of there. And leaving either situation is rarely easy. It's more along the lines of escaping.

There is perhaps no greater damage that can be done to a person than when they go to a therapist, and that therapist doesn't identify that they are in an abusive relationship and instead treats the situation as though the issues are relationship issues instead of an individual issue, or that the dynamic is a dysfunctional relationship instead of an abusive relationship. This would be like a cult member finally getting to the point where they work up the courage to talk to an outsider about what's going on, and then being told that they either need to "just leave," or that their issue is a relationship issue with the cult leader and that they just need to go back and keep working on things.

If there is a dynamic where one person is continually using manipulation and deceit to physically or emotionally hold someone hostage, either physically, emotionally, or mentally so that they can get what they want, then it's an abusive dynamic. It doesn't matter where that dynamic is found, it's still a big (and very real) problem—regardless if the dynamic is between a religious cult/cult leader, a hostage/terrorist situation, a partner/abusive partner "relationship," a child/abusive parent "relationship," manipulated masses/megalomaniac political leader (the Hitlers of the world); you name it. It's important that we see abusive dynamics at play when they are happening and not have our thinking about what we consider abusive or problematic become totally derailed because this person is a family member.

"I grew up with parents who were abusive and neglectful. My brothers and I were continually yelled at, put down, or ignored growing up. When I began dating, I was so desperate to be loved, but didn't realize it. I dated all the wrong people and wound up marrying a man who treated me a lot like my parents did. I think I stayed in that marriage for as long as I did, because how I was treated was on many levels, normal, and I didn't realize that there was a problem or that I should leave. My ex-husband was the one who ended up leaving me, and even though I was miserable being married, I was terrified at being alone. But, actually, him leaving me was really a blessing, because all that pain that I felt when that relationship ended helped me to discover that my boundaries, standards, and self-love really needed work. Now my new level of normal is much healthier. I am no longer starved out for love or validation from a man or from anyone really, and I for sure don't tolerate being abused by anyone."

— *Katie*

"Every relationship I've ever been in has been very different. Some were abusive and some were great. I didn't stay in the abusive relationships because I felt they were normal. I knew what I was experiencing wasn't normal, but I thought it was still workable. With all the abuse I endured, I was led to believe that it was either not happening, not that big of a deal, or somehow my fault. I guess what I'm saying is that I didn't realized I was being abused when it was happening. I always thought that commitment was forever, and that people should always try and work through everything. My parents

had a great relationship, and were married for close to fifty years before my dad died. I wanted to stay married too, and felt like if I left it meant I was a failure. What was normal for me was to stay married no matter what. I now realize that's where I was going wrong; I had no deal breakers and thought I just needed to work harder on the relationship, and that eventually he would change and he did change. He got worse. It took me thirty years, but I finally left, and it breaks my heart to think I stayed for as long as I did, and that I ever thought it was okay to be treated so horribly."

— Rachel

What People Tend to Think the End of an Abusive Relationship is Like vs. What the End of an Abusive Relationship is Really Like

What People Tend to Think the End of an Abusive Relationship is Like

Many people, including the person that was in the abusive relationship, tend to think that once an abusive relationship ends that the person who was in it should be thrilled that it's over. After all, they are finally free from this abusive person and can have their life back.

What the End of an Abusive Relationship is Really Like

The end of an abusive relationship often leaves the former target with a wide mix of emotions from confusion, anxiety, fear of their partner finding them, fear of being without their partner, concern about what others will think, feeling addicted or "craving" their partner, love, depression, guilt, despair, relief, a deep distrust in others, shame, regret, remorse, anger, rage, and embarrassment.

This wide range of emotions is, in large part, because an abusive relationship is a confusing relationship. It's one where the person in it is continually trying to reconcile why their partner has two very different sides to themselves and loving the good side while fearing the bad side. This confusion is especially strong if they've been continually told by the abuser that there is nothing problematic, let alone abusive, going on—and if there is, that it's not that bad, or that it's somehow their fault. All of this denial, minimization, and justification erodes not only a person's self-esteem but their perception of reality, leading them to feel responsible for how they are being treated, and powerless over leaving and so ground down that they don't think they are worth being treated with dignity and respect.

Added to this confusion, memories were made, routines were created, and strong bonds (called trauma bonds) were formed. These trauma bonds are forged through the highs of the really good times which often follow the lows of the really bad times and can feel incredibly intense.

And when the fog of manipulation starts to lift, and the person starts to see their former partner's abusive and manipulative behavior clearly, they either become numb or they become enraged. And even though they may feel angry and outraged, they may still struggle with missing the good times with this person—or they may be really struggling with being alone (because a relationship with an abusive person is an isolating relationship.) It's one where the dysfunction of the abuse warps their sense of normal, and this degree of chaos and crazy-making wears out others around them—to the point where their support system has to distance themselves because the target's toxic relationship is sucking the life out of them too.) Because of this, the target may feel (and actually be) painfully alone or around people who don't understand. And oftentimes those that try to be helpful come armed with well-intended bad advice from opposite ends of the spectrum ranging from, "You need to quit talking about all this and move on," "You need to try and work things out for the children," or "You need to forgive them."

And during all this confusion and wide mix of emotions, they may also find that they have overwhelming urges to contact this person. And when they do find themselves missing this person, they generally have tremendous amounts of mental anguish about why this is, and what's wrong with them that they would miss or even have feelings of "love" towards this person who has hurt them so profoundly and in so many different ways. They may think that any sane or reasonable person should be glad to get away from someone so destructive and dangerous, and then wonder what on earth is wrong with them for not being glad that things are over, or for missing someone who treats them so terribly.

When this shame spiral takes hold, it serves to further isolate a person because they become uncomfortable with reaching out—and understandably so if their feelings are misunderstood, minimized, or invalidated. So if and when the abuser circles back around with either promises of change (aka hoovering and future faking), or threats of making their life hell (by dragging them through a long and costly divorce, threatening to go for full custody, and so on), if they don't come back, it can then be really hard to not get sucked back in—either out of hope that this time things will be different, out of fear of what they might do, or out of overwhelm with the feelings they are experiencing with trying to leave.

"Leaving my abusive ex was so incredibly hard in so many ways. One of the hardest things was struggling with missing him even though he was so abusive. I guess it was because when things were good between us, they were so good. I missed the good times, and I missed coming home to someone. When I found myself missing him, I felt a mix of shame and embarrassment. I couldn't talk to other people about that because I knew how crazy and messed up that was. Everyone kept telling me how relieved I should be, and I knew that they were right, but we were together for five years, and there were things I missed about him. It took a while for those feelings to pass, but they did pass. It's hard for me to even understand how I could have ever

been attracted to someone like him. I guess hindsight is always 20/20."

— Sharon

"I would add to this list my own experience of a feeling of excruciating emotional pain that was experienced in a very physically felt manner. I truly understand what the word heartbroken means as that is exactly what it felt like. And it was almost unbearable. I had to take antidepressants for quite some time to alleviate the pain. It simply wasn't bearable, in fact it was so painful that I considered suicide as a very serious and viable option just to try to end the pain. Fortunately I had enough sense left to get to my doctor immediately, and to get a prescription when I started debating the merits of a razor blade versus pills as a method to execute myself. Within three days of starting the antidepressants the pain lessened and began to recede. I also experienced this same exact pain when I ended my relationship with my sister, so it is not confined to romantic relationships. The only thing that helped each time was at least six months on antidepressants."

— Luci

What Most People Think Abuse Is vs. What Abuse Actually Is

What Most People Think Abuse Is

Most people tend to think that the only "real" forms of abuse are extreme physical or sexual abuse, and that verbal, emotional, psychological, financial, or spiritual abuse aren't really *that* big of a deal, let alone abuse. It's the whole "sticks and stones may break my bones, but words can never hurt me" line of thinking. And this line of thinking couldn't be further from the truth.

What Abuse Actually Is

Abusive behavior is *any* behavior that is designed to get and keep power and control over someone. Abusive behavior usually comes across as manipulative, controlling, hurtful or harmful, and includes any and all behaviors that are disempowering, demeaning, defining, diminishing, destructive, dangerous, or deadly.

Abusive behavior falls within seven main categories: verbal, emotional, psychological, spiritual, sexual, financial, and physical, and can be overt (outright) or covert (hidden or subtle). More often than not, more than one type of abusive behavior is used to get and keep power and control over others. The vast majority of the time physical abuse is preceded by verbal, emotional, psychological, spiritual, financial, or sexual abuse.

In addition, while physical abuse may leave physical signs of harm such as bruises, broken bones, or scars, it's the verbal, emotional, and psychological abuse that a person undergoes that is often the most damaging, because it profoundly impacts their ability to trust and relate to others, their ability to discern the difference between what is a safe or dangerous person or situation, their perception of reality, their self-image, and their self-esteem. It can even drive a person to suicide.

"I didn't realize that I was in an abusive relationship because I wasn't being hit or even called names. All of his abuse was much more subtle, and all of it had a kernel of truth in it. For example, one time he began yelling at me because I forgot to pick up the dry cleaning on my way home. I felt like his yelling was justified because after all, I did forget to pick it up. Or he'd make subtle putdowns about how ignorant or uneducated I was, which, again, I felt were justified because I never went to college. Or he'd mention how concerned he was about my weight if I'd gained a few pounds, and then he'd start talking about how attractive other women were. It was always something. There was always some truth to what he was saying, but whenever I'd tell him I didn't appreciate his approach, he'd either start raging at me or I'd get the silent treatment. Our whole relationship was me trying to walk on eggshells trying to avoid being further ground down by his "brutal honesty," and it never worked. After I finally broke up with him, I was left with chronic anxiety and terrible self-esteem. I've since realized that there is no excuse for abuse, and I will never tolerate being in a relationship with someone who continually points out everything wrong with me or tries to plant seeds of insecurity."

— Janelle

Covert Abuse vs. Overt Abuse

Covert Abuse

The word "covert" means anything that is hidden or less outright or obvious. And so in terms of abuse, covert abuse is abuse that is often hidden, less outright or obvious. Some more common examples of covert abuse would be emotional or psychological abuse—or subtle forms of verbal abuse. Even physical abuse that doesn't leave a large mark can be viewed as covert.

Some examples of abuse that commonly fly under the radar of most people might be name- calling, teasing, sarcasm, being "brutally" honest, minimizing or denying a person's reality or experience (also known as "gaslighting") especially if they speak up and have a problem with how they are being treated by saying things such as, "That never happened," "You are crazy," or spinning things back around blaming them for "misremembering," or baiting a person into circular "conversations" that are designed to show intellectual superiority, humiliate a person, frustrate, grind them down, exhaust them, or provoke a reaction so that the narcissistic partner can point at them and exclaim how abusive and manipulative their partner really is. Physical abuse can also be done in covert ways, such as pinching, spitting, shoving, slapping, or even hitting or leaving bruises in areas that will be covered by clothing.

Overt Abuse

The word "overt" means anything that is outright or obvious. And for many people, overt abuse is anything that is more outright or obvious—usually physical abuse that leaves visible marks such as bruises or broken bones, or intense verbal and emotional abuse where name-calling, yelling, or belittling is involved.

The more informed a person becomes about abuse, the more their awareness increases, and what was once covert is now much more overt—and you can't help but see it. (I will warn you that when this shift does start to happen for you, you will most likely start seeing abusive/highly problematic behavior pretty much everywhere, and it can be very overwhelming. You may even find yourself doubting your sanity and your perception of what you are experiencing, because abusive behavior is rampant, and what's really upsetting is that many people don't even see this type of behavior as problematic, let alone abusive.)

"I stayed in an abusive marriage for close to thirty-two years, because I didn't realize I was being abused. I know that must sound so crazy, but I always thought that an abusive marriage was one where someone was being hit on a regular basis, and that wasn't me. He never called me names, yelled, or cheated that I know of, but his abuse was either brutal honesty or constant criticism. Both of which were often cloaked in an "I'm concerned about you" kind of way. According to him, pretty much everything I did was wrong—especially if I did things

different from him, or disagreed with him in any way. I learned early on in our marriage to never share my hopes, dreams, or insecurities with him, as he would use those against me whenever we fought. I knew that I felt ground down and like I was 100 years old, but I never thought that was abuse. It makes me sad to think how much I tolerated from him and for how long. If I could go back and do it over again, I would have left much, much sooner. "

— *Laura*

Normal Problematic Behavior vs. Normalizing Problematic Behavior

"Normal" problematic behavior in a relationship depends on what the person is used to experiencing. It may include abuse, addiction, adultery, or to being lied to, manipulated, deceived by a partner, belittled, degraded, yelled at, or to feel ignored or ground down—or to be treated in any other ways that show a lack of respect or regard for your feelings. While these things might be "normal" they for sure aren't healthy—which is why I'm not a fan of having "normal" be a measurement of what's workable.

Normalizing problematic behavior is what we do when they try to justify and minimize (normalize) problematic behavior (generally some form of abuse, addiction, adultery) and try to convince ourselves that what our partner is doing is somehow justifiable and workable. The first sign of problematic behavior is always confusion. We are confused not only because we are being manipulated, but because on some level we know what we are experiencing is a problem, but we don't want to believe it.

We normalize problematic behavior if staying is meeting some sort of need—and especially if we have a strong emotional or physical investment in staying. If we are lonely, or scared to be alone, or overwhelmed at the thought of being single or starting over, have children with them, if they are family, or if it would mean quitting a job, or otherwise making a major change that potentially means rocking our emotional (or financial) boat, then we have a strong emotional investment to stay.

The stronger the emotional investment is, the more a person tries to normalize what they are experiencing so they can convince themselves to stay. *In short, a hungry heart will eat lies.* And they will continue to eat these lies, until either they get fed up with being treated this way (which usually involves the abuser's behavior becoming so outrageous that the target feels they have no other choice but to leave), they find a healthier way of getting those needs met, or the abuser ends up leaving them.

Cognitive dissonance is the mental distress we feel when we have two conflicting thoughts about the same topic at the same time. The reason this is distressing is because we all need our thoughts to line up with our actions. If they don't, then we are acting in a way that doesn't make sense.

So in order to ease that mental distress, one of two things needs to happen: we either need to change our thoughts to match our actions, or change our actions to match our thoughts. This mental distress starts off as a feeling of confusion, and over time it progresses to feelings of mental anguish, anxiety, depression, anger, and rage.

So, in order to resolve this confusion, we often seek out clarification or advice as to what we are experiencing. *But it's not their behavior that's confusing to us (even though we think that it is)—it's that we are trying to convince ourselves that what we are experiencing is not as problematic as it is.*

And so in an attempt to make sense out of all this confusion, we start looking up their behavior on the internet, or asking friends and family, or maybe eventually, getting into therapy. *But none of this will help if we don't want to acknowledge that there is a problem.* We will cling to crumbs of hope that what we are experiencing really isn't a problem, or if it is a problem that it can be resolved— especially if we don't want to leave. So we start distancing ourselves from people who continue to point out that, yes, what we are experiencing is in fact a big problem, and instead we start surrounding ourselves with other people who have skewed standards and boundaries for what is acceptable or workable behavior, or perhaps we might even get tangled up with a well-intended therapist or people at church who tell us what we want to hear, especially if they tell us to keep working on things. Because in an even more twisted way, if we can make the issue our issue, then it gives us a false sense of control that maybe we can save the relationship by working harder on it. And work harder on it we do.

We often double or triple up our efforts at making our relationship work. And during this time our partner (who is used to getting away with everything short of murder— and in some cases even murder or attempted murder) continues to feed us crumbs of hope or perhaps even grand gestures of romance such as being a great spouse or even wanting to renew their vows …all the while just getting better at hiding their behavior and getting better at manipulating their partner.

If we are experiencing "confusion," or cognitive dissonance about our relationship, but want to stay in that relationship, then we will need to rationalize ("normalize") what we are experiencing. At first, the rationalizing is a series of small jumps in logic, most of which are within the realm of being a reasonable explanation. For example, a person might try to normalize text messages that their partner is getting from the opposite sex late at night by telling themselves that their partner did say that they have a lot of female/male friends, or if their partner is hiding their phone, they might believe them when they say it's because they can't trust us—or that we are too jealous and so they have to hide their perfectly normal behavior (yeah right), or that if their partner drank more than we were comfortable with on a second date that maybe they were nervous or had a hard day at work, or that maybe we are just too uptight.

But the more problematic behavior we put up with, the more the person with that problematic behavior realizes that they can get away with, and so their behavior tends to get worse and worse over time. And for the person who is trying to rationalize it, their partner's behavior gets harder and harder to rationalize to themselves and to others.

So in an effort to avoid any more mental distress about our situation, we begin to distance ourselves from people who have an issue with our relationship, because deep down we *know* it's a problem, *but we wish we didn't.* And if we don't want to leave, then we are going to have to do some intense mental gymnastics to convince ourselves that things aren't that bad, or that they can be fixed—even if our reality doesn't come close to matching our misplaced optimism.

When a person continues to try and normalize problematic behavior, three things happen: the person with the problematic behavior realizes that they can get away with whatever they are trying to get away with; the person experiencing it now has what would normally be deal-breaker behavior as their new normal for how they will be treated and what they will put up with; and the person who is experiencing it has to go to ever growing greater lengths to normalize what they are experiencing—the whole time feeling more confused and questioning of their partner, relationship, sanity, and reality along the way. This level of ongoing confusion leaves a person feeling anxious, depressed, insecure, and overall physically and emotionally worn out.

Because the fog of confusion and manipulation is so thick, and gets thicker the longer a person is in it, it often takes an extreme situation to cut through that fog and to "snap" a person out of it. The person will continue to stick around until either things get so outrageously bad they can no longer justify what they are experiencing or until their partner leaves them.

A great way to tell if a situation falls within the realm of normal behavior, or if it crosses the line into normalizing behavior, is to imagine telling the healthiest, most well-adjusted person you can think of what's going on, and then imagine their response. If it would sound problematic to them, then odds are it's a problem and you are trying to normalize it.

Another way to test what you are experiencing is to imagine the advice you'd give to someone you deeply cared for (such as a good friend, or perhaps a younger sibling) if they were in the same situation.

The reason you can think more clearly by imagining what you'd say if it were someone else is because you are giving yourself the emotional distance needed in order to make a healthy decision. (And if you want to get deep for a second, now think about what that means that you'd give someone else you cared for different advice than you'd give yourself...because if we truly care about ourselves, the advice would be the same.)

"It's amazing to me how much of my marriage I normalized. All of the lies, the yelling, the belittling, the racism and sexism, the cheating, all somehow became normal. When I did have problems with what he was doing, he would spin it back around to me to make it seem like I was making a big deal out of nothing, or that I had the issue because I couldn't accept him for how he was. I was always concerned about what he was going to say or do to not only me but out in public. His behavior was embarrassing, hurtful, and sometimes flat-out cruel. While I knew it was problematic, I kept thinking he'd change and that our issues were somehow within the realm of normal relationship issues—which I now realize they were not."
— Sharon

"Here's the way I rationalized EVERYTHING:

I would tell myself:

I must have misunderstood.

I must not have heard that right.

I must be a terrible communicator.

I must be imagining things.

I must not have a very good sense of humor because surely they were only joking.

I am being needy, and that's wrong so I must be careful to not need anything ever.

I am being jealous, and that's wrong so I must be careful to never want anything ever.

I am being too judgmental, I need to loosen up.

He/she is just tired, had a bad day, doesn't mean that, and I need to be careful and not say things that upset them.

I must have given them the wrong impression, so I must try harder to be clearer, and to do better.

What am I doing wrong? I have got to try even harder here because I am being completely misunderstood!

In all cases I always took all of the blame, and I always decided that it was always something that I was doing wrong, and that it was always something I needed to fix about and within myself.

Be funnier, be quicker, be smarter, be prettier, be happier, be more agreeable, be less needy, be less jealous, be thinner, be stronger, be more understanding, be more compassionate, be more empathetic, and it was always all on me.

I've known for at least 30-40 years: You cannot control anyone except yourself, so I went to war against myself, and tried to control, mangle and corral myself into being perfect, and into being able to tolerate and to accept anything, without needing or wanting anything, and without judging or discerning anything about anyone ever. And it STILL wasn't enough."

— *Luci*

Who You Attract vs. Who You Are Attracted To

Who You Attract

It's very common for people who have gotten out of a narcissistic abusive relationship to feel that they are continuing to attract all of the wrong people, especially if more people with problematic behavior seem to keep showing up. They might start reading up on how abusive people pick their targets, and they might even work towards dressing differently, smiling less, walking with their shoulder back, and so on.

However, who we attract is something that is largely outside of our control, because we

all attract a wide range of people. Not to mention that different predators prey on different types of people for different types of reasons. Some go after quiet, pleasant, agreeable people, because they are easy to dominate, and some go after confident and aggressive people because they are a challenge, or because they might have more money or social status.

Some of the people you will attract (as friends, coworkers, or partners) most likely are normal, decent people, some are highly problematic, and some fall somewhere in between. *Just because we attract certain people into our lives doesn't mean that we need to let them in—or keep them in our lives once we realize that their behavior is problematic.*

Emotional manipulators are often master manipulators, and the ones that are really good can be difficult to spot in general, let alone right away. You don't need to twist yourself into an emotional pretzel trying to change your appearance or how you present yourself. All any of us can do is to go slow, only give another person trust that is earned (which happens over months, not days or hours), and really get to know a person *before* we get emotionally invested in them. Because 10% of the people out there are really destructive or dangerous, 10% are great, and of those 10% great people, only 1% will be your kind of people. The other 80% of people out there fall somewhere in between. The only way to tell who is who is to give the dynamic enough time for a person's true colors to surface and to give yourself enough emotional distance in order to see their true colors clearly.

Perhaps the biggest part of steering clear of people with problematic behavior is to realize that you can break up with someone, or distance yourself from a person for any reason whatsoever. You don't need to justify, argue, defend, or explain yourself. Having a feeling that something is "off," or feeling like you aren't ready to date, are both very valid reasons to call things off. Stating what we need and not feeling bad, wrong, or guilty about it is something that those of us who are learning to develop healthy boundaries often struggle with. We often feel the need to make absolutely certain this person is cheating, stealing, abusive, or otherwise is dangerous or destructive before we leave. And that's where we tend to go wrong. You've seen this movie before. You don't need to sit through it to the end to know you don't like it. You don't need to wait until the bitter end to have the validation that the end is in fact bitter. It's okay to get up and walk out. Yes, other people may be annoyed. Yes, other people may tell you that you need to date again, or that you are being too picky or hyper-vigilant, and that's okay. Let them be annoyed or have their opinion—this is your life, and they don't get to decide what you do or don't do. It's okay to do what you need to do to feel safe and sane, even if very few people around you agree.

Who You are Attracted To

Who you are attracted to, *and more importantly, who you allow to stay in your life is more within your control.* And again, while we may also find ourselves attracted to a wide range of people, some great and some highly problematic, just because we are attracted to them doesn't mean we need to befriend them or date them.

This is where examining our vulnerabilities comes into play. It can be really hard to walk away from problematic people if we have an "empty bucket" as far as getting some sort of basic need met, whether that need is safety, security, or significance.

Meaning, if we are concerned about money, housing, transportation, food (all basic safety and security needs) or if we are feeling lonely, or unloved or unimportant (all basic significance needs), then odds are we will not make decisions that are in our highest and best interest, but rather we will make decisions based around getting these needs met. We may move in with a creepy person we met on the internet, just because they had a cheap room for rent, or we may fall for someone who is love-bombing us even though we aren't even physically attracted to them.

This is because many of our decisions (and behaviors) aren't made consciously; they are made at a deeper subconscious level, and all of our default behavior is an attempt to get our needs met in the quickest way possible. The emptier the bucket, the more of a scramble we will be in to fill it…and odds are we don't even realize we are in a scramble, or that we are making poor decisions. It's hard for any of us to think straight if we have a basic need that's been unmet for any length of time.

Have you ever heard of the advice that it's a good idea to not make a major life change for at least a year after a major life event such as a divorce or death? The reason this advice is given is because the odds of a person making some impulsive bad decisions is really high. But when a person is caught up in the scramble of getting their needs met, they have a really hard time seeing that their decision is impulsive and not founded on good judgment. If anything, decisions made during this time often feel so incredibly right (when they are so incredibly wrong)...which is why these decisions at this time can be so problematic.

If you find yourself reliving a pattern of relationships (or behaviors, in general) that are causing you hurt or heartache, it's time to slow down and examine what could be driving this behavior. This is not to say that being abused or exploited is your fault, it's not. This is to say, that when there is a pattern of similar people that start showing up in your life, that there is also something subconsciously going on there—that is worth exploring.

It's really important for us to examine our "buckets" and see which ones need filling so we don't keep finding ourselves in problematic situations or with problematic people time and again. Because when our buckets are empty for a prolonged period of time, they become vulnerable—and narcissistic people exploit vulnerabilities in others in order to get what they want. It's the lonely widow (or widower) who gets caught up in the online dating scam and loses their life savings. It's the child whose parents aren't around who gets caught up in a gang. It's the person who recently went through a divorce (or who felt ignored or unloved as child) who falls for the love-bombing and moves in with their "perfect" partner a few months later, only to find out they cheat, lie, manipulate, steal, abuse, and so on. I know this may feel like victim-blaming, but please believe me, that is not my intention—I've been in more than my fair share of toxic relationships and friendships too. And these buckets aren't the only piece in the puzzle; becoming familiar with what manipulative and abusive behavior is and how it feels is another big piece in the puzzle. It's the same with online scams. When they first began happening, people were falling for them right and left. Now that more people know about them, they don't fall for them as easily.

Having vulnerabilities is a part of being human, and we will always have them—and they will be forever changing as we go through life. We can't get rid of our vulnerabilities, nor would we want to, as they are one of the main ways that we bond in healthy ways with others. But it's important for us to be aware of our vulnerabilities as much as possible, as we run the risk of them being exploited otherwise.

Outside of identifying our vulnerabilities and being familiar with what manipulative and abusive behavior is, the other big thing we can do is to make sure we have healthy boundaries and deal-breaker behavior and make sure that our choices in people and in situations are filtered through those boundaries and standards. This is easier said than done. I encourage you to take some time and write out not only a list of qualities that you are looking for in people in your life, but also how you've felt around the problematic people in your life—as well as to examine if all of those friendships or relationships started off in a similar way (because usually they do). The more you can spot how your vulnerabilities have been exploited, the less likely you are to have that happen in the future.

Healthy boundaries and having deal-breaker behavior will get the wrong people out of your life and they take practice. Be kind to yourself during this process, as it's a lot like learning to ride a bike: odds are you will fall and get scraped up, but it's part of learning. Keep at it, and you'll get the hang of it.

"I had an abusive childhood, and that pattern of abuse continually repeated itself in my adult life. I couldn't figure out what it was about me that seemed to attract such abusive people. I tried changing the clothes I wore, smiling less, trying to be nicer and forever trying to keep the peace. And that worked to an extent, but it was exhausting, and I felt like I was forever walking on eggshells just trying to keep peace in my life. It wasn't until I started going to Codependents Anonymous (CoDA) meetings that I really learned about healthy boundaries and that it wasn't so much who I attracted, but how long I kept the wrong people in my life. I've since learned to be assertive or if need be, to leave a friendship or a relationship once I began to be mistreated. I don't waste my time on all the wrong

people hoping they'll change. I've taken my power back and realize that life is too short to be around toxic people. Of course, my whole family thinks I'm the mean and unreasonable one because I won't have anything to do with my abusive mother, but that's okay. They don't need to be okay with my decision."

— *Faye*

Commitment vs. Codependence

Commitment

Commitment is a conscious dedication, a voluntary obligation to a relationship — to be inclusive of the other person's needs, desires and viewpoint, because the mutual bond is your priority and it is mutually rewarding. You expect the other person to feel the same way, and most of life's challenges are met together, agreeing to stand by each other's side through the highs and lows of *life* together. Some of the normal highs and lows of life include: starting or ending careers, sickness or health, financial ups and downs, raising children, moving, exploring new hobbies, learning how to make time to work on the relationship, navigating boundaries with extended family, and overall learning to work together as a team.

Codependence

Codependence is beyond a healthy commitment. It is a state of being dependent on another person for more than just a mutual bond — but for your very sense of self. It feels like you need that person to exist, and without them you can't exist. That may sound romantic, but, regardless of what the movies and media teaches about love, it's not. At the most basic level, the need to please them, or earn their attention or approval comes from a place of "I don't know what I'd do without them" or from the fear that if we don't become what they want us to be, that they will abandon us. To live like this, is a life full of walking on eggshells and never fully being ourselves—or never getting to the point where we even know who were are, because we spend our lives sacrificing our wants and need, our identity, to please someone else. The need also blinds you to whether the other person feels the same way, or is even capable of providing what you want. It's the nature of this kind of need, that other people can't fulfill it entirely — because it's something within ourselves.

Unlike a commitment, codependence is a one-sided dynamic in which one partner tends to have a lot of destructive behavior and the other clings to them and to the relationship for dear life, while they are being dragged through hell and hoping that one day things will get better. This is not a healthy commitment, this is codependency. There is no value in being committed to someone whose behavior is destroying you.

Many people who are codependent don't realize it—and they often don't realize that their partner has been manipulating them. They often think of their behavior as being caring, compassionate, and concerned, and they often value commitment at all costs. They also tend to struggle with being able to tell the difference between a healthy relationship and an abusive relationship. They tend to not have deal-breaker behavior and instead believe that given enough love, understanding, patience, therapy, religion, or rehab that this problematic person can change.

Codependency tends to come out in three main ways: clingy, caretaking, or controlling.

- The "clingy" type of codependent behavior is full of people-pleasing, and doormat types of behavior. It's where a codependent person has a hard time walking away from problematic people or situations and stays until things get so bad they are forced to leave, or until their partner leaves them.

- The "caretaking and coddling" type of codependent behavior is full of justifying and enabling problematic behavior, being easily manipulated into thinking that this problematic adult doesn't understand the basics of adult behavior and that they are responsible for teaching them It's also putting everyone else's wants and needs ahead of our own, feeling like a perpetual parent or therapist to their partner or friends, and having weak, poor, or nonexistent boundaries.

- The "controlling" type of codependent behavior is full of acting like a parental figure, being overly involved, making threats to leave, being passive aggressive, or continually trying to "fix" someone's problematic behavior instead of walking away from people who continue to hurt them.

Many people who find themselves in a relationship with a difficult, abusive, or narcissistic person will have their commitment tested, and more than likely, their fears of abandonment triggered. If you already have an emotional need for validation (and most of us do), and are involved with someone who can't regulate their emotions or self-esteem, and who oscillates between pumping up your ego and then devaluing it, it is very common to double-down on your commitment. Your instinct tells you that if you can just *try harder*, if you give them *all* your love, you'll finally make that connection with them. But this is often a attempt of desperation to hang on to the other person, because your self-worth is tied to them. Losing them implies losing yourself.

More often than not, this extra effort does not result in stronger bonding or validation — because the other person doesn't have the same capacity or ability to form a mutual bond. If they did you likely wouldn't feel that desperate need. And so you can make a rational decision to break your *conscious* commitment and get out — however, you may still *feel* codependently attached. You may still have a deep emotional *need* for that person, for your sense of self, and *feel* as if you can't exist without them. This is an exceptionally difficult time, because part of you knows you have to let go for your sanity, and part of you won't let go for fear of losing yourself.

Many people refer to this contradictory feeling as "cognitive dissonance" (perhaps a more accurate term would be emotional dissonance). For most, the underlying need keeping you in the unhealthy attachment, is actually a childhood (or child-like) fear of abandonment. If you can realize that you don't need this toxic person they way you needed a parent, the attachment will loosen its grip on you.

With awareness of this distinction between commitment and codependence in oneself, it is equally important to learn to evaluate what drives attachment (or lack of attachment) for the other person — for all the people you have relationships with — by their pattern of behavior over time. All of us have instincts and needs we are unaware of, some triggered more than others. This is why awareness is so important — not only of others, but of our own emotional drives.

It's important to acknowledge that there is an aspect or degree of codependence that is part of our instinct to form strong bonds — we have a better chance of survival by sticking together even when things are difficult, and not just giving up at the first sign of imperfection. However, we can't let any single emotional drive dictate our behavior — we must regulate all of our emotions, take in to account all factors, including what we observe about other people, their behavior and abilities, and include our emotions and rational observations in our decisions about attachment.

"I thought that marriage was forever. I took vows, and I took them seriously. I thought that everything could be worked out—even his lying, cheating, and abusing. The last time I went back, a friend told me that I really needed to work on my codependency issues. I had no idea what she was talking about and was really offended. I didn't see how me being supportive and staying committed was bad or wrong. I began reading about codependency online and a lot of things began to make sense. I never thought of myself as codependent, but I guess I also never thought I was in an abusive and exploitative relationship either. The more I read about boundaries and deal breakers, the more I saw where I had been going wrong for so many years. I had some really skewed beliefs about what love towards myself and others looked like. I'm not sure if that necessarily makes me codependent, but it did for sure mean that my boundaries needed work and that I had been very naïve about other people and how relationships worked."
— Andrea

"I always thought of a codependent person being female, and because I was a guy, I never thought the term could apply to me. In addition, I

was independent, had no problem being single, made my own money, had my own house. However, what was me was that I had a pattern of intense and toxic relationships with women. I realized that while I was independent, level-headed, and strong in these other ways, when it came to relationships I had a pattern of falling quick and hard for charming women who were quick to want to make me their whole world. Each time this happened, I felt so loved. But it was more than that, it was like I'd been lost in a hot desert and they were this cold, ice water that I couldn't get enough of. Each time, I always thought that this woman was the one, and each time they'd end up hiding major things from me, lying, cheating, or were just flat-out controlling and dramatic, pretty much threatening that if I didn't make them my whole world, that they'd leave. My last relationship lasted four years, and it four years of an intense emotional rollercoaster, and my friends and I used to joke that I was in an abusive relationship—and actually, knowing what I know now, I was, but at the time I didn't realize it. I think it's because I was a guy, she was a woman, and she never hit me, but the elements of control were there. If I didn't give into her, she would make my life a living hell. I'm embarrassed that I put up with her for as long as I did. I had tried leaving her before, but each time I felt this insane clingy neediness which felt like it was going to destroy me if I couldn't get her back, or at least talk to her. I felt like an addict chasing that next hit. She was all I could think about, and I couldn't imagine my life without her—even though life with her was awful a lot of the time. I started going to CoDA meetings, and realized that I had a very similar pattern with my mother, who left when I was a kid. I'm not blaming her for my behavior, but now I can see where I got this skewed sense of what love and healthy behavior from."

— *Michael*

"I would just like to comment that I still to this day struggle with the label of codependence. I don't "feel" like I fit the label, then I resent it when it is applied.

If anything, I feel like I am more of a pathological optimist. My hope springs eternal from a well deep inside of me. And I cannot explain it any better than that. There simply was no shut off valve for my hopefulness. The ONLY way I ever ended ANY of these relationships was to deliberately and intentionally turn my back on my core being, and that core being is one who is eternally hopeful, and to deliberately and intentionally wrench the valve to the OFF position with all my might, and to force myself to just stop hoping.

It was and remains one of the hardest things I have ever had to do in my life. It went directly against the grain of who I truly am at my core. And it is also because my hopefulness has served me extremely well in my professional life, and in my personal life in almost all of my interactions with most people. Except of course, with the disordered and the destructive. It is my very deep bottomless well of hopefulness that keeps me going, and that keeps me being the solutions oriented person that I am. I don't give up and I don't stop searching for solutions. Ever. That is simply not who I am. It is extremely difficult for me to ever put a puzzle down and to admit there is no solution. I believe so strongly in myself and my problem solving abilities that I simply cannot admit there is no solution.

So to summarize, in my opinion it is dangerous to call a character trait that is generally and usually of tremendous value, and is one that usually brings so much joy, and solutions, and answers, and profit, and beauty, and abundance to one's life, and to make it sound like it is something "bad." This is why I don't like the label codependency.

I am in some strange way evenly matched up to and with the disordered. I am as intent and committed to making the relationship work, as they are to being disruptive, and destructive without concern to me or the relationship. Being determined, or developing what I call, "True Grit" has gotten me far in life, but has been destructive as far as relationships go. I can tolerate an incredible amount of pain if I am doing it to reach a loftier higher goal. I can simply shrug off injuries in order to reach a better final destination, I am easily able to delay gratification to reach a better place. I can wield incredible self-control and rule myself with an iron hand. And I have used these very traits to build a very successful life for myself that is exactly how I want it to be, exactly where I want it to be, and I am as completely and totally independent and free of reliance on anyone else as I possibly can be.

There is with almost every rule, always also an exception to that rule. So I would have to say it like this: In general, a hopeful optimistic nature, and dedication and commitment to being problem solving and solutions oriented is a good character trait, and is one that will serve you well throughout your life. Except in interactions with the destructive and the disordered. In those cases your stubbornness, dedication, hopefulness, optimism, and your commitment to finding solutions will be turned against you, and it will eventually cause you to implode in a most spectacularly devastating and destructive manner.

The reason your true grit won't help is because they are not receptive to solutions and finding solutions goes against their core being. Their goal is: chaos, confusion, disruption, destruction."

— *Luci*

Caring vs. Caretaking

Caring

Acting in a caring way towards someone involves *empowering* them to be their personal best by empowering them to take action that will lead them to become their highest and best self. Caring involves encouraging others to troubleshoot their own problems and to be proactive in seeking solutions. Caring about someone involves setting healthy boundaries, so we aren't jumping in to rescue them, because then it becomes caretaking, and when we are taking care of another otherwise capable adult, that's a problem. It's important that we let them make mistakes and to suffer the natural consequences of their actions if they continue to make poor decisions. This can be really hard to do and a really thin line to walk, but it's important for us to not get in the way of them learning the lessons they need to learn, because pain is the catalyst for growth and change, and self-esteem is built when we overcome adversity.

Caretaking

Taking care of a person in a way that doesn't match their age or ability level is considered rescuing and enabling behavior, because it doesn't allow the person to grow into their personal best. Caretaking involves jumping in and fixing things in order to prevent the other person from suffering the consequences of their actions. It's doing a child's homework for them, it's calling in sick to work for an alcoholic spouse. It's paying an adult child's bills or doing their laundry.

Caretaking behavior tends to come from a well-intended place, but it is damaging to both the caretaker (it can be exhausting and builds resentment). It is also damaging to the one being taken care of because they aren't learning how to figure things out for themselves and handle difficult situations in life.

A caretaking dynamic is an unequal, one-way dynamic that leads to the caretaker feeling angry, resentful, and worn out at having to always be there when the other person needs them, and they are usually the one who is continually focused on trying to fix their partner, or fix the damage to their relationship caused by their partner. Many caretakers feel that taking care of others is a deeply rooted part of their personality, and they have a hard time having friendships and relationships with others that are equal. If this describes you, I highly recommend taking some time to examine the different friendships and relationships you've had in your life to see in what ways you were acting as a caretaker—and to try to slow down that often knee-jerk reaction so many of us have with wanting to jump in and rescue others.

"My ex was an alcoholic, a womanizer, and a thief—stealing tens of thousands of dollars from his company. I continually believed all of his lies, excuses, and fake tears, and made excuses for him. It's to the point now where our adult children want nothing to do with him, and they are angry with me. I guess I can't say I blame them. He's destroyed this family, and I let him, not realizing the damage that was being done, and thinking that my love and support could change him."

— *Sarah*

Fairness vs. Growth

Fairness

Many people who go through abuse of any kind struggle with feelings of anger and rage when the relationship is over—especially when they realize that what they went through was abusive. They often (understandably) feel that what happened to them isn't right or fair, and they want to know when karma is going to come to settle the score so that their abuser suffers as much (or more) than they do. It's hard to watch the abuser move onto their next target and live out this perfect life or seemingly skip through life with no consequences while the target is left with their life and sense of self blown apart.

However, and this is a hard truth to hear, the reality is that life isn't about fairness; life is about growth. And growth is usually sparked by pain that pushes us out of our comfort zone into doing something different. It's important to realize that many people's comfort zones aren't comfortable—especially if they are in or recently out of an abusive relationship. A comfort zone is nothing more than a way we are accustomed to doing something, and a person may be in a comfort zone of depression, anger, isolating themselves; you name it. While watching an abuser suffer some sort of consequences can be satisfying and very validating, this may never happen. What you do have control over is to focus on making what happened to you somehow work for your highest and greatest good. The best way to get revenge or to "win" is to not let what they did destroy you; the best revenge is to dig deep and find your fight, and to decide that you are going to have a great life in spite of what they did to you. This isn't easy, but it is possible. And setting the intention that this isn't going to ruin your life is a big first step.

Growth

To cling to ideas of what we think is fair and how things should be will only cause you pain and it will keep you stuck. This is especially the case involving any kind of trauma. I can understand wanting justice, and wanting to be heard. I can understand wanting them to suffer like how they made you suffer. To feel that way is normal, but please don't let your feelings of rage and anger keep you stuck in wanting them to suffer. There is a lot of growth that can happen in your life because of what you went through. I realize it's growth that you didn't sign up for, but here we are...and what's the other option? To stay angry and pin your happiness on them suffering? No. You've been through enough, and although this may be the hardest thing you'll ever have to, I encourage you to lean into this pain and realize that it has a very important message for you. That message is, "You deserve better." Love doesn't hurt. It's a lack of love that hurts. You are worthy of love, and the best person that can give that to you is you.

All trauma is transformative, and it can either make us or break us, but the good news is we don't have to wait around passively and see how the chips may fall. We can decide that we are not going to let this destroy us; and that instead, we will squeeze out as much personal growth from this as we possibly can. Like I mentioned before, life is not about fairness; it is about growth. And in order to survive under harsh conditions, we must learn to adapt—and if we don't, we will die either physically or emotionally. Now I realize that you might be thinking to yourself that you are a million miles away from thriving. Hell, right now, a good day for you might be getting out of bed or not contemplating suicide. I get it. I've been there. But please know that the pain of this isn't always this intense, it doesn't last forever, and that many of your best days are still ahead of you. And perhaps most importantly, you can overcome this. You don't need to have all of the answers today, but I encourage you to dig your heels in and decide that you are going to take what happened to you and use it towards your highest and greatest good.

Life isn't happening to you, it's happening for you, and this may sound really hippy woo-woo, but I also believe that life, and especially events like these are happening for us as a species. See, on a micro level, pain happens so that we grow from it, and on a macro level, it's happening so that each species evolves. And this might sound really out there, but I fully believe that those of us who have been through an abusive relationship of any kind become a lot more in tune with our intuition. These hard-earned skills that we can dig out from being abused, take a bit to refine, but in time you may come to realize that you are a lot more awake to problematic behavior as well as to your own emotions than other people who haven't gone through something similar. In addition, if you are in a support group, you are probably shocked by how many other people are going through the same things as you. I fully believe that not only is abuse an epidemic that no one seems to really know about, but that it's part of the next stage in human evolution, which is an emotional evolution—one that you are on the leading edge of.

"I really felt like my life was destroyed beyond repair after being involved with a narcissist. It wasn't until I came across some people in a support group talking about how they were able to get so much personal growth out of this experience that I began to get curious. I really felt like my life was blown apart and would never be the same. I've since shifted out of the mindset from being angry that things aren't fair and that I wasn't treated fairly (which is putting it mildly) to squeezing as many personal growth lessons out of this as I possibly could. Although I wouldn't want to repeat what I went through, in many ways I've learned a ton about myself and really feel what happened to me was a big wake up call. I had been going around instantly trusting everyone and taking them at face value—even when my gut instincts were warning me not to. I had no deal breakers and continually gave people chances until they caused me so much harm I couldn't handle it anymore. I thought that's what normal people did, and I think a lot of normal people do, which is why so many of them are living lives of silent desperation. I didn't realize that I was being nice and accommodating to a point that I was continually hurting myself. Today I am so much more in alignment with my feelings and boundaries, and my life is so much smoother today because of that. I feel like I'm seeing things clearly for the first time ever. These experiences we have in life truly are about growth, especially if the other option is to let them destroy us—which is not a good option! I've learned that some of the most intense growth comes from the most intense pain."

— *Marie*

Trauma Bonds vs. Healthy Bonds

Trauma Bonds

Trauma bonds are the result of the good times being really good (the idealization phase), and the bad times being really bad (the devalue or discard phase)—which is what tends to make up the highs and lows of an abusive relationship. This emotional coaster ride is a type of intermittent reinforcement. These trauma bonds are the bonds that are forged between the captive who empathizes with their kidnapper, the prostitute who loves her pimp, the abused spouse who loves their partner, the cult member who defends their cult leader, the hostage who befriends or defends their captor, or the abused or neglected child who defends their abusive parent's behavior.

Five elements are often present during the creation of a trauma bond:

1. There is a one-sided dynamic where one person is controlling and the other is being controlled (but may not realize it).

2. The abusive behavior is sporadic and is characterized by intermittent reinforcement, where the good times are really good, and the bad times are really bad.

3. The target experiences extreme mental distress and confusion (cognitive dissonance) and (at a subconscious level) denies what is going on to themselves in order to convince themselves that the relationship can survive, as well as so they can protect themselves emotionally to avoid an emotional collapse. (Because it's a very hard pill to swallow to realize that their relationship with this person was never real, is never going to be what they need, and that they need to leave. It's hard for any of us to leave a situation when we are getting some of our needs met, especially when we have a high emotional investment in things working out.) During either psychological or physical abuse, disassociation is often present, where the target feels like this isn't happening to them. They might feel as if they are in a movie, or in a state of shock. Disassociating from what's going on allows the target to compartmentalize the abusive aspects of the relationship in order to focus on and stay for the positive aspects. This is done by rationalizing or normalizing what they experienced, which many targets do by telling themselves, "It could always be worse," "No one is perfect," "It's due to their childhood," or "It's partly (or completely) my fault."

4. The more invested (physically, emotionally, financially) a person is in the relationship, the

more driven they will be in order to stay, and in turn, the more driven they will be to defend what they are experiencing. So in order to smooth over the mental distress and resulting confusion they are experiencing from their heart and head not being in alignment, they might tell themselves that they are staying because this is what commitment is all about, and they might further reinforce this belief by becoming more invested in their faith. They might also go to therapy, delve into self-help books, or sign up for a marriage retreat trying to figure out how they can learn to trust again or be a better partner, thinking if they just changed, then the relationship can be saved. (Because if leaving is out of the question, then they are going to have to justify to themselves why they are staying. The easiest way to do that is to make the issue their fault, because at least that way they have some sort of control over things changing— even though this is a false sense of control, because they aren't responsible for their partner's treatment of them.)

5. The worse they are treated, the more they will have to justify to themselves (and to others) why they are staying. They do this by avoiding others who have issues with their significant other, because this contributes to their mental distress (cognitive dissonance). They also will be inclined to surround

themselves with people who support their decisions to stay with an abusive partner, thereby creating a support system full of people with very dysfunctional, damaging, destructive, and potentially deadly beliefs about what commitment is.

While trauma bonds are commonly associated with *extreme* situations involving harm or the threats of harm, to where the person being controlled is attempting to "survive" the situation, however, I'm going to assert that I think *any* type of one-sided unhealthy bond between two people that is forged through *any type* of abuse or exploitation to *any* degree that results in a target defending the person who is using, abusing, exploiting, or neglecting them is a trauma bond. This is a big problem.

In terms of trauma bonds with abusive people, "surviving" this relationship often means having the relationship, friendship, job position, internship, etc. continue, and thinking that things can and will change. During this time, in an effort for the person to keep the relationship going, they often start walking on eggshells, thinking that if they can just change themselves and their behavior that this will have a positive impact on their partner's behavior. Like any other type of intermittent reinforcement, however, sometimes it seems to work and sometimes it doesn't seem to work. This thinking is reinforced if a narcissistic partner has bouts of decent or even ideal behavior, and leads their partner to think that finally things are turning a corner—

only to realize down the road that they are up to the same things again—which leaves them emotionally devastated...again. What the targets of abusive people don't realize (due to all the ongoing manipulation, false promises, lies, blame, or triangulation) is that their partner's behavior has nothing to do with them (even though it really feels like it does). Abusive people are only driven to do what they want, and sometimes that falls in line with what their partner wants and sometimes it doesn't.

Trauma bonds deepen when we gloss over the bad, focus on the good, and then continue to reassure ourselves that everything will be okay (that this relationship can be saved) even though to any sane outsider, things are really bad and we need to get the heck out of there. The thinking for a person who is wrapped up in those trauma bonds is that the relationship or dynamic can work if they can just please their "captors" enough.

In terms of hostage situations, it's common for hostages to start "ingratiating" themselves towards their captors by proving their worth by being quiet, running errands for them, helping to calm down other hostages, or otherwise becoming a part of the same team as their captors. In terms of abusive relationships, it's common for partners of abusive people to start ingratiating themselves by walking on eggshells, being people-pleasing, thinking that if they can just somehow prove their worth, or stay out of the way that their partner will eventually treat them right—or at least will stop physically or verbally abusing them. When crumbs of kindness, attention, or affection are given, the partner reinvests themselves into this team dynamic as an attempt to make things work. They think that things have *finally* turned a corner, and confuse all the pain that the abusive person is putting them through as somehow a positive bonding moment, and something that they can get through as a couple.

These highs and lows are directly related to what's known as "intermittent reinforcement." Intermittent reinforcement is a psychological term that was developed from an experiment involving rats, where the rats were trained to pull a lever in order to get food. At first, their environment was predictable, and there was a direct correlation to their behavior and getting their needs met; pull the lever, get the food. Then the researchers changed the dynamic to where the rats weren't getting the direct reinforcement, but intermittent reinforcement. So sometimes they'd pull the lever, and there would be food, and sometimes there wouldn't be. The rats continued to pull on the lever, much more frequently now, because they weren't sure if they were going to get fed, and they still held onto the hope that their actions could somehow still have some control over their environment.

When people encounter trying to navigate the same type of unpredictable environment, they start trying to pull on that lever to figure out what they need to do in order to be treated with kindness, faithfulness, and honesty. So they may make sure not to confront their partner about them messaging strange people at all hours of the night, or they might not bring up any of their partner's past problematic behavior in an attempt to keep the peace, or they may get into really great shape in order to try and keep their partner faithful. And these attempts might seem to work for a while…until they find that their partner is cheating, lying, "siphoning" funds, yelling, name calling, or hitting them again.

In an abusive relationship, trauma bonds are forged through the good times that often involve attention and affection and then are reinforced through the bad times which involve abuse, fear, neglect or terror. The effect that a trauma bond has on a person is the feeling of this "us against them" dynamic where it's the abusive person and their partner against the world—and in their partner's eyes they've "been through so much together" when in fact, they've really been put through so much by their partner.

My guess would be that most people who find themselves in a one-sided marriage or relationship oftentimes tend to have similar types of trauma bonds with other people in their life—most likely their parents, friends, and many of the other significant relationships in their lives. Trauma bonds in motion tend to come across as, "I love you, I'll do whatever needs to be done so that you stop hurting me, just please don't leave me…we can get through this." This is toxic and dysfunctional thinking at its worst.

Let me stop for a moment and address the difference (as I see it) between trauma bonds and codependency, because not everyone in an abusive relationship is codependent. The way I see it, the difference between trauma bonds and codependency is that trauma bonds can be forged during a one-time event (for example, if they were held hostage in a bank robbery, or got caught up in an online dating scam). However, the distinction here is "one-time event." If the person *in any other* situation with friends, family, and significant others has healthy boundaries, then there aren't codependency issues present. However, if there is a long-standing pattern of being bonded to hurtful people, or a series of one-sided friendships, work dynamics, familial relationships, and relationships with significant others, then this is a red flag that there is some codependency going on.

Many people who struggle with codependency also struggle with knowing what healthy bonds (aka relationships) are, and what healthy boundaries are. They have usually lived a life where they are used to settling for crumbs from others—crumbs of kindness, affection, attention, and often crumbs of loyalty, honesty, and being treated with dignity and respect from their partner, because somewhere along the line they realized that in order to get attention and affection they had to earn it, or they had to put everyone else ahead of themselves.

And because it can be really hard for any one of us to see our own issues, many people don't realize that they have issues with boundaries, codependency, or trauma bonds as they've been this way as long as they can remember. It's like the saying goes, "The last thing the fish notices is the water." Please know you are not to blame for what happened. Most normal, decent people tend to think that other people have the same morals and values as they do, and because of this they take others for face value. Healthy boundaries, what manipulative and abusive behavior is, and paying attention to our gut instincts are things that very few of us are taught. And once you realize what's going on, odds are you'll start working to get more in alignment with what is healthy for you—and you'll be shocked by how fast your life starts to change for the better.

Signs that you are trauma bonded to someone:

1. You believe in commitment at all cost and think that being treated poorly isn't a reason to leave. You don't have deal-breaker behavior. You consider everything to be workable—even lying, cheating, stealing/siphoning household funds, active (and destructive) addictions, or abuse of any kind. The more you go through, the more you feel that this speaks to your level of commitment. If others see a problem with you staying, you tell yourself that they just don't value commitment like you do, or that they are jealous that you've been able to make things work. You realize that you are sinking yourself in order to save them, or in order to keep the relationship afloat, but this doesn't seem problematic—it seems compassionate and the right thing to do…even if doing so feels like it's slowly killing you.

2. You minimize or deny what's going on. If you tell your friends and family how your significant other speaks and behaves toward you, or that you caught them lying, cheating, stealing, etc., they are concerned for you. Yet you think this is just how you fight—or that *they* aren't the problem—it's the other woman (or man) that's the problem, or their childhood, or their addictions, or their anger issues, or that they just don't know how to communicate—or that you are somehow the problem. They've done worse in the past. That if only you could get through to them, or if only given enough time, understanding, patience, rehab, therapy, or religion that they could change into being a good partner.

2. Things never change for long. You have repetitive fights about the same thing, over and over, and no one ever wins; there's never any insight. If you do feel that you "got somewhere" with the fight, that's all wiped out when you have the same fight about the same thing again— probably the next day.

3. You defend their behavior, and distance yourself from people who have a problem with your relationship or your partner. When something major does surface, you find yourself complaining to others about what they did this time, but as soon as they get upset, you backpedal and are quick to justify and minimize their behavior. After all, you don't want to leave—you just want them to quit lying, cheating, stealing, manipulating, and otherwise treating you so poorly.

4. You feel addicted to them. Everything in your mind tells you to leave them, but the thought makes you feel panicky—really, really panicky. If you do stop talking to them for a few days or weeks, you find yourself "craving" them and wanting to do whatever it takes, or wishing that they'd offer up any crumbs of an attempt to get you back so that this relationship can continue.

5. You keep holding out hope that this time things will be different. You often feel like Charlie Brown, who repeatedly kicks the football that Lucy holds, only to have her pull it out at the last minute. The idea that THIS TIME he won't pull the football continues to have power despite his *always* pulling the football and you *always* landing on your back.

6. Walking on eggshells. You keep trying to convert your spouse into someone who treats you right, convince him to behave differently, or prove yourself to him. You think if only you can prove yourself, everything will be different. You try to get him to understand that what he does/says is hurtful to you. If only he would understand!

7. You don't like your significant other. You might feel like you love them, or even that they are your soul mate, but you don't like or respect them, and you are embarrassed and ashamed of their behavior and of how they treat you and your children.

8. You'd be upset if you found out your child, friend, or sibling was dating someone like them. Although you can't leave your spouse and even say you don't want to, you'd be horrified if your child brought home a new partner and declared they were just like your significant other.

9. You feel confused, devastated, angry, and exhausted. You want to leave because they treat you with such a lack of respect and dignity, but you also don't want to because you feel they are your soul mate. You are angry with them but feel guilty for leaving. You feel like you give and give but it's never enough. You wish you knew what it took to get through to them or to make them value this relationship for good. You can't tell if this relationship is a fairy tale or a total nightmare.

Healthy Bonds

Healthy bonds develop between two people over time as two people go through the highs and lows of life together. Healthy bonds are based on mutual trust, support, dignity, and respect, and include open, honest, sincere, and solutions-oriented communication and behavior. Healthy bonds are formed when both individuals are able to get their wants and needs met both by themselves and within the relationship or dynamic. There is a feeling of certainty, clarity, and calm around the other person, because appropriate trust has been established and maintained. There is a feeling of deep appreciation and admiration for the other person. There is no hidden selfish agenda or behavior. There is no using, abusing, or exploiting the other person. There is no manipulating another person's emotions in order to keep them around. There is no being dragged through hell hoping that someday the other person will treat them right. There is no hiding their partner's mistreatment of them or their relationship from others because they are embarrassed by how they are being treated. There is no "I love you, but I hate you."

"I was married to a man who lied, cheated, and manipulated me since the day we first met. Of course, it took me over ten years to realize this and another five years to really, fully end that relationship and to stop getting sucked in by more of his lies and false promises. I kept thinking that if he said he was sorry that I owed him another chance. I dropped domestic violence charges on him multiple times

because I felt sorry for him. It took me years to realize he was just saying and doing whatever he needed to say and do in order to keep me around. And what's so sick and sad is I somehow thought all these highs and lows, and all the other women, the abuse, the lies and him continuing to come back to me somehow meant that he must have really loved me. Wrong! It was just that I was the one who was the biggest sucker for his lies. Now that I see it clearly, I realize that feeling jealous, insecure, distrusting, angry, depressed, anxious, needy, and full of rage isn't what love is about. I can't believe I ever thought that feeling emotionally tormented or blown apart was even in the same ballpark as love. That's not love; it's trauma bonds."

— *Susan*

Someone Who is a Friend vs. Someone Being Friendly

Someone Who is a Friend

The word "friend" tends to be one of those catch-all words that refers more to someone who is friendly. However, just because a person is friendly, doesn't mean that they are a friend; it simply means they are being friendly. Just because a person is friendly, doesn't mean that you have enough in common with them to work towards building a friendship with them—*and it also doesn't mean that they have friendly intentions.*

For many of us, the word "friend" starts being misused in childhood. It's common for many parents to ask their child after their first day of school if they made any new friends, or a child may refer to anyone who was friendly towards them as a friend. As children get older, they often continue this thinking that anyone who is friendly is a friend, or that they feel guilty or obligated to be friends with people who are friendly towards them—*even if that person is hurtful to them.*

It's very important to be able to distinguish the difference between a friendly person, an acquaintance, a friend, and an enemy.

A friendly person is someone who is friendly. You may or may not know them or have anything in common with them. They may or may not have good intentions. All you know about them is that they are friendly. You can be friendly back—if you feel comfortable with that, but if you aren't comfortable with them for any reason, it's also okay to distance yourself from them.

An acquaintance is not a friend, and they may or may not be friendly. They are simply someone you are acquainted with. Most acquaintances tend to be someone that you know on a more surface level, such as a neighbor, a coworker, or a great-aunt. The level of sharing is usually kept at a minimal level, and the conversation usually stays at a pleasant and polite level, or what I like to think of as "dinner party manners."

The next level of an acquaintance might be a "work friend" or a "school friend" where the level of sharing and time spend is greater than that of an acquaintance but not to the level of depth of a friend. You might find yourself talking about your relationships or personal health issues but mainly because you spend a lot of time with this person and feel relatively safe in opening up around them. They might be someone you'd invite over for your child's graduation party, but they aren't someone you'd go on vacation with.

A friend is someone who is kind, compassionate, considerate, and who has your best interest in mind. A friend is someone who has consistent actions over time that show that they are trustworthy, and someone you feel safe being emotionally vulnerable with. A friend is someone that you enjoy being around, and someone who is there for you, and who can celebrate your successes in life, as well as be there to support you through the down times. Friendship is a state of mutual trust and support between two people. If that's not there, then it's not a friendship, and if you are the one who continues to give trust and support when they don't do the same, you will forever experience hurt and heartache by the imbalance. There is a history of mutual trust and support between the two of you.

Friends are people that are in your inner circle, and it's really important to make sure that you *only* have people that have your best interest in mind in your inner circle. Once you make the shift to having people in your inner circle *based on how they treat you, instead of how you feel about them,* your life will radically begin to change, as you are now seeing things clearly. As it really doesn't matter if you love them, or if you feel guilty for not continually being there for them, or obligated to stay in touch because they are a parent, or because you've known them since high school or fearful of what others might think. If they have a pattern of being hurtful or harmful to you, or the dynamic is one-sided, you might as well let go of it, *because there's nothing there anyhow.*

Someone Who is Being Friendly

One of the biggest tools in an abuser's tool kit is charm. Many highly problematic people out there tend to come across as friendly, and their friendly behavior is how they get people (both children and adults) to lower their guard so that they can use, abuse, or exploit them.

A friend is *not* someone who actively controls, uses, abuses, or exploits you in any way—or has a history of treating you this way. A friend is *not* someone who gossips about you, sabotages, undermines, grinds you down, has behavior that leaves you doubting your sanity, or feeling like they are toxic or an energy vampire. Friends don't cause intentional hurt or harm to each other, and they for sure don't treat each other with disdain, aggression, hostility, or contempt. Friends don't tease you about things you are sensitive about, put you down, pressure you into having sex with them (or spend time with you hoping that if they are nice enough to you for a long enough period of time that you will break down and have sex with them). Friends don't send each other sexy pictures, or secretly hope for a relationship with the other person. Friends also don't run hot and cold to where they are really nice and fun to be around some of the time and then other times are cruel or rude.

It's also worth noting that narcissists are notorious for having a harem of former, current, and future sex partners around them—whether they message these people online, or actually see them in person. They often claim that these people are "friends" and spin their outrageous flirtatious and inappropriate behavior to blame their partner for being jealous and insecure. It's not jealous or insecure if you have an issue with your partner messaging sexy "friends" for prolonged periods of time—especially if they are hiding their phone, not wanting to message that other person in front of you, not wanting you to meet these other people, or are willing to end your relationship because you aren't okay with their "friendship" with this person. *This is not what friendship looks like; it's what cheating looks like,* and frankly, you'd be better off figuring out how to leave them instead of arguing with them trying to get them to see how outrageous and inappropriate their behavior is because they know it's wrong. They just don't want to stop or to be bothered about it. Make no mistake, if you were to act in the same way, they'd be mad as hell.

An enemy is someone who not only doesn't have your best interest in mind, but who is also actively working against you. Enemies use, abuse, exploit, manipulate, lie, deceive, steal, create chaos, and undermine you in whatever way they want to in order to get their needs met. Enemies can often come across as friendly, but don't mistake an enemy being friendly as them having changed, or as them being a friend. Like the saying goes, don't mistake an enemy's smile for them baring their teeth. If someone has a hidden agenda, or is abusive or cruel towards you—they are not your friend, they are an enemy and someone you should steer clear of as much as possible. …It can feel harsh referring to someone as an enemy, and by all means you don't need to refer to them as such if you aren't comfortable doing so. What's important here is that you understand the difference between a friend and an enemy, so you don't get guilted back into being friends with someone who acts friendly but whose actions are intended to harm you. These "frenemies" are some of the most destructive people out there, because they'll cause a ton of damage in your life and pretend to care about you the whole time.

"Learning what a friend really is was such an aha moment for me. Before, I was always friends with people because we had certain things in common, or because they were friendly or funny or what have you, and I kept finding myself in friendships that either fizzled out or those friends turned abusive, or that they weren't there when I needed them. I realized that there was never that state of mutual trust and support; it was always one-sided, and that I had this pattern of

rescuing people—friends, family members, total strangers, men I dated, you name it. I was always there to listen to them when they had issues, but they were never there for me. What's interesting is that I've since realized that my healthier friends felt the same way about me! That I would only call them if I was single or in crisis. Now that I realize how out of balance my life was, I've made some major steps to get things more in balance. I no longer make the man I'm dating my whole life and no longer put my friendships and hobbies on the back burner. I make sure to keep my real friendships and hobbies going, and my life is so much better."

— *Pauline*

Respecting vs. Respectfully

Respecting

True respect is a deep state of appreciation and admiration that's *earned* over time. Not everyone out there is deserving of our respect, especially if they behave in a morally reprehensible way.

Respectfully

Treating a person respectfully is the basis of pleasant and polite interaction and is usually how people with manners treat others. It's also the basis of what most people would consider the foundation of appropriate interaction with another person and a basic human right. Even the laws for murderers and child molesters abide by the concepts that they will not be treated in ways that are cruel or unusual. There is the expectation that no matter how vile a person's behavior is, that as a society, they will be given basic rights. They have the right to food, clothing, shelter, safety, and being treated with dignity and respect. So while we don't respect their behavior, or even them, they do have the right to basic human rights, simply because they are living beings.

Abusive people will often tell their targets that they treat them abusively because the target isn't worthy of being treated respectfully, because the target hasn't earned it. This is the typical abuser's mentality, and please don't get caught up in thinking that you need to somehow earn the right to be treated like a human being.

I also want to clarify something, because I could see how an abuser could twist this concept into insisting that the target reopens contact, or is somehow obligated to keep them in their life, and if they don't then the target is treating them with a lack of dignity and respect. Please know that you are not obligated to keep a toxic person in your life, and that you setting these boundaries is not you being disrespectful to them—you doing so is self-protective and a reasonable consequence to their actions, and is you treating yourself with dignity and respect.

If you are in a relationship, friendship, or any other dynamic that is costing you your dignity and self-respect to stay in it, you are in an abusive relationship.

"My ex-husband used to always tell me that he treated me the way he did because respect was something that was earned, and that I hadn't earned it. And instead of divorcing him (which is what I wish I would have done sooner) I kept trying to prove to him that I was worthy of being treated respectfully. I realize now that treating another person respectfully is how normal, decent people treat each other— and that isn't something that needs to be earned. Having respect for someone is something that needs to be earned, but that's not required in order to treat someone respectfully. I will never again tolerate being ground down or treated with such disrespect, and I've made damn sure that my children understand that how they were treated wasn't okay either, and for them to not tolerate or justify ever being treated like that by someone, let alone their spouse."

— *Molly*

A Parent vs. A Predator

A Parent

Anyone who is fertile can have a child. It's not a crowning achievement to have a baby or to get someone pregnant; it's a biological function. Where the crowning achievement part comes in is the parenting skills after the birth of the baby happens.

For many people, their true parent is the same as their biological parent, but this isn't always the case, and I think it's important to separate out these concepts. A true parent is someone who actually does the job of raising, nurturing, taking care of, and loving a child. A biological parent is one that brought the child into the world. They may or may not play an active part in that child's life. Many times outsiders will insist that a child go the extra mile to keep communication open with a parent who completely abandoned them, or who they do know but who has made little to no effort to be in their life because they think, "Well, but that person is your mother or father." Just because a person has a child doesn't make them a parent; it's their parenting of that child that makes them a parent. Many times children who have been adopted feel a driving need to find their "real" parents, oftentimes much to the hurt and heartache of their adoptive parents who actually raised them. It's one thing for a person to want to find their "bio parent" but it's another to totally discount the job that adoptive parents did and to think of it in terms of them just being long-term baby sitters—especially if they were loving parents. The same goes for children who seek out their "real" father or mother after a step-parent has raised them. There is a difference between a biological parent and the one who does the job, and it's important to see this difference so people aren't inadvertently pushing people into staying in contact with an abusive parent out of guilt or obligation, as doing so only sets up the target of abuse for further abuse.

A Predator

Many abusive parents are either not involved in their child's life, or if they are involved it's only so they can use, abuse, and exploit them. There are many children out there who have been used, abused, exploited, and neglected by these predators, and yet still keep in regular contact with them because they are holding onto the hope that this predator can become the parent that they always wanted or needed. It's hard to give up this hope and to see these kinds of hurtful actions clearly. ...I once asked an abusive person why he thought target's kept going back. His answer was that "hope dies last." Predators rely on their targets continually forgiveness. They exploit their target's hope, love, guilt, and sympathy. I know it's hard to give up the fantasy of having a loving relationship with an abusive or neglectful parent, but it will be harder in the long run to continue to live in denial of what's really going on. Parents don't steal your identity and rack up debt; predators do. Parents don't molest their children; predators do. Parents don't put their children in harm's way (such as making them sick) in order to get attention; predators do. Parents don't use, abuse, or exploit their children in order to get their own self-esteem needs met; predators do.

"My father molested both me and my younger brother growing up, and all the adults in our lives ignored it. I cut off contact with my father the moment I moved out of that house, but my brother still not only talks to him, but has his kids around him on a regular basis. I don't know what's wrong with my brother and why he's risking his children this way when he knows what our father is like. Actually, I do know why he does this. It's because our whole life we were pushed

into thinking that we needed to forgive him, and that he was our father so we should have him in our lives unconditionally. Sick, sick, sick. And I've gotten to the point where anyone who defends my father's actions is cut out of my life too. I don't know how people justify the actions of a child molester or why they'd have them around their children. A parent doesn't target a child like that, but a predator does."

— *Scott*

Wanting a Person in Your Life vs. Needing a Person in Your Life

Wanting a Person in Your Life

Wanting a person in our life is where we are being choosy about who we let into our inner circle, based on how they treat us and the positive emotions we feel when we are around them. The people in a healthy inner circle are those who are empowering, encouraging, and have our best interests in mind. There is open, honest, sincere, and solutions-oriented communication, and they love and accept us for who we are. These kinds of people enhance our life, and if we are in their inner circle too, then the benefit to them would be the same. Being choosy about people you let into your life and especially into your inner circle is what an abundance mindset looks like in motion. It's making the shift from hoping to be chosen by someone and that they will like us, to realizing that there are a lot of great people on this planet, and realizing that having great people in our life is something that we can have too. When we make this mindset shift, we stop making other people our whole life, and instead build up a life we love, and make other people the candles on the cake—instead of making them the whole cake. And because this other person isn't our whole life, if they start mistreating us, then we are able to either address it, reset boundaries, or walk away (even though it still hurts like hell). We aren't in a state of desperation trying to keep a toxic relationship or friendship afloat, because we've raised our standards and expectations for how we are to be treated.

Needing a Person in Your Life

Needing a person in your life is making the other person "the whole cake." Needing other people is a sign of scarcity (and often codependent) thinking. This is the kind of thinking that often comes from being lonely or being afraid of being alone and thinking that we need another person to feel complete. If a person is continually clinging to people in an effort to not be alone, then odds are they aren't being choosey enough about who they are clinging to. And the irony is that if they are clinging to a person, regardless of how that person treats them in an attempt to stave off being alone, they will usually find themselves continually hurt, abandoned, and alone, because they are clinging to either all the wrong people, or needing too much from all the right people—which pushes all the right people away.

Needing someone is the equivalent of "you complete me," which feeds into the destructive and disempowering mentality that it takes two halves to equal a whole. In reality, when two incomplete people come together hoping that the other one will complete them, what happens is that they join into a codependent relationship and cling to each other out of a dysfunctional blend of clinging (fear of being alone), caretaking (enabling), and controlling (trying to fix the other person so that the other person will treat them loving)—because they don't know how to treat themselves with love.

If a person is relying on someone else to *make* them feel loved, safe, or secure, then if that person leaves or starts to become abusive, they will have a hard time leaving because there is no solid sense of "them" that can readily leave or move forward. This isn't to say that having needs or expectations of your partner is somehow wrong or bad. It's not. It's okay and normal to have needs, and for you to try to get these needs met. However, this becomes a problem if we get tangled up with a person (or people) who continually try to use guilt or shame into making us think that wanting anything more than their crumbs of kindness, loyalty, attention, or affection is somehow us asking too much.

A healthy relationship is one where two people are already whole, know how to meet their own needs, consciously choose the other person to be in their life because of who that person is and the emotional value they bring into the relationship.

"I had always gone through life feeling unloved and unimportant. I was quick to cling onto anyone who showed any crumbs of kindness towards me, and the vast majority of the time those people turned out to be abusive. I now don't look to others for approval or love; I've learned how to love myself. And I now love myself enough to walk away from the wrong people instead of clinging to them hoping they'd change because I needed them to love me or because I needed a friend."
— *Sandra*

"I did NOT feel loved, safe, or secure. Since all of my toxic relationships were very long term, (father, sister, brothers, long term boyfriend) once I began to awaken from the fog, and to experience this awareness of not feeling loved, safe and secure, I began to try to set boundaries in effort to save these relationships. My boundaries were promptly annihilated, smashed through, or ignored. And to request better treatment when my trust was broken, or when I felt unfairly or abusively treated was where the REAL games and the REAL pain began. My CPTSD flashbacks were almost constant. All of these problematic people were masters of telling me that it was my expectations that were the problem, and that I was trying to control them, and that I simply had to accept them as they were: warts and all. And the abuse continued to escalate with each boundary I set and with each request for better treatment I made.

Anyway my point is, and I have been struggling with this concept myself lately, and I've been trying to come to grips and to terms with the idea that: It is OKAY if I have needs. It is NORMAL to have needs. And there is nothing wrong with NEEDING to feel safe, secure and loved. What is not okay is to try to get those needs met with someone who is INCAPABLE of meeting those needs. That's the real problem in my opinion. Needs are normal, but we have to find the right people when we try to get our needs met. We have to find people who deserve our trust, and who can be relied upon to treat us with love, and who actually want us to feel safe and secure—and not just when it's convenient for them. And we have to learn to set boundaries with them, or walk away once we realize that they are incapable of treating us with the dignity and respect that we deserve."

— *Luci*

Problematic Behavior vs. A Personality Disorder

Problematic Behavior

Problematic behavior is usually viewed as any type of behavior that defies social and/or legal standards of conduct. This kind of behavior may be problematic in the sense that it creates interpersonal issues, or it could be severe, and they could have legal issues because of it. Any degree of problematic behavior can cause (at a minimum) major disruption, dysfunction, and destruction in a person's life and in the lives of those around them (whether the person with problematic behavior realizes it or not).

Many people who are in "problematic" or abusive relationships struggle with trying to get clarity as to what they are experiencing. If and when they come across the concept of a "personality disorder" it's very common (and understandable) for them to then want clarity as to whether or not this person "just" has a bunch of problematic behavior or if this person does indeed have a personality disorder. If they do have a personality disorder, they often (again, understandably) want to know which one they have and if there is any type of treatment for it, and so they agonize over trying to figure out if this person perhaps has Borderline Personality Disorder, Narcissistic Personality Disorder, Antisocial Personality Disorder, or what. However, keep in mind that a person doesn't have to have a full-out personality disorder to cause a tremendous amount of stress, chaos, damage, and disruption in your life.

"Fleas"

The term "fleas" is a slang term for problematic behavior that is "picked up" in an environment "infested" with dysfunction. It's very common for people who have been in a relationship with a narcissistic person (especially for several years or more) to start to see problematic behavior within themselves—and for them to become terrified by this realization. They might wonder if narcissism is contagious, or if they've become a narcissist. If this describes some of your fear about your own behavior, please know that you can get rid of your "fleas," and that your problematic behaviors can be changed, if you have the awareness that there is a problem, the desire to change it, and take action to behave differently.

If we come from a dysfunctional home or relationship (which estimates are around 85% of us do—and frankly, I think it's higher than that), then odds are we have some problematic behavior that we either learned from our parents or that we developed as a defense or a coping strategy being around an abuser.

In addition, it's very common for an abuser to accuse their target of being a narcissist if they stand up for themselves, try to set a boundary, have a problem with how they are being treated, or question a narcissist in any way.

Personality Disorder

According to the Mayo clinic, a personality disorder is defined as "a type of mental disorder in which a person has a rigid and unhealthy pattern of thinking, functioning, and behaving, and has trouble perceiving and relating to situations and people." Generally, personality disorders are apparent by the time a person reaches adolescence and causes a person difficulties in personal relationships as well as how they function in society.

What makes a person with a personality disorder so difficult to change isn't so much that they have problematic behavior (because we all do to some extent); *it's the degree, frequency, and their ability (or desire) to change that's the problem.*

The challenge with getting absolute clarity as to whether or not a person has a personality disorder is that most people with manipulative and abusive behavior don't often want to go to therapy (they don't think they have a problem—or they think their partner has the problem). And if are especially manipulative, and they do go to therapy, there is a very high chance that they can and will manipulate the clinician into thinking either they don't have a problem or that their partner does. In addition, please realize that a person could go to a handful of different clinicians and get a handful of different diagnoses. This isn't to say that any of these diagnoses are necessarily inaccurate or that the clinicians were necessarily manipulated; it's that a lot of symptoms and diagnoses overlap, and it means that the diagnosis given is largely a combination based on the clinician's experience diagnosing personality disorders, as well as the behavior that they saw from that person at that time.

But frankly, I think trying to sort out problematic behavior from personality-disordered behavior is losing sight of the bigger picture. Meaning, if a person in your life has behavior that is problematic *for you,* then it's a problem, and you don't need to stick around and spend time with someone who drains your energy or who is hurtful or harmful.

This is where having a clear idea of what your deal breakers are, and also being clear about how long you are willing to stay and what kinds of changes you'd need to see happen in order for you to stay, are important. If leaving is not an option, for whatever reason, then I'd encourage you to redirect your energy from trying to get them to change to focusing on how you can make your life as tolerable (ideally enjoyable) as possible with them in it. Because to spend your life trying to get them to change, will only exhaust you and annoy them.

The following comes from Luci, a co-leader of our book club, friend, and valued member of the support group, who so perfectly sums up her experience with this:

"If you have a problem with anything at all that they are doing, and you point it out, you are told that YOU are the narcissist. Now they may not use that word, and you may not know that word, or the concept, or the DSM description, but whenever they behave in ways that you find triggering, rude, uncompassionate, non-empathetic, cruel, judgmental, attacking, predatory, or anything less than a normal humanitarian, mature, adult manner, and you point it out and ask for better, you are promptly reattacked and are drowned in a deluge of justifications for their behavior. They might blame you, and accuse *you* of having caused them to behave in this manner in the first place, and that their actions are simply defensive actions that they are taking to protect themselves from *you*. In addition, you learn quickly either through their rage or their silent treatment, that you have NO RIGHT to call them on ANY of their behavior ever. You are told that you are selfish, self-centered, self-serving, want too much, expect too much, are delusional, unrealistic, self-seeking, self-aggrandizing, and just plain full of yourself about what sort of behavior you deserve and how you deserve to be treated…and that you haven't earned the right to be treated with respect.

In short you are made to feel that you are selfish, grasping, greedy, entitled, self-serving, self-centered, boundary-busting, uncharitable, unchristian, unreasonable, unforgiving, wrong, crazy, bad, weak, too needy, and you are in fact asking them to become superhuman, asking for too much, and more than a human can bear, to ask them to make ANY change in their behavior at all.

The very fact that you even ask for ANY behavior at all to stop makes them turn on you, and what you receive back is entirely and completely disproportional to the request made. But in their mind there is not a shred of doubt: YOU are the one who is and has The Problem.

You may have asked for one thing: you may have said, it is not okay to yell at me. And in response you get a dissertation on how and why you made them yell at you and how awful, horrible, and selfish you are to ask them to change anything about themselves, because, after all, in their mind, it's all your fault they had to yell at you in the first place. If you hadn't forgotten to buy milk, they wouldn't have had to yell at you. If you hadn't worn so much make up, they wouldn't have called you a whore and accused you of cheating. If you had only been home more, lost weight, dressed sexier they wouldn't have cheated. If you had only made chicken salad for dinner instead of pizza they wouldn't have beaten you because you made the house too hot by using the oven.

In response to your single and simple request for them to not yell, call you names, or hit, they start World War III in retaliation for you making any request at all for them to change. And over time you begin to think that you really are the problem, and if you could just do or be better that they would stop abusing you. But it never stops. Because their abuse isn't caused by you, and it can't be stopped by you. It's a reflection of them and their pathologically distorted mindset.

And while all this is going on, your boundaries have been eroded and washed away without you even realizing what and how it is happening. Now you begin to wonder if you are the narcissist. Even if you do not know the word, over time you begin to feel and to be convinced that you are the problem, you the person who is expecting too much, you are the selfish and self-centered one.

You are so BUSY sorting through their response to you that contains a million elements, a million moving parts, and all of the accusations that are leveled at you, that your mind simply becomes so confused, that you lose sight of the original subject. Your mind does not have the ability or the capability of sorting through all of these accusations that are leveled against you, and evaluating their veracity or truthfulness, or the accuracy of these accusations, so you completely lose your ability to get back to the original subject of what caused you to raise this issue in the first place.

You become engrossed and enmeshed and mired in sorting out answers to questions like: Am I too demanding? Do I expect too much? Was I being uncharitable? Am I too judgmental? Was I being selfish? Am I being controlling? What rights do I really have? What do I deserve?

Then next you get lost in rationalizing their incomprehensible, response to you. The response given to your simple request that was then rebutted and retorted to with World War III proportional tactics. And BECAUSE of the extreme depth and breadth and level details within the response you receive, just the fact that it is so very, very detailed, then it appears at first glance to be something well thought out, so you in turn begin to think: Maybe I am being too hard on them. Maybe I am asking for too much. Maybe they cannot control themselves as well as I can. Maybe they don't understand because they have never had children. Maybe they've had too much to drink. Maybe they had a bad childhood. Maybe they have been abused, maybe, Maybe, MAYBE... A million maybe reasons, possibilities and potential "reasons" float up into your mind and it is at this point that you totally lose the battle.

I have heard this scenario referred to as doing mental gymnastics when dealing with one of these characters, and that feels like a very, very accurate description. You end up having to do mental gymnastics in order to try to keep up with:

- Their astounding chutzpah, bravado and entitlement at exhibiting the bad behavior in the first place.

- The mental fortitude you summon to make your original protest to the human rights violation that just occurred, when you try to set the boundary that it is not okay to yell at me, or I don't take orders, I don't date cheaters, It is not okay to steal from me, it is not okay to lie to me...

- The dizziness and confusion that ensues when their response deluges you and sucks you under like being overwhelmed by a tidal wave with its sheer volume and level of details and explanations and rationalizations for how and why you caused them to behave and to speak or act towards you in this manner in the first place.

- Your own sense of guilt and responsibility that arises based on the return volley and level of details given as your very sense of justice and fairness starts to bob and weave about, and is tossed upon the waves, and then you begin to backtrack and start to question your own experience and your own expectations, and begin to try rationalize their unacceptable behavior.

- The stabbing concern and sense of responsibility you feel when told with confidence and assertion and with no uncertainty or wavering at all, and like it is a well-known, widely known and accepted fact that you are the root cause of all of the problems that you are experiencing between the two of you.

- Often this will be followed up with assertions that many others, many unnamed others, have also experienced this same exact phenomena within their interactions with you, and that it is a deep and abiding cause for concern, and that possibly mental health assistance could be helpful to you in seeing your own HUGE contribution to this dilemma. There is an assertion made with great bravado and with great confidence that it is very distressing to them that you cannot see and grasp and know how in reality it is YOU who are causing and are the root cause of all of these conflicts and YOU are the reason and the root cause and responsible for all of their bad behavior.

- If very lucky you MIGHT get an admission from them of something like: yes I should not have screamed, cheated, lied, or stolen from you. But I just want you to know that you caused it. That you need to work harder on your personal interaction skills because make no mistake about it you are the one who is pushing me beyond my tolerance levels and making me lose my cool and making me act this way.

If this is your experience, I want to make it absolutely 100% clear, this is NOT how a mature, emotionally healthy adult responds to a request for better treatment, better behavior, or a request for a halt or stop to destructive, damaging, unproductive behavior. EVER.

This may indeed be your normal experience with them and with how they fight, but this isn't healthy or even workable. This is what crazymaking behavior looks like in motion.

But make no mistake about it: This is the farthest thing away from healthy and normal as one can possibly get. Repeat, this type of behavior is about as far away from normal and healthy behavior as one can ever possibly get. EVER.

And I can prove it right here, right now very, very simply and very, very easily. I can prove who is the perpetrator, who is the narcissist, who is the instigator, who is the aggressor, who is the predator, and who is the prey, who is the victim, who is the target, and who is the scapegoat.

If I come to you and I say to you one of two things: If I say to you:

1. When you yell at me I feel hurt and scared and I feel like you don't care about me. What is your response? What do you DO with this information? How do you use it? Do you stop yelling, apologize and do your very best to do better? Do you vow to consistently do better and to stop yelling moving forward? Or do you attack even harder and start justifying your yelling and try to beat your "opponent" into the ground and try to convince them that they caused you to yell at them in the first place? Or do you make and give a lip service only, surface level shallow apology, but secretly store the information up in your mind as a weapon to be used against them in the future? Do you store up and save the fact that yelling at them makes them feel hurt and scared and unloved, and do you save it up, not as reminder to yourself to be careful and to not hurt them, but rather the opposite, store it up and save it in a weapons arsenal, as an excellent and valuable tool and weapon to be used at a later date for power and control over them?

Or

2.   If we are talking and I say: It is not okay to yell at me, I will talk to you but it is not okay to yell at me. (Or, it is not okay to lie to me. It is not okay to steal from me. It is not okay to attack me in front of my friends. It is not okay to put me down. It is not okay to mock me. It is not okay to give me orders, etc.) What is your response?

Do you deny that you yelled and rationalize it and blame me, and tell me that I am responsible for you yelling at me, and do you tell me I caused you to yell, and in fact forced you to have no choice except to yell? Or do you take responsibility for yelling and agree it was wrong to yell and stop yelling? Do you accuse me of trying to control you, and tell me I am bad person for trying to control you? Do you tell me I have no right to tell you how to act?

In both cases, your response is most likely: Please, tell me exactly what I am doing wrong. I care about you. I cannot stand for you to feel that way. I feel so bad. Please tell me what I can do and how I can change to make you feel better. I want you to feel safe and happy around me, and it breaks my heart that I have hurt you. Let's work this out together, and I promise I am going to work very hard to not make you feel this way anymore. This is what being solutions-oriented and working as a team looks like in motion.

So I think that we FEEL like we are the narcissist because they tell us that we are being uppity, and getting too big for our britches, when we ask for fair and decent respectful treatment from them.

This is a theme from my childhood, requests for fair and decent treatment are met with responses that we are being selfish, controlling and narcissistic. We are told that we believe we are better than we are. We are told that we are asking for better treatment than we deserve. We are told we have to earn the right to decent respectful fair treatment. And that we are not there yet and must just try harder.

And harder we try, because we are STILL making them blow their cork, and we are making them slap, hit, yell, shove, scream, attack, mock, insult, belittle and hurt. So they "know" for a fact that we don't deserve better treatment yet, because WE are STILL forcing THEM to behave badly, and that is how they KNOW for a fact that we don't deserve decent kind respectful treatment. *And that is CRAZY talk.*

But if you try to remain and try to continue to listen to it, you will end up losing your sanity, and you will come to believe that you are in fact worthless, and crazy. This is what life is like with a narcissist or a sociopath/psychopath."

"When I first came across the term 'sociopath' I realized that was my ex. I then spent a lot of time trying to figure out what the other

toxic people in my life were—if they were sociopaths or if they were 'just' lying, cheating, rude, and so on. I've since realized that I don't want anyone with problematic behavior in my life. I got rid of all the crazy-makers, controllers, and people who ran really hot and cold towards me, and my life is so much calmer."

— *Ben*

"I grew up in a home with an incredibly narcissistic and abusive mother, and I've always been concerned that I would be like her. The more I learn about abusive behavior, boundaries, and what is healthy, the more I see a lot of problematic things I do. I was scared for a while that I was a narcissist, but then someone in a support group told me that I most likely had "fleas" and that I could change these things if I really wanted to. I'm happy to say that I've gotten rid of a lot of my "fleas," and the relationships in my life are much better."

— *Diana*

A Relationship vs. A "Manipulationship"

A Relationship

A relationship is a dynamic between two people and is based on *mutual* trust, dignity, support, and respect and includes open, honest, sincere, and solutions-oriented communication. If one person makes a mistake or has an issue, it is brought up, discussed, and a resolution is reached. Problems come up, feelings might be hurt, and fights happen, but both people are able to "fight fair" and not seek to destroy each other in the process. However, if you are a target of abuse, it's important that you realize that this isn't a relationship—because the dynamic isn't based on mutuality, it's based on control, and that by having open, honest, sincere, solutions-oriented communication will only make things worse.

A Manipulationship

A manipulationship is a one-sided dynamic between two people that is based on manipulation, and includes deceitfulness, lies, control, (and generally a lot of cheating, siphoning funds, and other types of "squirrelly" behavior). It is based around one person (the emotional manipulator) continually doing whatever they want, with whomever they want, as much as they want, and if and when they get caught they often deny their behavior, blame others— which can include accusing their partner of being jealous, crazy, insecure, or overly emotional, giving empty promises that things will change, all the while they are not changing—they are just getting better at hiding their problematic behavior.

In a manipulation-ship one person works out of their self-interest, has no *sincere* regard for the devastation that their behavior causes to their partner or to the relationship, and uses guilt, obligation, intimidation, fear, and control to get the other to stay. All the while the other one is resigned to continually doing damage control and "forgiving" them, giving them a second (or twenty-second) chance all with the hopes that maybe this time things will be different. Narcissists and other types of emotional manipulators are often nothing short of emotional terrorists, and their targets are their captives. Please do not confuse this for love. Love isn't abusive. It doesn't cheat, steal, lie, exploit, or neglect the other person, and it for sure doesn't leave the receiver of that love feeling emotionally devastated and ground down.

"Once I heard the term 'manipulation-ship' it was like I saw what was going on clearly. I kept holding on thinking we were in a relationship, and that everything could be fixed if I could just get through to him. However, he kept lying, cheating, and refusing to be accountable for anything he ever did. So while I was trying to fix things, he was content on breaking them and then making me seem like I was at fault for why everything was broken, or he'd deny that things were broken and tell me I was crazy."

— *Serena*

Real Intimacy vs. Rushed Intimacy

Real Intimacy

Real intimacy happens over time and is mutual. It's based on trust that is *earned* by a person having consistent, appropriate behavior (their words and actions matching up) over a reasonable amount of time, and *cannot be rushed.* Building trust consists of sharing some information about ourselves and then watching how a person handles what we've shared with them, and then adjusting accordingly—whether this means slowly revealing more to them over time because they have proven themselves to be safe and trustworthy, or pulling back and not revealing any more to this person because they are acting in a way that is untrustworthy or that makes us feel unsafe.

Rushed Intimacy

Rushed intimacy is a shallow interaction or superficial connection between two people. These intense connections often happen when an emotional manipulator rushes intimacy, as they often create an intense soul mate connection with their target by becoming a charming, likable, perfect partner that is so interested in them. They mirror back all of their target's likes and dislikes, and so, for the target this intense connection doesn't feel rushed at all—if anything, for their target, it feels incredibly right, like they've finally met their perfect partner, or have won the relationship lottery.

Some examples of how emotional manipulators rush intimacy:

- Excessive communication, which often includes wanting to talk, text, or Skype with the person for hours on end every day.
- Excessive compliments, to where they are continually reinforcing to their target how perfect they are for them, or how it's so nice that the

target is so different from their ex. They might go so far as to specifically address areas that their target is insecure about in order to make them feel safe, secure, and significant—and seemingly loved for who they are...when really they are telling them everything they want to hear.

- Excessive "mirroring." This is where they "mirror" their target's hopes, dreams, mindset, interests, etc. back to them. This creates a very deep connection quickly, as human beings are wired to like and trust other people that are similar to them.

- Telling the target deeply personal stories or secrets (which are most likely not even true) during the first few times interacting with them.

- Pushing boundaries and trying to get sex out of their target as quickly as possible (and trying to make the target feel insecure, paranoid, or guilty if they don't).

- Having *a lot* of sex. Sex is a very common "weapon" of manipulators, as it often creates an intense chemical, physical, and emotional bond— especially if the narcissist is having a lot of sex with their target as well as giving them false flattery, and talking about their ideal life together (future faking).

- Hinting at, or talking about moving in together, marriage, or starting a business with someone they've known for less than a few months.

- Being overly helpful and coming to the rescue (any "free" help from an emotional manipulator *always* comes with a huge cost in the long run).
- Pushing for forgiveness or for you to trust them when they've done a bunch of deal-breaker things and have acted in an untrustworthy way.

For emotional manipulators, rushing intimacy is usually done to obtain some source of "supply" (sex, money, housing, transportation, social status, public image, or ego boost), and they do this by creating a manufactured soul mate type of connection, and assessing and exploiting their target's vulnerabilities along the way. They will tell their target everything the target wants to hear, which usually includes false promises, false flattery, and giving false hope that they can change.

It's important to remember that pretty much everyone (narcissist or not) is on their best behavior during the first ninety or so days of knowing them—especially the more charming ones. So what you see during that time isn't who they are, *but who they want you to think they are.*

"Our relationship moved at light speed. Right away, we were talking for hours every day, and within the first few weeks, he began talking about us moving in together and hinting about marriage. I thought these types of whirlwind romances were romantic and only something that happened in a movie. Looking back, I trusted him because he told me that he grew up with an abusive father, and I could relate as I

grew up with an abusive father too. I felt sorry for him, and thought we could help each other heal. Fast forward, we did get married, and shortly after the honeymoon my life became a living hell. I found out about a ton of lies and other women, and frankly, I'm not even sure he was ever abused. If anything, I think his father cut off contact with him because he's a total sociopath and his dad had enough. When I did finally kick him out, he drained my account, including my child's college fund. I can't believe I trusted him or that I fell for any of it. It was about ten years before I dated again, and I am now happily married to a wonderful man. We moved super slow in the beginning, and what we have is built on something real."

— *Laura*

Love vs. Love Bombing

Love

Love is a deep bond between two people that is built on mutual trust and support and includes being treated with honesty, respect, and appreciation, and grows deeper over time. In a loving relationship, a person feels a sense of safety and security.

Love Bombing

Love bombing is an intense and almost immediate artificial bond manufactured by an emotional manipulator. It is built on manipulation and lies, and usually involves constant communication and compliments, false flattery, future faking, mirroring, and rushing intimacy. The goal of love-bombing is to get the target to trust the narcissist so that they can use, abuse, or exploit them for their own selfish desires.

Love bombing is most commonly associated with cults and online scams (especially dating scams). However, it works very much the same way with any emotional manipulator that has their sights set on any type of target for any reason (usually money, sex, public image, social status, convenience, or sadistic fun).

It's common for those who have been in an abusive relationship to mistake love bombing for love, especially if their ex was selfish, unaffectionate, inattentive, or outright rude, abusive, or inconsiderate. If anything, for a person who has been so emotionally and physically starved out, love bombing not only does not come across as problematic, *it can feel incredibly healthy and ideal*—as though they've met Prince (or Princess) Charming, when in fact they've met their worst nightmare and don't realize it yet. Love bombing tends to come on fast and furious, and to the target, it often feels like either things are too good to be true—as if they were fishing, and the fish just jumped into the boat, or they may feel a deep sense of relief and excitement as if this person is the answer to all their problems or that they've *finally* found their soul mate.

What's also common is if a person has been the target of love bombing in the past, for them to then use that experience as their baseline for what love bombing is. Please know that love bombing, just like any other type of problematic behavior is on a spectrum, and it can (and often does) come across differently with each emotional manipulator. So just because your narcissistic ex texted you five hours a day and began talking about marriage during that first month, doesn't mean that this new person isn't problematic if they are only texting you two hours every day and haven't mentioned marriage. There are a lot of factors that come into play, and it's important to see them as a whole instead of trying to break them down into their individual parts. Many narcissists love bomb, and some don't. Some push for sex, and some aren't interested in sex. Some yell, belittle, and name call, and some don't. It's important that we see a person's actions for what they are, and to have healthy boundaries and deal breakers in place, so we aren't using another abusive person's actions as our baseline for what's a problem.

"When I first heard the term 'love bombing' everything made sense. That's exactly what happened to me. He came on so strong, and even though it felt like too much, too soon, I was so flattered by all the attention. I was recently out of a relationship with an unaffectionate man, and I didn't realize how starved out I was. I realize now that's why I 'ate up' all the love bombing and mistook it for love."
— *Rochelle*

"It's weird to think of love bombing in terms of a friendship, but that's exactly what it was. Within the first few times of talking to her, we

became fast friends. Over time, all that intensity turned into her becoming controlling, demanding, jealous, and possessive. I used to joke with other people that I felt like I was in an abusive relationship, because that's what it felt like. The reality was that our friendship was abusive, but it never dawned on me that a friendship could be abusive. I thought only relationships could be abusive. It's taken me years to connect many of these dots and to realize that I had been falling for love bombing with friends and men, but now that I see it, I no longer fall for it. I have some friends and family that think I'm being too hypervigilant, but they've never been through something like this, and I've gotten to the point where I no longer try to explain why someone coming on so intense like that is a red flag. They just don't get it, which makes sense because a person couldn't understand this until they've lived it."

— *Shannon*

Infatuation vs. Idealization

Infatuation

Infatuation is the first stage in the beginning of most relationships and is very normal. It is an intense period of time, usually lasting a few months, that includes wanting to be around someone as often as possible or thinking and talking about a person seemingly nonstop. However, *in a healthy relationship, boundaries are still set and respected*, and both people still have their own individuality. Meaning, they keep up with their hobbies, friends, job, etc. While they may spend a disproportionate amount of time with this new person, they do not make them their whole life.

Infatuation does not include professions of love or talk of marriage within the first few days or weeks of knowing someone (although both people may fantasize about these things). While there may be a lot of rushing of intimacy going on, there is no whirlwind that kicks up and no major life decisions (like moving in together or marriage) are discussed or made during the first few weeks. Both people are able to be grounded enough to realize that while they might feel that they've met their perfect partner, they are in the "love is blind" phase, and they don't let their passions get the best of them. While moving full steam ahead isn't always a sign of abuse, it is usually a sign of either immaturity or an empty emotional bucket (loneliness, feeling unloved, or fear of being alone). Regardless of what's driving it, it's never a good idea to go full-speed into a major commitment without truly knowing a person, because everything is easy to get into, and much harder to get out of.

Idealization

Idealization is the first phase in a cycle of narcissistic abuse (which is then followed by the devalue phase and then the discard phase), and often involves boundary pushes, love bombing, rushing intimacy, heavy amounts of mirroring, and the feeling of a soul-mate connection shortly after meeting this person. The idealization stage leads to a whirlwind romance which seems (and feels) "too good to be true," or it might come across to you or others as problematic with how fast things are moving, or because the behavior seems really rushed, "crazy," or immature (because it is). These whirlwind romances often grow into tornados which cause massive amounts of destruction and devastation to a person and their life.

Idealization slowly starts to turn into the devalue stage, which generally moves from intense amounts of communication and compliments (love bombing), to outbursts of anger or silent treatment that is given if the emotional manipulator is questioned or challenged (in any way—either real *or perceived*), subtle put downs or name calling, continued boundary pushes, "squirrelly" behavior, "strange" or seemingly rude or inappropriate comments out of the blue, things that don't quite add up, and other signs of problematic behavior, all of which leads a person to feel more and more confused the further the relationship progresses.

It's important to note that not all narcissistic relationships have a heavy idealization phase. Sometimes there isn't much of one at all, outside of the emotional manipulator throwing crumbs of attention or affection to their target, but for some targets, this is all that's needed to get sucked in.

"I'd been in love before, but never like this. Which is why I stayed for so long, and which is why I had such a hard time leaving. When I did finally leave, he moved on at light speed, and quickly became the seemingly perfect partner for the next woman. I realized then that

that's what he does. He is an emotional con artist and goes around pretending to be his target's perfect partner, when really he's mirroring all of her good qualities back to her. He doesn't love. He loves the high he gets from getting others to love him. It's so sick. I wish I could warn his latest target; she seems so sweet and innocent, but I know she'll never listen to me. I wouldn't have listened to someone had they tried to warn me either. After all, it's hard to believe your soul mate is actually Satan on his best behavior."

— Audrey

"Normal" Bad Behavior vs. Devalue Phase

"Normal" Bad Behavior

"Normal" bad behavior in a *healthy* relationship is behavior that might be insensitive, frustrating, or annoying, but can be discussed and resolved. Normal bad behavior isn't intentional, provoking, or sadistic, and it does not include abuse, or destructive, dangerous, or deadly behavior of any kind. It does not involve treating the other person with a lack of respect or dignity, and it does not include treating the other person with disgust, contempt, or aggression. It does not include chronic lies, deceit, chronic cheating, double lives, hidden accounts and racking up debt the other partner doesn't know about, name calling, belittling, screaming, hitting, threatening, etc.

Even though normal bad behavior isn't abusive behavior, this doesn't mean that it's not problematic or worthy of being a potential deal breaker—only you can decide what your deal breakers are.

The Devalue Phase

The devalue phase in a narcissistic abusive relationship starts off with "confusing" and hurtful behavior that tends to come across in three main ways:

The Sweet/Mean Cycle. The sweet/mean cycle involves seeing two very different sides to a person, to where a person might think to themselves that they are dealing with a Dr. Jekyll and Mr. or Mrs. Hyde type personality (aka Prince/Princess Charming and Prince/Princess "Harming.") These two sides of this person lead to an emotional roller coaster for their partner, which tend to involve good times that are *really* good—often over-the-top good (which is the idealization stage again)— and bad times that are *really* bad (devalue/abuse and discard stages).

During the "sweet" times, this person can seem like the ideal spouse or ideal parent and have a charming/romantic/attentive/intense soul mate connection re-established, and have considerate, compassionate, caring behavior. They generally have this grand behavior in front of others or post it on social media so as to protect their public image (and their self-created illusion) that they are in fact a great person.

149

The Hot/Cold Cycle. The idealization stage can also lead into the hot/cold cycle, which is where things get really intense (which could involve lots of attention and affection/soul mate connection type feeling) and then all of a sudden communication stops or dries up to almost a trickle. When this happens, the target often finds themselves in a scramble to get that attention and affection back, wondering what happened, what they did wrong, or what's wrong with them that made this person vanish in a flash when they seemed to have such a deep connection.

The Fairy Tale/Lifetime TV Movie Cycle. This is where a relationship goes from feeling really healthy, good, comfortable, and overall ideal to then finding out their partner has been chronically lying, cheating, mishandling/syphoning household funds, double lives, hidden accounts, long-term affairs/hidden families, etc. So much drama starts to be revealed that the person feels like their life has become a movie, and they have a really hard time understanding how this could have happened when there didn't seem to be any major problems in their relationship.

The common threads between each of these cycles is that at some point they are exposed to or come across their partner's manipulative and/or abusive behavior (which can manifest as verbal, emotional, psychological, financial, sexual, spiritual, or physical abuse.) When they confront their partner about how they are being treated, they generally witness their partner's cruel or calloused "indifference" (lack of sincere empathy or remorse) after they experience (or uncover) the abusive behavior and/or what they've *really* been up to.

"I stayed for as long as I did because I thought our fights were just the normal highs and lows of a relationship. It wasn't until someone told me I was in an abusive relationship, and that feeling perpetually confused, having ongoing emotional anguish, and living with someone who had a Dr. Jekyll and Mr. Hyde personality wasn't normal that I got the validation I needed in order to leave. I left feeling like I'd been in an emotional meat grinder. I can't believe I ever mistook any of that for being normal, or for love."

A Bad Breakup vs. A Grand Finale

A Bad Breakup

A bad breakup often involves some degree of drama, lies, cheating, hurt feelings, name-calling, blame, guilt, or immature or petty behavior. While bad breakups are still incredibly painful and problematic, they don't spiral into such extreme behavior where the other person feels like they are living in a Dateline episode or a Lifetime TV movie.

A Grand Finale

A "grand finale" is often high drama and includes a lot of over-the-top chronic lying and a jaw-dropping level of deceit and lack of empathy and remorse, and ends with the person realizing they weren't a partner with this other person, but they were instead a target, and that they weren't in a relationship, but that they were in a manipulationship. A grand finale usually involves a narcissist's "mask" slipping—and them trying to get it back in place to "save face" and then it ends with their mask completely coming off. When a narcissist's lies and deceitful behavior are found out, this is when they start getting into a scramble to either do damage control or to get control back over their target. As more and more of their outrageous behavior is uncovered, the more lies and outrageous behavior are used in their attempt to regain power and control.

This is the time that double lives, secret pregnancies and families, long-standing affairs, hidden bank accounts or credit cards, hidden cell phones, fake names, stalking, harassment, secret online accounts, breaking into their ex's home, gaslighting, manipulating the children, the therapist, people at church, threats of suicide or murder, rage, verbal and/or physical abuse, claiming to have cancer or some sort of other illness, claiming that someone their target knows is sick or dead, and all sorts of dramatic, destructive, dangerous, and even deadly behavior reaches a height the person didn't know was even possible.

"A double life, a pregnant mistress, debt I didn't know about, thinly veiled threats, and on and on.... The kicker is that we had been in

couples' counseling (for other issues) on a weekly basis for close to six months and doing seemingly great when I accidentally found out about his double life. When the truth began to come out, I realized our whole twenty-year marriage had been nothing more than a string of lies, women, manipulation, and debt that I will be forever paying off. The big lesson in all of this has been once a person shows their true colors to believe what you see. Don't justify it, don't try to fix it; just run."

— *Janice*

Healthy Skepticism vs. Paranoia

Healthy Skepticism

Healthy skepticism is when a person doesn't take everything at face value. They have a healthy degree of skepticism of others—*especially* with regard to things that don't add up, or that seem unreasonable, questionable, far-fetched, too good to be true, or otherwise "off." For example, I wouldn't invite a stranger into my home just because they are a spiritual leader, nor would I immediately trust a person who is a therapist, teacher, doctor, nurse, in the military, who is elderly, female, or whom I have a pleasant conversation with. This isn't because I have issues with trust; it's simply because I don't know this person, and all I have to go on is a single data point (age, gender, profession, a conversation, etc.) and at this stage appropriate levels of trust haven't yet been *earned.* Trust is something that takes time to develop, and appropriate trust is developed slowly over time and through consistent, appropriate behavior during that time.

Paranoia

Paranoia is when a person has a lot of mistrust or suspicion of others for reasons that are *unfounded,* such as thinking that people are watching them, talking about them, spying on them, or out to get them.

After a person gets out of an abusive relationship, it's very common (and normal, and understandable) that they would be distrustful of others—especially if they experienced covert psychological abuse (which the vast majority—if not all—targets of abuse do experience to some degree).

An abusive relationship is like an emotional meat grinder, and by the end of it, a person generally feels ground up into a million little pieces and completely disoriented and confused by what happened, how it happened, how they didn't realize it was happening, and most importantly: how to prevent it from happening again.

And when a person has been hurt (especially in ways that aren't easily identified by them or by others), they go into self-protection mode. This usually involves isolating themselves, avoiding others, feeling anxious in general, and feeling anxious and/or distrustful of others. When a person starts feeling like this, they also question their judgment and overall sanity, as it can really feel like they are losing their mind. Many people have a hard time opening up to friends, family, and even therapists and doctors because they may feel that they aren't going to be believed, or that what they went through is going to be minimized or totally invalidated.

Unfortunately there is a lot of well-intended bad advice given to people who have been in an abusive relationship for them to get out there and start dating again—that what they've been through is a "bad breakup" and that they've isolated themselves for long enough. This is some seriously dangerous advice. If a person doesn't trust their judgment and if they doubt their intuition about people or situations, they need to be encouraged to not make any major decisions, and not to date, and to overall go slowly when going about trusting people and situations so that they can learn how to build trust in a healthy way. Trust is earned and not blindly given. To make the shift from hypervigilance (which is usually related to Complex Post-Traumatic Stress Disorder) to healthy trust takes time—and it should take time. For a person to not easily and openly trust others isn't paranoia; it's appropriate and shows a healthy degree of skepticism.

"After being in an abusive relationship, I had a really hard time trusting people. I felt broken and angry that I could no longer take people at face value and instantly trust them. It took me awhile, but then I realized that instantly trusting strangers was never healthy to

begin with. I now go a lot slower when meeting new people, and I no longer talk to men I've met through dating sites for hours before I meet them. It's a great feeling to finally have my power back and to take things at a pace I'm comfortable with, and if someone else wants me to move faster, well, too bad!"

— *Rory*

A Relationship Issue vs. An Individual Issue

A Relationship Issue

A relationship issue is a shared issue between two people that involves communication and negotiation about how to effectively work as a team. Some examples of relationship issues would be getting on the same page with developing a budget, how to "fight fair," how to divide household duties, or how to discipline or reward children. Relationship issues do not involve abuse, addiction, adultery, or being treated with a lack of dignity and respect. These aren't relationship issues, *these are individual issues*—and people who have unresolved individual issues to this level have a lot of work to do on themselves before they can be in a healthy relationship.

An Individual Issue

An individual issue is one in which one person has unresolved personal issues that is leading them to behave in ways that are disempowering, destructive, damaging, or deadly to themselves or others. It is impossible to have a healthy relationship with a person who has unresolved individual issues, and only they can fix themselves—we can't do the work for them. So you can drag them to rehab, therapy, church, or give them love and understanding, but *if they aren't ready, willing, or able to do the work of changing, they won't change.* Even if they are ready to do the work of changing, please realize that true change takes time, consistent effort in the direction of change, and the emotional insight to continually examine their behavior and to work towards improving it. And just because one person has problematic behavior, doesn't mean that they are motivated, or consistently motivated to change it.

Unfortunately, people get into couples' counseling with the goal of "fixing" their relationship, which usually means "fixing" their partner. And if you encounter a therapist who takes everything at face value, doesn't realize when they are being manipulated, and isn't able to separate out the difference between a character issue and a communication issue, as well as is also determined to make your relationship work (perhaps because they have their own unresolved codependency issues, their own ego needs, or perhaps because they think all issues are relationship issues and are rooted in communication problems), then this can cost you a lot of time, energy, and money—not to mention it will continue to put you in harm's way and is incredibly re-victimizing.

Because the individual needs to fix themselves first, and the other partner needs to realize that there is no relationship. This is what the whole "meeting people where they are" comes into play. If a person has manipulative and abusive behavior, then it's important to see that they in fact are being manipulative and abusive—and to not treat it like it's a relationship issue. Mistaking a character issue for a communication issue is like getting caught up in an online dating scam where the scammer cons you out of your life savings, and then thinking that going to couple's counseling will help. The same goes for trying to reach a solution with anyone in your life who does destructive or exploitative things. Now I'm sure the scammer or abuser or whomever has a whole host of reasons as to why they do what they do—after all, we all have reasons for why we do what we do, but that doesn't mean that there is a valid reason for conning someone, or that what they are doing is somehow workable, or that you should tolerate being treated that way.

Having an excuse, no matter what it is: if they had a bad childhood, are addicted to something, were abused before in a previous relationship, are not valid reasons for hurting other people. I know that might sound cold and calloused, but it's the truth. If a person has unresolved individual issues that are negatively impacting you and your relationship, it's a mistake to give them a free pass to continue to hurt you because of their past. It can be easy to get caught up in guilt and obligation and to think we are somehow responsible for healing someone else, and true healing doesn't work this way. Only they can do the work of healing their old wounds, so please don't lose sight of the larger picture and try to justify deal-breaker behavior into workable behavior because you feel guilty or because you are tired of being single, or because you want to hang onto the fantasy that your parent can one day be that kind and loving parent that you so wish they would be.

"I thought that any issue between two people was a relationship issue, and could be resolved with better communication, or me being more compassionate and being a better son. It wasn't until I heard the terms "narcissist" and "sociopath" that my mother's behavior began to make sense. That's when I realized her behavior was never my fault or my responsibility to fix, and that any communication with her was just setting me up for further abuse—which is why I finally cut her out of my life. Of course, my family thinks I'm a jerk for doing that, but she doesn't have a right to abuse me just because she's my mother."

— Roger

"My husband had been lying, cheating, and abusing me verbally, emotionally, and physically for years and blamed me for all of it. What's worse is that I believed him. I really thought that all his issues were somehow my issues too and that if I could just be what he wanted me to be, then he'd stop cheating and treating me like crap. It wasn't until his abuse put me in the hospital that I really realized it was a serious problem, and that next time he might kill me. We had relationship issues, but his behavior was 100% his issue, and I'm

*sure he'll treat every woman in his path the same way. Of course, if
you listen to him tell the story, he'll tell you how all of the women in
his life abuse and use him. What makes me sick is that so many other
people believe him! He even participated in a march against domestic
violence last month. It's like he doesn't get that he's an abuser. It's so
crazy."*

— *Barbara*

Being Choosey vs. Being Chosen

Being Choosey

Being choosey means to have high standards and to be
highly selective about whom you choose to be in your
inner circle. As far as dating goes, being choosey means to
be highly selective about what kind of partner you are
looking for and to spend your time with them figuring out
if they are a good fit for what *you* are looking for. Since
everyone's criteria is different, it's important to be clear on
what yours are. Some examples of important criteria for a
partner or a friend are: kindness, compassion, openness,
honesty, sincerity, solutions-oriented communication (and
actions), and someone who has a good attitude about life
in general, and who is responsible and accountable for
their actions.

Being choosey is an attitude of abundance coupled with a
healthy degree of self-love, and a clear idea of deal-breaker
and deal-maker behavior. It's the belief in knowing what

you are looking for in a partner and, while a person may be open to compromising, they are not open to settling.

Being Chosen

Being chosen is a mindset that involves an attitude of scarcity—that this other person is the only one out there for us. With an attitude of scarcity, a person is in a scramble in order for the other person to "choose" them for a partner, without them considering if this person is the kind of person they want in their life.

"My whole life, I'd always been so focused on wanting to be liked, and dating was no exception. It was a major turning point when I realized that I was more focused on wanting people to like me than I was seeing if they were what I was looking for in a friend or a significant other. I don't even think I had criteria for what I was looking for, I was just so desperate to be loved—and didn't even realize it. I've done a lot of work on building my self-esteem, and a life I love. Now I'm really picky about who I let into my life!"
 — Candy

Setting a Boundary vs. Threatening Consequences

Setting a Boundary

Boundaries are the bodyguards to our standards, and they are an important part of how we value ourselves. In order to understand boundaries, I think it's helpful for me to back up a bit and talk about standards. Our standards are often largely subconscious beliefs about what we expect out of life, out of relationships, and how we deserve to be treated by ourselves or others. It's worth the time to examine your standards and the thinking that led up to those standards, as most of the time our standards come from "programming" from parents, religion, friends, school, etc. that we received when we were young. The best way to examine your standards is to look at what's shown up in your life (your relationships, job, income, car, etc.) because everything in your external environment is a physical manifestation of your internal environment. The tricky part about standards is that they might be healthy in one area, and really low in another. And because our behavior is our normal, it can be difficult to see where our low standards are. So for example, you may have a car you really like, pay your bills on time, eat healthy foods, and have friends that enjoyable to be around, but you find yourself continually dating controlling, rude, crazymaking, cheating men. It may look like on the surface that you have high standards, but if you are tolerating being treated poorly, then somewhere along the way you developed the standard that being treated like that (and staying) was somehow workable and allowable. Whether this standard was something you picked up from abusive parents, society, religion, or from friends, or all of the above, somewhere along the line you picked up a faulty message about your self-worth. ...And while it may seem that the abuser was the one who ground down your standards, those weak spots in your armor were already there. Because boundaries and standards aren't taught, and worse, because unhealthy ideas of love and codependency are what's taught, it's no wonder that people don't have healthy standards.

If you want to change your life, the fastest way to do so is to examine the people, places, and things in your external environment, and then to examine the standards you have in those areas. Bringing awareness to a problem is always a big first step. The next step in all of this is to decide that you are going to raise your standards. Get clear with yourself as far as what you won't tolerate, and if it ever happens again, you'll be out the door. Once you raise your standards, your boundaries will follow suit, because our boundaries are what we say and do in order to make sure that are standards are met. So for example, if my standard is that I will not tolerate someone yelling at me or treating me with hostility in any way, my boundary would be to distance myself from that person, and then either cut ties completely, or let them know that I refuse to be treated like that and if they do it again, I'm done.

Drawing a boundary with someone involves letting someone know what is and isn't okay with you, and then having some sort of enforceable consequence if they cross that line, or if they cross it again.

You shouldn't need to discuss the basics of adult behavior with another adult; meaning, you shouldn't need to explain to your boyfriend why flirting with the waitress isn't okay, or why "friending" sexy strangers on the internet isn't appropriate, or why yelling, hitting, or belittling you isn't okay. A person doesn't need to be given multiple chances to behave according to your standards. If their behavior falls within your deal-breaker behavior, it's okay (and healthy) to distance yourself from them. How many chances you want to give someone is up to you, but keep in mind that if they keep doing whatever it is that they are doing then they aren't really sorry (they're just sorry they have to suffer the consequences of getting caught!)

Threatening Consequences

Threatening consequences are what many people who struggle with setting a solid boundary do. They might yell and scream, or threaten divorce or to cut another person off, but they don't mean it—and they and their partner both know it. The reason they do this is because they want their partner to know they are upset, but because they really don't want to leave, threatening to leave and holding onto hope that their partner will change is all they really can do.

"It took me close to fifty years to realize that me threatening to leave wasn't setting a boundary. I figured because I was letting him know

how upset I was, that was somehow setting a boundary. I put up with being abused and cheated on for thirty-two years, the whole time thinking he'd change if I could just get through to him or if I could just become a better partner. And he didn't change, he just got worse. I will never again tolerate being treated like that. I come across a lot of the younger women in the support group who have a hard time being alone, and that's a big reason as to why they stay, but really, there is nothing lonelier than being married to an abusive person."

— Rachel

"My mother has a pattern of dating abusive men, starting with my father who left us shortly after I was born. It was always the same type of guy, but with a different name. I remember thinking when I was a child how weird it was that she kept finding all these abusive men, especially since we lived in such a small town and all my friend's dads were so nice. Now that I'm much older, I realize that her standards, deal breakers, and self-worth were also big parts of the problem. And since she doesn't realize that her boundaries and standards are an issue, she only—she only sees their abuse as the problem, she'll continue to date abusive men until she does. She told me a few months ago that she feels cursed, and doesn't know why she attracts such horrible men. It's so frustrating because I can try and point out that there is a pattern with the types of men she dates, so there must be something more going on, but she won't hear it."

— Mandy

"I recently discovered I had double standards. A standard to me is what behavior I require and expect of myself and in turn that I actually exhibit it, and live that way. How I require and expect me

to comport myself, how and what I find acceptable behavior within and of myself. What I would tolerate and not tolerate and find acceptable as far as my own behavior goes. My standard list for myself is a mile long!

What I finally had to accept and finally determined the "problem" to be was: I had a completely, totally and radically different set of standards for others. And I rationalized this easily. Since I could not control other people or their behavior, then who was I to set standards on them or requirements for their behavior? So while I held myself and my own behavior to a very, high, high set of standards, I had NO STANDARDS at all for other people's behavior towards me. It was completely laissez faire, live and let live, anything goes.

And I had to do this to be able to keep the people who I believed I "should" keep close to me and in my life and in my inner circle. Like my father, brothers, sister, son, long term boyfriend, etc.

What has finally had to happen within recovery is to loosen the stranglehold on myself of my own standards for myself, and to simultaneously tighten up the reins a significant amount on the standard of behavior I expect from others towards me. And in particular the standards for people who are allowed to be within my inner circle."

— *Luci*

Boundaries vs. Fortressing

Boundaries

Boundaries are the bodyguards to our standards for how we expect to be treated. Boundaries involve knowing what is both deal-breaker and deal-maker criteria, and are set *and then acted upon* in order to keep a person safe and sane. Boundaries involve three steps: 1. Deciding how you expect to be treated. 2. Asserting yourself if someone crosses that boundary. 3. Taking action if they continue to cross the line (which usually involves distancing yourself, or if a child crosses the line, a consequence would be implemented.)4. Continually checking in with yourself emotionally to see if any boundaries and standards need to be evaluated. (If you are feeling angry, resentful, irritated, or hurt, these are generally signs that you've had a boundary violated.) While it's true that no one else knows what your boundaries are, and that it's important that you assert yourself, it is reasonable to expect that another person would (and should) understand the basics of adult behavior (don't hit, yell, cheat, steal, lie, etc.) Trying to set boundaries with an abusive person can put you in danger. They know what they are doing, and they are using force to gain power and control over you. You would be wise to distance yourself from this person, *especially if they are or have ever been physically abusive, as the odds of them killing you are significantly higher than the odds of them ever changing.*

Your boundaries will grow and change over time as you grow and change, and your boundaries are an extension of who you are and an important part of treating yourself with dignity and respect. *So while you may love the abusive person in your life, it can't be at the expense of loving yourself enough to keep yourself safe and sane.*

If a person has a solid enough sense of who they are and what they are about, they will not be swayed by the negative opinions of others—and for many of us, developing a solid sense of self takes time and practice. Setting boundaries, at first, might feel exhausting—like you have to fight a bunch of battles and continually be the bad guy by saying no or putting your foot down and not allowing others to walk all over you or to mistreat you. But over time it really does get easier, and eventually you will get to the point where you agonize over setting boundaries. Having healthy boundaries will just be an extension of who you are and will come as naturally as doing any other type of self-care like brushing your teeth in the morning.

Fortressing

Fortressing is a very common stage that most people go through when they first learn to set boundaries— especially if they have been hurt multiple times. Instead of drawing lines in the sand in order to keep problematic people or situations at bay, they build high walls in an attempt to keep everyone out and to keep themselves safe and sane. This may happen for a number of reasons; perhaps they've been hurt too many times, or perhaps they don't know what a healthy boundary is so they take it too far. Learning to navigate the difference between a healthy line in the sand and building a high wall takes time and practice.

"After I got out of an abusive relationship, I didn't trust anyone. I realized I also had a lot of abusive friendships and family members in my life too. It was like pulling a string on a sweater, and my reality was unraveling. It was terrifying, and I just wanted to be alone. I isolated myself for about a year, and I still keep people at arm's length. It took me awhile to even be okay with the idea of meeting new people and building trust, and this time around my friendships and relationships have been much better. The key really is going slow and realizing that it's much easier to leave when you see red flags early on if you aren't so quick to make someone your whole world. Once I realized I could take things at my own pace, I stopped fortressing so much, and began easing into having healthier boundaries. It took me awhile to figure out what healthy boundaries were and how to make them, but I'm slowly getting the hang of it. It's very exciting."

— *Kim*

Sincere Communication vs. Insincere Communication

Sincere Communication

Sincere communication involves being open, honest, accountable, and solutions-oriented *to the degree that the other person has earned your trust.* When two people engage in open, honest, sincere, solutions-oriented communication, there is clarity, understanding, and the ability for the relationship to strengthen and grow. *There is no healthy relationship without sincere communication.* There is only learning how to twist yourself into an emotional pretzel and to try and cope with someone who isn't ready, willing, or able to have the relationship grow.

In addition, it is not only a mistake, it can be dangerous and possibly even deadly to have open, honest, sincere, and solutions-oriented communication with someone whose actions have shown you that they are actively working against you and your relationship when you aren't looking, or if they are dangerous or destructive in any way—especially if they have hinted at, threatened, or have a history of aggression, abuse, or violence of any kind. Having sincere communication with an abusive person will only serve to set you up to be used, abused, and exploited. It is wise to see a person's actions for what they really are, instead of justifying them because of how you feel about them, or because you hope they could be different someday...just given enough love, understanding, rehab, religion, or therapy, or thinking that you need to be open with them because they are your parent or your spouse. There is no shortage of emotional manipulators out there who can say all of the right things and can pretend to have healthy communication and can pretend to work towards the greater good of the relationship…especially after they've been caught actively working against their partner (lying, cheating, stealing) when their partner wasn't looking.

Many targets of abusive people often feel a lot of guilt for not having open and honest communication with an abusive person. They often feel that they are doing something wrong by not responding to their text messages, or with planning to leave. Please know stopping sincere communication with an abusive person isn't problematic, it's healthy, and it's time you go into self-protection mode. It is a mistake to have open communication with someone who has been actively hurting you, especially if they take what you tell them when you are being open and then later use it against you. Leaving an abusive relationship can be a lot like leaving a hostage situation. Think of it this way, it would be a mistake to explain to your captor that you are planning on escaping because they are too controlling and you don't like being held hostage.

This is why it's important to see if the communication is sincere. The only way to tell is if the actions line up with words over a consistent period of time. If they don't, then they aren't being sincere.

It's a mistake to be in a relationship or dynamic where you are being sincere while the other person isn't. This isn't a relationship; *you are being manipulated*—and the best manipulators out there will act sincerely and friendly the whole time while they are plotting to work against you. As the saying goes, "don't confuse an enemy's smile with them baring their teeth." So while you are being sincere, they are gathering information against you.

So while you are holding onto hope that this time will be different, they are working on furthering their own selfish agenda, to which you will pay the price—which may be financially (with them draining the accounts or putting you in debt you don't know about), or physically, psychologically, and emotionally by potentially exposing you to diseases if they are chronically cheating—not to mention stress, anxiety, depression, or other physical harm.

Insincere Communication

Insincere communication is closed, dishonest, and self-serving. It's where a person's words do not match their actions consistently over time, and with most emotional manipulators, this is the only type of communication they have—although it takes most of us awhile to realize this. They are chronic liars—even if the truth would work better.

Insincere communication involves anything that is designed to gain and keep power and control over their target, which usually includes the silent treatment, stonewalling, gaslighting, pot stirring, triangulating, circular conversations, false promises of change, future faking, diverting, blame shifting, and overall conversations that are designed to frustrate, confuse, upset, provoke, blame, mislead, or push their target over the edge.

Insincere communication brings about chronic confusion, and serves to leave the person who is working towards a solution feeling distrusting of their partner, insecure in the relationship, and frustrated that any issue they have never seems to get resolved. It also creates a situation where they feel they have to walk on eggshells and that they cannot bring up any concerns or issues about their partner. In the long run, this lowers their self-esteem and their feelings of shame and embarrassment for staying in a relationship like this.

As a side note, people who have codependency issues may also have unhealthy communication. So while they may also give the silent treatment or not be willing to face issues that the relationship has, the driving force behind their behavior is very different. An emotional manipulator is driven to get (and keep) power and control over their target so that they win, whereas a codependent person is driven to get (and keep) their "relationship" together at all costs because they feel incomplete being single.

"I kept thinking that all of his yelling and put downs would stop if I could just get through to him about how hurtful he was being. I finally

*filed for divorce, and that's when he said he'd go to therapy. Big
mistake. After the first few sessions, I opened up about how I felt and
really made myself vulnerable, and during our next fight, he turned
and used everything I said against me. I didn't even realize another
person could be so hateful. He said that I was such a loser, that it
was no wonder why my mother committed suicide. That hurt me on
so many different levels, but it was at that point I realized that not
only did he not love me, he didn't even like me, and that I needed to
leave."*

— *Victoria*

An Attitude of Cooperation vs. An Attitude of Competition

An Attitude of Cooperation

An attitude of cooperation is one of mutual support and
trust and is based on open, honest, sincere communication
where both people are sincerely working towards a win-
win solution. It's what true teamwork looks like in motion,
and it can only exist if both people have the same goal.

An attitude of cooperation does not mean that you are the
one who continually needs to try and fix the relationship
or work as a team when the other person's actions are
selfish and continually show that they are not working
towards being a team. If you are the only person on the
team, then there is no team; this is you being manipulated.

An Attitude of Competition

An attitude of competition is not one of teamwork. It's a one-sided, win/lose dynamic in which one person seeks to get their way at the expense of the other. There is a time and place for an attitude of competition, but to have that kind of attitude in a relationship will kill it, because it is no longer a team. An attitude of competition is a "me vs. you" dynamic, where one person seeks to get their wants and needs met regardless of the damage done to the other person (and if one person is sadistic, then they are intentionally damaging the other person, and *enjoying* the process.)

Narcissists are driven by a blinding degree of selfishness which comes out as them needing to have power and control over others or how others perceive them. Their "me vs. you" attitude really shows itself if they are challenged in any way—in ways that are either real *or perceived*. When a person is operating with a "me vs. you" dynamic, they are not looking to reach a solution, they are looking to win.

For a person who is abusive, this usually means they will do whatever they need to do to keep getting their way (aka "win.") They might become intimidating or threatening in order to get and keep power and control. This usually means them yelling louder, giving the silent treatment, making subtle (or not so subtle) put downs, planting seeds of insecurity, devaluing, diminishing, or degrading their partner, making threats, or becoming physically aggressive.

Or they might go the exact opposite way and play the part of really wanting to work as a team. They might come across as sincerely remorseful, saying and doing all of the right things—including going to therapy, being nice, compassionate, considerate, involved, and caring. It's like a light switch was flipped! For their partner, this *instant* great behavior is such a relief—because they're given the (false) hope that perhaps their partner has *finally* seen the error of their ways and has turned a corner. They may feel really optimistic, reaffirming to themselves that they *knew* if they just held onto hope long enough that their partner would change, and would stop all of their lying, cheating, stealing/siphoning funds, abusing, or lack of empathy and remorse.

But yet they often can't shake this feeling that this long-awaited change seems *so* easy for their partner. And if it was so easy, then why didn't they change a long time ago? How come now their partner has suddenly been able to develop so much insight into their behavior and seems so invested in the relationship. And while they feel relieved that things have turned a corner, they often feel that something about the speed of their partner's change feels…off. But they don't want to rock the boat, because they've been waiting for this miracle for a long time, and now that it's here, they don't want to live in the past or question things too much. ....And that's exactly why this manipulative person is doing all these things—it's to continue giving their partner false hope, so that they will stick around, and so they can use them some more. Also playing the part of the repentant partner is a great way for them to rebuild their public image, and to get others to rally around in support of them.

I will tell you that it's been my experience that when someone's behavior changes so radically, it's usually not sincere. It's usually them acting the part in order to keep the game going on their terms. Even though movies and the media would like us to believe that people's behavior can change so radically in the blink of an eye, the reality is that a person doesn't go from a nightmarish soap-opera type behavior to a fairy-tale perfect partner generally ever, let alone over the span of a few days. True change takes time, effort, and sincere accountability for wrongdoings.

What's usually going on is that they've gotten better at hiding what they are up to, and when they think no one is looking, they are up to the same old deceitful tricks. Narcissists hate it when the game doesn't end on their terms, and it's not uncommon for them to beg for forgiveness and to act like the perfect partner, only to break up with their partner a few days or weeks later. And if they do leave, they might give some sort of pity-inducing apology, saying, "I don't want to hurt you anymore," or blaming their leaving on someone else by saying something like, "I have to leave because my ex/child/parent has cancer and I have to take care of them," (which is probably not true) or them saying nothing. Then their partner comes home to an empty house and bank account.

When you are on the receiving end of this, it can be really difficult to wrap your mind around what you are experiencing because *they can seem so sincere.* They might convince their partner to renew their vows, have another baby, adopt a pet, or buy a house—things that would register to a normal person as sincere, committed action. But to an emotional manipulator, there is nothing sincere about what they say and do; it's all about saying what they need to say in order to get what they want, and it's all about them.

When you are dealing with someone who has a pattern of deceitful behavior, it is a mistake to assume they are telling the truth when their actions have shown that they are lying. To deny what is really going on is only going to make you vulnerable. And no, you don't have trust issues that need to be worked out. *You would be wise to have trust issues with a person who has lying issues.*

"Even though we were married, I never felt like we were on the same team. The cheating, the lies, the manipulations...they were never-ending, and they were all designed for him to get his way. I stayed married until I couldn't hang in there anymore, because I thought

that's what commitment was. Being committed to a person who isn't on the same team, and who has no desire to work as a team, is a mistake, and one that I'll never make again."

— Bobbi

Doing All the Right Things vs. Saying All the Right Things

Doing All the Right Things

Doing all the right things means the person who has damaged the relationship is doing the work to repair that damage and to repair the relationship.

It does not mean that you need to do the work of fixing the relationship or trying to become a better partner in an effort to avoid abuse or to try and keep them faithful. If you are twisting yourself into an emotional pretzel to make things work and are taking responsibility for their destructive actions, this isn't healthy, and you are being manipulated.

Saying All the Right Things

Saying all the right things means saying whatever someone needs to hear—but generally not having the consistent actions to back up the talk. Remember, talk isn't just cheap; it's free.

A manipulative person will say all kinds of things in order to get what they want. They will apologize, suggest that they go to therapy, promise that things will be different or that they will change. Talk means nothing if the consistent actions aren't there—and by actions I mean them willing to live a life of total transparency and be fully accountable for the damage they've done *and to not only never have it happen again*, but to also rebuild the trust that was broken. If a person continues to say all the right things, and have all the right actions, but you catch them doing the same things again, then they aren't truly remorseful, and they haven't truly changed.

"Looking back on things, our relationship ran a pattern. I could always tell when he was cheating because he'd either pick a fight so he could break up with me or grow silent for a week, or he'd announce out of the blue that he wanted a divorce. I'd catch him cheating, and then he'd rage at me, blaming me for finding out. I'd leave, and then he'd start promising change. He really did a great job at saying all the right things. He had me believing that he was a sex addict, so then now the problem was his sex addiction and so it wasn't his fault. Then he promised therapy. Then he promised I could look at his phone or his computer whenever I wanted to. Each time he cheated I thought it would be the last, and it never was. The only thing that changed was that he got better at hiding his cheating. He had multiple email accounts, multiple phones, credit cards I didn't know about; you name it. Talk is cheap, and these kinds of people lie, lie, lie. They lie when the truth would work better. It's a mistake to trust anything that they ever say. Focus on their actions, and also realize that whatever you do know is only about 10% of what's really going on."

— *Victoria*

Persistence and Commitment vs. Power and Control

Persistence and Commitment

Persistence and commitment are two important qualities at making a relationship work—but persistence and commitment are only healthy if *both* people treat each other and the relationship with dignity, respect, honesty, and sincerity. Without those foundational pieces in place there is no relationship, there is only a "manipulationship."

Power and Control

Power and control are two qualities that are often confused for persistence and commitment. The qualities of persistence and commitment are exploited by a narcissist when their target finally has had enough and either wants to leave or wants to start drawing boundaries.

What tends to happen is that if the emotional manipulator gets caught doing something (yet again), and if they want to keep their target around because they want to continue using them, then they will often use guilt, obligation, pity, sympathy, blame, shame, fear, or intimidation to keep them around.

They will generally insist that this time will be different, and then when their partner holds the line that they want to break up or want a divorce the emotional manipulator will spin the situation, making themselves the victim and blaming their partner for not wanting to work on things or not being committed enough!

Now that they've spun things around, they play the baby bird with the broken-wing card, and exploit their target's emotions of guilt, sympathy, and hope.

They will often say things such as:

"I need help; how can you leave me now?" (Translation: You are supposed to feel sorry for me and then feel obligated to stay. Ideally, you will chalk up all of my problematic behavior to my alcoholism, drug (or sex) addiction, mental illness, or because of a communication issue between us. This way I can shift the focus off of my accountability and onto your feeling sorry for me and ideally, taking care of me while my bad behavior destroys you.")

"I can't believe you are giving up on us so easily." (Translation: "I can't believe you are trying to leave me! I know I lie, cheat, siphon funds, and manipulate you, but you are supposed to continue to stay with me until I decide to leave you.")

"I'm willing to change for you, the least you can do is give me another chance." (Translation: "I am in control here, and I say when this relationship ends. So for the time being I'm going to be on really good behavior, and I'm going to hide my problematic behavior even better.")

"I don't deserve you. I'm tired of causing you pain." (Translation: "I really want you to think I'm a great person with empathy, remorse, and compassion. I'm also saying this to punish you, so that you'll feel extra bad because you now think I have the insight, caring, and concern that you've always hoped I've had. So when I do come back around (after I've got my fill of cheating on you, you'll gladly take me back because you'll be holding onto hope that I do care about you. But I don't. I was just out cheating, and didn't want to feel guilty about it, so I broke up with you, planted the seeds that I'm a good person, and set the stage for you to work harder at making the relationship work when I do come back.")

This is all smoke and mirrors designed to confuse you and to pull you back into the fog of manipulation. Don't fall for it. This is not what persistence and commitment look like; this is manipulation, and it's the main way narcissists gain and keep power and control over their targets.

A narcissist's behavior, especially when they are trying to regain control, often comes across as *really persistent*. They will double or triple their efforts at making things work and to their target and the outside world, it can really come across as though they are truly sorry, because for those of us who aren't highly manipulative, we wouldn't dream of being that persistent if we weren't sincere.

Our mistake is projecting our thoughts and morals onto them. However, the good news is that once you see manipulative behavior for what it is, you'll have a hard time unseeing it. Remember, emotional manipulators want what they want, when they want it, as much as they want it, and feel entitled and justified in getting it—regardless if it hurts their children, their spouse, their family, even themselves in the long run. Your value system is not their value system. After all, look at their behavior! Would you ever treat them (or anyone else) like that?

So what does power and control masked as persistence and commitment look like? It can be them apologizing, crying, begging, pleading, being on their best behavior, going to church, or therapy or both. They may send flowers to their target's work, or call friends and family in an attempt to get them to encourage the target to stay in the relationship. They may call or email their target fifty times, just wanting them to pick up so they can say they are sorry. They may call their target's parents and tell them they are sorry for how they behaved.

But don't mistake this grand show for anything other than the idealization phase of the cycle of narcissistic abuse. It's all future faking, and it's where charm meets intensity. And all this intensity and future faking can really suck a person back in—because after all, it's designed to.

The only comparison I can make to a person who really hasn't ever experienced this is to think of how a small child acts when he or she really wants a toy. The child sets his or her sights on a toy, and then goes into overdrive trying to convince their parents to get it for them. If the parents say no, the child will up the stakes of the game. They will use guilt, charm, and manipulation. They will promise the sun and the moon if that's what it takes to get that toy. They will tell their parents how much they love them, and then if that doesn't work, they will tell them how much they hate them. They will try to be cute, and then they will pout and be mean. They will beg, cry, plead, yell, slam doors, throw a temper tantrum, and go on and on—and they don't let up—especially if their parents have given in before. They know that if they just say the right things long enough, they'll eventually wear them down.

If the parents are trying to set boundaries with the child and vow to themselves that this time they are going to hold the line in the sand, the child's behavior will continue to escalate. They will try every angle until they either wear the parents down or they give up; they will beg, plead, cry, yell, threaten, tell the parents they are mean, or that they no longer love them. They may run crying to the grandparents or whoever else might take pity on them and give them what they want. If there is any little negotiation or sign of weakness from the parent, the child knows they've hit a weak spot. When they do, they focus on that weak spot and triple their efforts to get them to cave.

They might seem like such a sad and lost puppy without you that you might have all kinds of guilt for shutting the door or turning out the lights on that puppy that your heart breaks into a dozen pieces as it scratches and whimpers at the door. And while this is the hardest thing you've ever had to do, there's a part of you that is angry. After all, you didn't want this relationship to end, but damn, you can't stay if they are going to keep doing what they are doing! You feel like you are between a rock and hard place. You feel like you are the one suffering the consequences. You never wanted any of this. You just wanted to love them and to be happily married. But you can't be treated like this. You know you can't be treated like this. This is beyond workable stuff. …Or is it? Maybe things could be fixed. Maybe you could give them one last chance. After all, you've been through so much with them already. But…you promised yourself last time that you'd leave if they did this again. You wonder if you are codependent. You wonder if you are crazy. You wonder why they continue to cheat and lie. You wonder why you can't seem to get through to them, and why they seem to have no moral compass when you aren't around. You wonder if any of this is normal. And the whole time you are trying to sort out what to do and how you feel, the whimpering puppy gets louder.

But stop for a second and really think about this. They aren't a scared puppy, or a small child, or a baby bird with a broken wing. They are a full-grown adult who does whatever the hell they want to do when you aren't looking. Who is this person? A baby bird with a broken wing, or a manipulative adult who has no moral compass?

And you love them. But do they love you? You can't help but wonder, because a person who loves you wouldn't do this. Deep down you know this isn't love, that what you are experiencing is not even in the zip code of love.

And yet you feel guilty for wanting to break up with or cut off contact with them. This is a person who lies, deceives, cheats, steals, treats you and your relationship like an afterthought. You feel like the mean one, and the one who isn't really committed to working on the relationship. Wait. What? How did things get so spun around?

You were being manipulated; that's how.

And the intensity of their actions is often mistaken by others as persistence and commitment and the actions of a person deeply in love and sincerely remorseful. They are not. These are the actions of someone trying to regain power and control over their target by wearing them down and manipulating them.

"Normal" people don't have behavior that destroys the relationship and then become insistent that their partner needs to "forgive and forget" and give them a second (or a twenty-second chance) at making things right, and if their partner is tired of all their lies, they don't blame *their partner* for having a problem with commitment. *Only manipulative people think and act this way.*

What can be especially crazy making is that others don't often see this behavior as problematic—even many therapists or church counselors often make the mistake of taking actions at face value and assuming that everyone is sincere in their desire to change. This is <u>*dangerous*</u> thinking and can (and often does) keep a person trapped in an abusive relationship for years or decades longer than they need to be.

How a person acts when no one else is around is who they really are. Do yourself a favor and don't try to change them. Doing so will only frustrate you and enrage them—not to mention cost you time, money, energy, and your sanity. *It's okay and healthy to walk away from people who cause destruction in your life.*

"I kept going back because he was so persistent. He'd call and text dozens of times a day. He'd send flowers; he would drive by my house. I mistook all of that attention for him caring and thinking he was trying to win me back, when really it was about dominance and him winning. He saw me as an object and our relationship as a game."
    — *Cheryl*

"The biggest turning point in my recovery was in asking myself if I would them (or someone else) how they were treating me. This is was such an important concept and piece of healing for me, and it remains so still today. If I'm ever find myself questioning how I'm being treated, and wondering who has the issue: if it's them or me, I begin to review every interaction, and I ask myself "Would I treat someone

else like that?" If the answer was no, then I know that one should be doing it to me either."

— *Luci*

A Fresh Start vs. Isolation

A Fresh Start

A fresh start means starting over in some way. It could mean starting a new job, moving to a new place, moving to a new city, or getting a makeover. A fresh start can be a very exciting and liberating time in a person's life.

In terms of an abusive relationship, a fresh start is often what the abuser convinces their target to do by either moving to a new area or cutting off contact with people who "know too much" about the abuse. Sometimes the target may be the one who pushes for a fresh start in order to ease their cognitive dissonance and distance themselves from all the reminders of the cheating, lying, stealing, and manipulation that happened. Together, they may build up this fantasy of creating a fresh start in a new town where they don't know anyone, or they will talk about starting over in life with just each other. The problem with this is that the abuser's past behavior isn't the problem. The problem is that the abuser is abusive, and that's not something that moving or cutting off contact with other people will fix.

Isolation

Isolation is the main tool in an abusive person's tool kit and is what many emotional manipulators often push for initially to secure their target, or after their bad behavior comes to light, some bridges are burned, and damage control no longer works. They may either insist on or offer a fresh start in order to escape the drama or chaos left behind by their former actions.

The problem with this is that the other people and all the drama and chaos aren't the problem—the person's problematic behavior is the problem. And they can't outrun themselves. As the saying goes, "Wherever we go; there we are." What makes getting a "fresh start" with a person who has no shortage of manipulative behavior is that "getting a fresh start" often involves either moving away from or cutting or reducing contact with former friends, family, a job or other types of support systems.

This romanticized idea of getting a fresh start often serves to restart the "idealized" phase of narcissistic abuse, as well as to further deepen the cognitive dissonance experienced by their partner, and in turn, further deepen their bond by creating this "it's me and you against the world" type of dynamic.

Due to cognitive dissonance, Stockholm syndrome, trauma bonds, and any potential codependency that's going on, it's very common for a partner of a narcissist to want to cling to them and to become very defensive and protective of both them and their relationship.

So if anyone in their support system has a problem with their relationship or with them moving away, those people are usually the first ones to have contact cut off, and have now become part of the perceived problem that they are trying to escape. The added challenge is that if the support system never mentions any concerns about their relationship, or that this other person is abusive or is narcissistic, then the person in the relationship may spend years or decades without the clarity or validation that there's a problem outside of what they are perhaps thinking are normal relationship issues. The target may then become resentful if others realized they were in an abusive relationship but never said anything. I've found that an effective way to walk this line is to drop a hint and leave it at that. So, maybe saying something like, "Google narcissistic abuse, and gaslighting." Odds are the target will eventually look up these terms during their search for trying to make sense of things.

"When I caught my now ex-husband cheating for the third time, we decided to move to a new town to get a fresh start. We sold our home, moved several hours away, and adopted a dog. What I didn't realize is that I was also moving away from my friends and family, and he had become my whole world. It wasn't a fresh start; he was isolating me from the people who were trying to encourage me to leave."
— *Bobbi*

Appropriate Guilt vs. Inappropriate Guilt

Appropriate Guilt

Appropriate guilt is when we feel bad for doing something wrong. For example, if you borrowed money from someone and then never repaid it, it would be appropriate for you to feel guilty.

Inappropriate Guilt

Inappropriate guilt is when we feel bad about our actions even though we didn't do anything wrong. Many targets of abuse tend to feel inappropriate guilt when they stand up for themselves and don't let someone else steamroll over their boundaries. This "inappropriate" guilt is very common when a target cuts off contact with an abusive person and that abusive partner begs for a second chance or claims that they "need" them.

In a relationship/dynamic with an emotional manipulator, it is very common for the emotion of guilt to be manipulated in order to keep the person stuck in the relationship. The abuser may claim that they:

- Didn't mean to act in a hurtful way.
- Didn't know they were being cruel or hurting your feelings.
- Now realize how hurtful they've been, and that with *your* help they can change.

- Have never met anyone like you before, and they feel that they are losing the best thing that's ever happened to them.
- Have really changed this time, or that this time they want to get into therapy/couples' counseling, rehab, or find God.
- That things will be different, just pleaseeeee give one more chance.
- That the children need both their parents there, and how that they've *told* you they are committed (even though all their actions when you weren't looking show the opposite); how can you just walk away?

Inappropriate guilt is also *often used to manipulate others* into become "flying monkeys" for a narcissist to do their bidding and to push the target back into the relationship. The narcissist will next go to others around their target, and then using these same pity ploys, will get other people involved in pushing the target to give them a second chance.

And to an outsider who isn't deeply familiar with abusive relationships, the target's symptoms may look like bipolar or borderline personality disorder, they may be incorrectly diagnosed as such—when really the core of the issue may be that they have **PTSD** from being in an abusive relationship, especially when there has been a high degree of psychological abuse present.

A great way to tell if you are experiencing inappropriate guilt is to ask yourself if you are feeling bad by holding a boundary, or otherwise acting in a way that you need to in order to keep yourself safe and sane. If this is the case, then odds are there is some manipulation going on, because normal, healthy people don't have a problem with other people's boundaries. They respect them and then adjust accordingly. If you're setting a boundary upsets someone in your life (especially a person who is crazy making, controlling, or otherwise abusive), pay close attention to this, because you just found the line for where their respect for you ends.

"Oh, I've been driven by inappropriate guilt pretty much my whole life, starting with my mother. I was always made to feel guilty if I ever said no, did something she didn't like, or tried to set a boundary. When I married my husband, he was very much the same way. I still struggle with guilt over divorcing him and no longer have any contact with him. He'll call or text me periodically, because he's bored, horny, or needs attention or money and tries to guilt me into talking to him, but I've done a good job of not caving into that guilt. He's a master manipulator, and I see him for what he is."
— *Sasha*

"I have experienced this with my own sister. She continues to occasionally push for us to go to therapy together through flying monkeys or letters, even after several years of no contact. She doesn't ever actually offer to change, but she sees no value or use in going to therapy alone. Nope. She needs me to go with her. At first I experienced

tremendous guilt and agonized over not agreeing to go with her because I really thought she might be sincere.

Since some time has gone by I am eternally grateful to my therapist who supported me, and helped me hold the line and tell her: "No, you need to go on your own. I've already tried to work with you, and it almost killed me so no. But, if you ever do decide to go, then have your therapist contact my therapist, and then at that point I will reevaluate whether joint therapy could be helpful after you've done your own work." So far, to my knowledge, she's never set foot in a therapist's office."

— Luci

Being Appropriately Emotional vs. Being Overly Emotional

Being Appropriately Emotional

Being appropriately emotional is when a person's emotions fit the situation. It's normal to be sad when something sad happens (or when thoughts of previous sad events surface). It's normal to be scared or startled when something scary, sudden, or strange happens. It's normal to have your feelings hurt or to get offended or upset if someone makes you the butt of a joke, teases you in a hurtful way, calls you names, or yells at you. It's normal to feel confused when you are being manipulated or when you have cognitive dissonance. It's normal to feel jealous if your partner is talking about how sexy or desirable someone else is. And it's normal to feel suspicious if your partner is being secretive about messaging other people, hiding their phone, or is acting in ways that are suspicious.

Normal Emotions During and After an Abusive Relationship

When a person is traumatized, it is very common for them to experience all kinds of psychological and seemingly neurological or medical issues, and to feel like they are being overly emotional—and in many ways they are, but this is because they have been traumatized. People who have been traumatized often feel like they are going crazy or losing their mind. They begin to feel anxious, paranoid, depressed, suspicious of others, nervous, jumpy, easily agitated, and want to isolate themselves. They may hear voices, have a hard time sleeping or sleep too much, or they may gain or lose a lot of weight. They may become easily irritable or lash out in anger/rage. They may stop talking for long periods of time. In short, they may truly feel that they are crazy, bipolar, or a total mess, and some people do have complete breakdowns and wind up in the hospital. And because to an outsider who isn't deeply familiar with abusive relationships, their symptoms look like schizophrenia, bipolar, or borderline personality disorder, they may be incorrectly diagnosed as such— when really the core of the issue may be that they have **PTSD** from being in an abusive relationship, *especially* when there has been a high degree of psychological abuse present.

A person might also have these other mental health challenges too, but it's important for a mental health clinician to screen for PTSD as well as to explain to the person that even if they have these other mental health challenges that it doesn't mean that the abuse was somehow their fault. Because what tends to happen is that if a person is diagnosed with some sort of mental illness, they become defeated and depressed, and often go into total emotional collapse, thinking that everything really *was* their fault and that they were the problem all along.

If you or someone you care about is on anti-depressants, anti-anxiety pills, or anti-psychotics, or mood stabilizers, and have experienced abuse or trauma, there is a very solid chance that much of your behavior is a very normal reaction to a very abnormal situation and is PTSD related. I encourage you to find a therapist who is familiar with PTSD and treatments for PTSD, such as Eye Movement Desensitization and Reprocessing (EMDR) and Emotional Freedom Technique (EFT) therapy.

Being Overly Emotional

Being overly emotional means to have an emotional response that is out of proportion to the situation. It is very common for abusive people to blame their targets for being "overly emotional" or "too sensitive" if they have a problem with being abused or have any issue with the abuser's questionable behavior. This is not being overly emotional or sensitive—it is normal.

It's also very common for abusers to minimize and justify their behavior. In their mind, their abuse isn't abuse; it's an appropriate reaction to the target stepping out of line—which is why the most common excuse for abusive behavior is some form of "look at what you made me do." And oftentimes an abusive person will intentionally provoke their target to cross that line just so they can start a fight or abuse them. They will often do this by planting seeds of jealousy that would make any normal person suspicious, and then when their partner does finally ask them why they are doing this, the abusive person flies off the handle accusing them of being jealous, manipulative, controlling, or abusive. Or the abusive person will focus on areas that they are sensitive about (their appearance, their parenting, their career, etc.) and then when the target stands up for themselves, the abuser either accuses them of trying to start a fight, or they will break up with the target making it seem like it's the target's fault for being so difficult.

However, even though they've justified their behavior to themselves, for most abusive people, they know on some level that how they are treating their target would not be socially acceptable. That's why they tend not to act this way in front of others.

If you are experiencing (or witnessing) abusive behavior in front of other people, then know that the abusive person has really done some major mental gymnastics to rationalize their behavior and they feel *completely* justified in their treatment of their target. This is really alarming behavior, as it shows a severe lack of empathy, regard, or remorse for their partner. (This is why partners of narcissistic people are often referred to as "targets," because a partner isn't treated this way; only someone who is a target of abuse is treated like this.)

And because they feel their actions are completely reasonable and appropriate, if their target confronts them about their behavior (or oftentimes even confronts them in general), a barrage of abuse (verbal or other kinds) tends to follow.

If the target in any way addresses how they've been treated, their concerns are usually met with being told they are some form of "too emotional," "crazy," "too sensitive," or even that *the target* is the one being manipulative or abusive by bringing up their concerns.

It is an exercise in frustration and crazy making to be rational with a person who is rationalizing their behavior to this extent. *If a person is continuing to rationalize their behavior, and they do not see a problem with it, then they will continue to have that behavior.*

These types of responses are abusive in and of themselves, as they seek to gain power and control over not only a person and the situation, but over a person's perception of their experience. This is the core of gaslighting—which is basically doing something problematic, and then denying it and blaming the target for not seeing the situation correctly. This is where the phrase, "Who are you going to believe, me or your lying eyes?" stems from. When a person is continually being told that the issue is with them, they often come to believe that they really are overly emotional or too sensitive, when in fact they aren't—they are having a normal reaction to abusive or problematic behavior.

Ask yourself how they would react if you acted like them. How would they feel if you were to hide your phone or to message someone and not tell them who or why? Of course, if you were to ask them this, they might say they have no problem with this because they trust you. They aren't telling you this because it's the truth; they are telling you this as a way to plant seeds of insecurity and doubt in you, and to make you question if maybe you are out of line with thinking something is squirrelly with their squirrelly behavior. ...And if their treatment of you is really no big deal, ask yourself how would they react if you mentioned their weight out of "concern," or made snarky comments, or yelled at them? My guess would be that they would flip out and begin yelling, give you the silent treatment, or stay cool, calm, and collected, and then a few days or weeks later start with snarky putdowns and twisting their verbal knives into old wounds that they know you have (wounds that you opened up to them thinking you could trust them with hurtful things that happened in your past). Emotional manipulators can dish it, but they can't take it—and that level of hypocrisy is a big problem, and shows their true level of pathologically- twisted thinking.

"If I questioned him about why he was hiding his phone, or who these women were that were texting him, he'd tell me that I was crazy, paranoid, or jealous. And I believed him, I guess because believing that I was crazy, paranoid, or jealous was easier than accepting that he was most likely cheating on me. I never did found out for certain if he was cheating on me, but I broke up with him anyhow, as I couldn't stand feeling like such a confused and anxious mess. A real relationship doesn't feel like that."
— *Shawna*

Being in Love with Them vs. Being in Love with Who They Pretended to Be

Being in Love with Them

Abusive relationships are confusing and intense relationships. There are often a lot of emotional highs and lows and making up and then breaking up. When times are good, they are often really good—but when times are bad, they are really bad. And because abusive relationships are not only intense, *but also confusing,* it's easy for a person to get lost in the manipulations, lies, intense emotions, and false promises of change that so many emotional manipulators create. This is why it's helpful to back up a bit to try and sort out what love really is and compare it to what we are experiencing.

Love is based on honesty and trust and involves a person being treated with dignity and respect. Love is a feeling of safety and security. Love is knowing where you stand and knowing that the other person is on the same team as you.

If these elements aren't present; then it's not love.

It's "love addiction," and this unhinged neediness is often created by the instability of an abusive person and is part of the trauma bonds manufactured by the highs and lows of an emotional manipulator who is giving you what you need, and then pulling it away (or having it pulled away when you realize what they've been up to) when you least expect it.

I'm not trying to minimize how you feel. I'm sure there are some people reading this right now who want to argue with me and ask me who am I to say what love is and isn't, and that all feelings are valid. Let me be clear; all feelings are valid, but let's make sure that we are all using similar definitions for those feelings. The words you use shape your thoughts and in turn your feelings. If you are calling two drastically different concepts by the same name, you will not only be confused, but also the way you go about understanding what's going on, and the resulting healing that comes from this will also be very different.

My point is that just because you feel intensely towards a person doesn't mean that's love. It might feel like love. I get that; believe me, I do. But it's really important that you get crystal clear on what makes up love, because doing so will make it that much easier to cut through the fog, and to determine whether you are in a healthy relationship or an abusive one. And separating out the difference between healthy love and dysfunctional love addiction will really help to clarify why you feel the way you do and will help you move forward and heal from all of this that much faster. It really messes with people's heads when they find themselves missing a person who treats them so poorly and then falling into a spiral of shame as to why that is. It's because that intensity, craving, and pull to go back to what's toxic is all part of a "love addiction."

I know you feel a level of intensity towards them that you've probably never felt before. I've been there...several times. I get it. It's as though you need them...you crave them, you think about them day and night. And deep down you are ashamed at the depths you'd go (or the depths to which you've already gone) to make this work.

Being in Love with Who They Pretended to Be

Once we get to the place where we can separate love bombing from love, rushing intimacy from true intimacy, intensity from sincerity, love addiction from love, codependency from commitment, then it makes it much easier to get some emotional distance and to see things clearly.

And once we can reframe and redefine our understanding of the intense way we feel, it will also help our brain to process what's going on—because it causes a person a lot of mental anguish to think that they are still in love with a person who treats them so poorly.

Loving who you thought they were, or hoped they could be, makes *a ton* more sense, and it helps your brain get out of that loop of trying to make sense of how you could love someone who causes you so much pain. Because odds are who you hoped they could be (or who they pretended to be) was probably a pretty likable person that you had a lot of good times with. And odds are most people would like the charming, likable, vulnerable side of them too (and that's what they are relying on.)

So if you find yourself missing them, gently remind yourself that you love who you thought they were or who you thought they could become. Shifting your wording will help to relieve a lot of the mental anguish, shame, and anger that can come from thinking you miss or love them.

There's an exercise that I encourage people to do that really helps to see their behavior clearly and to not get sucked back in, and that's what I call writing out your, "For When You Miss Him (or Her) List." List all of the hurtful, harmful, and hateful things that they did, (in bullet point format, so it's fast to read, because once those feelings of nostalgia kick in a chain reaction of feelings happen fast, that tend to be a slippery slope into reopening contact) so *when* "nostalgia" kicks in, and it usually will— you can go back and read your list. It will help to remind you that this person has two very different sides to themselves, and why you need to move forward and not go back to them or anyone like them ever again.

"One of the hardest things for me was to understand how I could love a man who was so cruel to me. I knew how sick this was, and I felt so ashamed that I still had feelings for him. Then someone in a support group told me that I didn't love him, that I loved who he pretended to be and who I wished he was, and that made a lot more sense. After all, the guy he pretended to be was a great guy and anyone would have liked that guy—but that's not who he really was…and that's why I left."

— *Sasha*

Workable Behavior vs. Deal Breakers

Workable Behavior

Workable behavior is any behavior that *you* decide is not a deal breaker for you—not me, not your parents, not your spouse, not your therapist, *you*. And while it's much easier to determine the difference between what's workable and what's a deal breaker *before* you get emotionally invested in a person or a situation, it oftentimes takes us being in really toxic situations for us to get the clarity that we never want to be in a situation like that again.

Deal Breakers

A deal breaker is any behavior that you decide is an instant "I'm out." Everyone's deal breakers are different, however, I think you'll find that for people who truly value themselves and the peace in their life, any type of behavior that would cause major destruction in their lives would be a deal breaker. At a minimum, this would be any type of abuse, active addictions, adultery, or a bad attitude (meaning either someone who is constantly negative, unsupportive, critical and criticizing, or who treats them with a lack of dignity or respect.

Outside of some more major deal breakers, here are some other potential deal breakers to consider:

- Opening up joint credit cards or taking out loans without your knowledge or consent (or breaking trust in some way).
- Differences with wanting (or not wanting) children.
- Differences in religion (and are differences in religion a big deal? Will they be a big deal if and when you have children)?
- Different ideas on how children should be disciplined or raised in general.

- Different ideas on what healthy boundaries are with family and friends.
- Different ideas on how money should be saved, spent, or invested.
- Different ideas on lifestyle and where (and how) you want to live.
- Differences with how to fight (Do they slam doors, give the silent treatment, and threaten divorce when they fight? Or do they ask for time to cool down and say that they'd like to talk about this more tomorrow night)?

To try to convince yourself that you can turn deal-breaker behavior into workable behavior will only frustrate you, and it will annoy the other person. Not to mention that trying to fix something that isn't within your ability to fix will most likely lead to all kinds of emotional and physical issues including anxiety, depression, headaches, constipation/irritable bowels/GI issues, fatigue or exhaustion, unexplainable pain, inflammation, and chronic illness. If you are experiencing any of these symptoms, first make sure that it's not your relationships that are making you sick.

If you are in a "relationship" (manipulation-ship) that involves behavior that falls within what would be considered deal-breaker behavior for most people, and you want to try to make things work, before you throw a lot of time, money, and emotional energy into "fixing" your relationship, I'd encourage you to get crystal clear on the following:

- Is this an event or a pattern?
- Do they have a pattern of acting in ways that minimize you or your concerns about things?
- Does this person have sincere and full accountability for their problematic behavior, or is it a continual struggle to try and pull the full truth out of them?

And most importantly:

- Where is your line in the sand? Do you have deal-breaker behavior for others, or is the plan to hang on until they've caused so much damage that you can't hang on anymore?
- What kind of changes would you need to see (and over what time frame) in order for you to stay?
- How much time and/or money are you willing to spend in therapy before you move on?

I'm gonna tell it to you straight. It boils down to this: does this person have a pattern of treating you with a lack of respect, a lack or dignity, a lack of regard, and an overall jaw dropping lack of indifference? If the answer is "yes," then you would be wise to make this deal-breaker stuff, because when a person continually shows you through their actions that they don't care about you or the relationship, it's a good idea to get away from that person. Normal, healthy adults don't have the moral compass of a sociopath, and to think that deep down they could actually have a moral compass will only lead to you being let down, disappointed, angry, and hurt in the long run. Because what tends to happen is that they don't change, they just get better at hiding their deceit. They might say that they care and promise to change, but look at their actions. Not their actions when they've been caught or when they claim to be sorry—I'm talking about their actions when they think you haven't been looking. That's who people really are. And while Benjamin Franklin once said that there are only two things that are certain in this life: death and taxes, I'm gonna add a third one to that list, and that is when a person is a chronic liar, what you think you know is only the tip of the iceberg.

So if you find out that they are acting single when you aren't looking, then you'd be wise to cut them loose and let them be single. It's a big fat waste of your time, energy, and money to be a spouse to a person who acts like they are single when you aren't around. And it's a mistake to expect loyalty from someone who won't even give you honesty.

"It wasn't until recently that I realized that I had the mindset that everything was and should be workable. I didn't even know people with such pathological behavior existed. Actually, I guess I did know, but I always thought I'd be able to spot them. I didn't realize that a

person could (or would) claim to be a Christian, go to church every weekend, go to such great lengths to act like the most amazing husband and father and live a double life. It took me over twenty years of being married to a man who was a chronic liar and cheater to fully realize that he was never going to change. I thought that commitment was forever, and that everything was workable. I didn't have deal breakers, and I didn't believe in divorce. I was the perfect target for him, and he knew it from day one. I had a pretty ideal childhood, and my parents were happily married for close to fifty years before my father died. I knew relationships were hard work, and I wanted to do whatever it took to have a relationship like my parents had. I kept thinking that my ex would eventually see the light and change. None of us realized just how manipulative my ex-husband was, and we all believed his excuses and lies for years. My ex "borrowed" I don't even know how much money from my parents which he never repaid, and recently I found out he has a child with another woman. The damage he's done to our family is horrendous."

— *Stacy*

Kindness vs. Weakness

Kindness

To really embrace the concept of kindness means for us to be friendly, considerate, and compassionate—towards others *as well as towards ourselves.* Kindness is only truly kind if our actions are considerate and compassionate to everyone involved. If we are considerate and compassionate to others at the expense of our own safety or sanity, then there is a problem. We are either being manipulated, or we have blurred the concepts of compassion and codependency, or both. At a minimum, if we are continually putting others ahead of ourselves to the point where we are being used, abused, exploited, lied to, cheated on, stolen from, or feel exhausted or crazy around certain people, then our beliefs about how we deserve to be treated as well as our boundaries need some work.

Many people who find themselves perpetually hurt or let down by toxic people tend to start to feel bitter and jaded. This is because they are operating from the standpoint that if they are nice to people that people will be nice back—and this isn't always the case.

Weakness

Weakness means to lack strength. In terms of interacting with others—especially highly manipulative others—it often means lacking strength of boundaries and standards, and letting others steamroll over us, while thinking that if we can just be kind enough to them that they'll stop, and will eventually treat us with all the kindness and support we have given to them. You can't people please your way into being treated well by an abusive person. All this does is make you more of a target.

Now I'm not saying that I think partners of narcissists are weak—they are not. They have been manipulated, and their kindness has been exploited. They have been through hell, and it takes a strong person to go through hell and come out on the other side. However, they often don't realize how strong they are, because once they leave hell, they often collapse and feel like they can't go on. What they don't realize is that healing takes time and it's more of a marathon and not a sprint—and that they don't have to go on the rest of this journey alone.

Once the fog of manipulation starts to clear, and they start learning about their standards and boundaries, that's when the magic really starts to happen, and over time they get in tune with their inner guidance and where their boundaries are. The result of this is that they learn to balance their kindness with boundaries, the result of which is that they become some of the most powerful, self-actualized people out there.

"Once I realized that my mother was continually preying on my kindness, I realized that the solution wasn't necessarily to stop being kind, it was that I needed to get comfortable with having boundaries with her and to stop feeling guilty because I stopped giving into whatever she wanted. At first, I felt really mean by standing up for myself, but if me being "kind" to her, meant that I wasn't being kind to myself, then something big was out of balance there. My family life with my husband is a lot more in balance, now that I won't let my mother continually borrow money, stay with us whenever she's been evicted, or yell at us whenever she feels like it. I would never have tolerated being treated like that by a total stranger, and it's sad that my own mother would treat me like that and that I thought that was

somehow okay. My kindness is no longer my weakness to be exploited by people like her."

— *Candace*

Acceptance vs. Allowance

Acceptance of Problematic Behavior

Acceptance of problematic behavior doesn't mean that you are okay with it, or that you have to continue to allow it in your life. It means that you are accepting that this is their behavior. You might still hope that they might change down the road, but you aren't holding your breath. When (and only when) we accept someone else's behavior for what it is can we start to see the situation clearly and then start anticipating how they will most likely act.

Allowance of Problematic Behavior

Allowance of problematic behavior is when we realize that a person has problematic behavior and then allow them continued and open access into our lives, even though their behavior is disruptive, disempowering, damaging, or destructive. Allowing problematic behavior to continue tends to either come from a place of feeling ground down and hopeless that things will ever change, or it is a sign that standards, boundaries, and self-worth need some work. Many people tend to keep toxic people in their lives out of guilt, fear of being alone, or fear of what they (or others) might say or do, or obligation. *However, your life will dramatically start to improve once you start keeping people in your inner circle based on how they treat you instead of how you feel about them or based on what relation they are to you.*

"I've become really picky about who I let into my inner circle these days. I've spent my life surrounded by abusive and manipulative people and I guess I thought that was normal. My brother has been in and out of jail multiple times for drugs and violence. I kept thinking I needed to keep him in my inner circle because he was my brother— even though he continually stole from me and caused a ton of disruption in our life. The last straw was that he made a general threat about hurting me and my family. Now that I see his behavior clearly, I 'accept' that he is who he is, and I respond accordingly. I do still have hope that he will change, but that's more for his sake. With him threatening us, that was the final straw, and I'm done. I'm not going to put my family at risk and let him cause more damage because he's my brother or because I hope that he might someday change. I accept him for who he is at this point in his life, and now I keep him at a safe distance. It's sad things have to be this way, but it is what it is."

— *Darrel*

Self-worth vs. Hurt Feelings

Self-worth

Self-worth is a person's confidence in themselves and in their abilities, and it makes up an important component of their self-identity. Self-worth is who we think we are and what we think we are capable of.

Hurt Feelings

Hurt feelings are what we commonly get when someone says something hurtful about us or about our abilities. There is no shortage of people with inconsiderate, rude, or abusive behavior out there, and hurt feelings will happen. However, we can make the conscious decision to let hurt feelings be hurt feelings, and to not let those hurt feelings negatively impact our self-worth. Other people can think and say what they want about us, and we don't need to accept their opinions about us as truth. Even if their opinions are truth, we don't need to let them impact our self-worth. Easier said than done, I know.

A helpful way that I've found to do this is to visualize keeping your self-worth and hurt feelings in two different buckets. This technique can also be a great way to undo a lot of what that abusive person said to you. So if you are hearing all of the hurtful things that they told you, imagine yourself taking that comment out of your self-worth bucket and putting it into your hurt feelings bucket.

It's important that we keep these buckets separate, and practice paying attention to what it feels like and how we tend to act if our hurt feelings bucket is full and has spilled over into our self-worth bucket. We can separate out the different marbles into the right buckets so we don't let another person's opinion of us negatively influence who we think we are or what we are capable of.

If we are getting feedback from a person who is abusive or a chronic liar, then it's important that we realize that their opinion isn't going to be accurate—because abusive people tear down others in order to make themselves feel better. As the saying goes, rudeness is the weak person's imitation of strength. Healthy, happy people don't go around destroying others, only abusive people do. Abusive people tend to focus on the qualities of another person that they are jealous of or that they know will foster the deepest insecurities in the other person so that their abusive comments have maximum impact. Please don't let these kinds of people determine your self-worth, because the only way they know how to feel secure within themselves is by destroying others. Don't give them the satisfaction of destroying you. Dig deep and find your fight to reclaim your self-worth, and remember, the best revenge really is living a great life.

"My ex continually put me down in ways that were very subtle. He'd plant seeds of insecurity about my weight, my job, and how attractive other women were. I never thought this was verbal or emotional abuse,

I always thought he was just being brutally honest, and that there really were all these things wrong with me. All his hurtful comments I took to be truth, and I allowed them to really impact my self-esteem and self-worth. I now realize that it's normal to have hurt feelings when someone is abusive like that, but that I can make the conscious effort to not let it impact my self-worth."

— *Janice*

Reacting vs. Responding

Reacting

Reacting to something means to give a "knee-jerk" reflexive reaction to someone's behavior or to a situation. They take an action, and then we reflexively take an immediate reaction. These reflexive actions happen without thinking, and it can (and often does) happen to most of us—especially if we are "emotionally triggered" by something (which we may or may not realize that we are being emotionally triggered by).

Responding

Responding to something means to give a thought out response to something. There is the action, then there is our planned out response. It takes a good amount of self-awareness, self-control, *and practice* to shift our behavior from a reaction to a response. Once you realize that you've been stuck in a loop of reacting to someone else's behavior, then you can work towards breaking that cycle. Doing so can be *so* empowering.

It's a great feeling to see when a person is baiting, provoking, or otherwise trying to drag you down into the mud to wrestle around with them—and it's incredibly empowering when you can sidestep their drama and dysfunction and not even miss a beat. It takes a lot of awareness of their behavior and practice anticipating what they are going to do and how we respond to it, but you can get there. If you keep practicing responding, it will eventually become your new normal, and then there will come a time when you will think it's strange that you ever did anything different. The added benefit to this is once you really get this skill down— awareness of what is—and anticipate their behavior and plan your response to it, you will be able to transfer that skill to every other situation that you come across, and you will be able to do this so quickly and possibly even effortlessly, that you don't even experience the situation as problematic. Because you've become so nimble, you are easily able to adapt and adjust your response. It's kinda like how an Olympic hurdler runs and jumps over those hurdles. It takes a lot of practice, but once they get it down, they really get it down, and they just sail through the air and jump over those hurdles like they are nothing.

"My ex-husband used to play this game with me, although it took me awhile to realize that's what it was. He'd provoke me with saying

things he knew would set me off (like blaming me for his cheating, or telling me that my father should have beaten me more when I was a child, for example), and then when I would explode in anger, he'd sit back and act cool, calm, and collected, and then play like the victim of me—that I was being so mean and abusive to him. For years, I thought if I could just get through to him as to how much he was hurting me that he'd stop bringing up certain topics and learn to 'fight fair.' Then I began learning about narcissistic abuse and realized he was hitting all my pain points intentionally so I would react, and so he could play the victim. Once I saw it as a game, I realized I needed to stay calm, stay in control of myself and the situation, and get away from him before he began pushing my buttons. Now when I have to see him, which is not very often, I respond to him, I don't react. It's kinda funny, because he gets all flustered and upset when I don't react."

— Samantha

"One thing I have discovered about myself is that being around disordered people, and becoming the direct target of their insanity will trigger me into an emotional flashback. And with this sort of experience there is no working through it, unraveling it, decoding it and then slowly over time learn how to stop going into the flashback experience.

Because I received the sort of advice that I could learn how to respond, then I actually believed I "should" be able to be around the disordered. I felt I "should" be able to be exposed directly to their attacks of rage and fury, their accusations, and their manipulations. And that I "should" be able to stand there, and respond calmly, and I "should" not go into a flashback that paralyzes me with terror and fear, and that cuts off my ability to communicate with my middle brain or my frontal cortex.

But being told that I "should" be able to learn how to do this – stop going into the flashback, remain completely in control of my emotions, and be able to simply and calmly respond - left me feeling completely and deeply shame filled, because I really cannot stop the emotional flashbacks when they occur. When someone starts yelling at me out of the blue with no warning and for no reason, then I am instantly hijacked into a flashback, and no amount of delving into the past, or into the underlying issues, or even spending millions of dollars on therapy is ever going to change this, or is ever going to help me. I will never be able to remain calm, take a step back, and cock my head to the side, detach emotionally, and wonder why they are acting so crazy. I am quite literally hijacked by my amygdala, and become mute and paralyzed and terrified with fear.

So what is the answer? What is the cure? I have had to learn to accept, and to be patient, and understanding, and forgiving of myself for not being able to get on top of these paralyzing emotional flashback experiences, and I have had to face full on with no flinching or avoiding it that I personally am not capable of doing or getting to the state you of not being triggered into reacting. My reaction being a sort of mute terrified paralysis.

The only thing I can do is to cut this person ruthlessly out of my life, and never ever see them or have any contact with them ever again. And to forgive myself a 1000 times a day for not being able to tolerate their behavior emotionally, and respect and honor that I simply cannot be around anyone who exhibits extreme disordered behavior towards me. And in particular anyone who exhibits unprovoked and unexpected rage. So just some thoughts on people who are permanently scarred with CPTSD is they may not ever be able to respond, and it's nothing to feel guilty about.

The wonderful news is that as long as I stay away from them, I live a peaceful, calm, flashback free life!"

— Luci

Feeling Appropriately Emotional vs. Feeling Emotionally Triggered

Feeling Appropriately Emotional

Feeling appropriately emotional is having a feeling that is in proportion to what's going on. It's normal to feel sad or depressed when a relationship is over. It's normal to feel anxious if we lose our job, or don't have enough money in the bank to pay bills. It's normal to feel happy when we come home and see our pet. It's normal to feel distrustful of others when you've gotten out of an abusive relationship (especially one that included emotional and psychological abuse). It's normal to feel angry and enraged at being used, abused, and to have had your good and trusting nature exploited.

Feeling Emotionally Triggered

Feeling emotionally triggered can come across in different ways for different people, but usually it's the feeling of being disproportionately emotional to a situation. My guess would be that the vast majority of people out there have some sort of emotional triggers. Perhaps they've never thought of them this way—most likely, because if these are long-standing triggers, we might think we just feel this way, and that there's nothing more to it.

When a person feels this way, they might not know why—they just know that they are experiencing intense emotion. For example, a person might feel really angry, "tightly wound" or depressed around the holidays, or they might hate being around children, or perhaps they get upset walking into a church or hearing other people discuss religion, or seeing a car that looks like their ex's and feeling sad or mad which leaves them in a "funk" that might last all day or even all week.

I want to point out that there's a difference between a preference and a trigger, and the difference is that a preference is more emotionally neutral. So for example, a person might not want children or they might not be a fan of religion, but if the mere mention of these topics brings out a fight or flight response, (feeling defensive, angry, and wanting to fight about it) then there is more there. Preferring one thing over another, such as preferring to not have children or to not be religious normally leaves a person feeling more emotionally neutral.

Although emotional triggers can be really unpleasant, and most of us spend our whole lives trying to run from them, they can actually be very revealing as they are a signal that there are some emotions a few layers deep that need to be resolved. The good news is that once an emotion is resolved, its power over a person dissolves rather quickly. Because we are rarely (if ever) truly upset by the events themselves—it's our *perceptions* of the events *and the meaning that we assign to them* that determine how we feel. If we want to instantly change how we feel, a great way to do that is to change the meaning we assign to different events. And the meaning we assign to different events in large part comes from new understandings that we can form. Oftentimes these new understandings come from getting new information, and in terms of narcissistic abuse, I highly recommend reading my first book called, "Start Here" which covers all of the basic terms, concepts, and frequently asked questions surrounding narcissistic abuse. It is a crash-course guide of sorts for getting people up-to-speed with figuring out what's going on and why.

Silent Treatment vs. Cooling Down

The Silent Treatment

The silent treatment is a form of verbal abuse and is designed to punish and "groom" a person into acting a certain way. The silent treatment involves withholding communication, affection, or attention from a person with the intent to punish them for acting a certain way, and grooms them to never act this way again. Generally a narcissistic partner will give the silent treatment if their partner questions or challenges them in any way and to any degree. Even asking the simplest of questions to which they don't feel they owe their partner an answer or explanation can result in the silent treatment. The person on the receiving end of the silent treatment is left to twist in the wind, wondering when and if the other person will reopen communication with them.

Freezing a person out like this is abusive, as it creates intense (and unnecessarily) psychological and emotional anguish in the person experiencing it. It damages trust, honesty, and communication, and leaves the person who is experiencing it to start walking on eggshells. From then on out they've learned they can't bring up concerns or certain topics, or else their partner will withhold communication and/or affection from them.

Cooling Down

Cooling down is when a person gets upset and needs their space. It may be seen as similar to the silent treatment in that one person is upset and doesn't want to talk to the other, but their desire not to talk isn't to punish the other person; it's either an effort to stop the fighting that is going on, or it's to collect their thoughts so they don't say anything they'll later regret.

Cooling down involves open, honest, sincere, and solutions-oriented communication, which includes letting the other person know they plan on reopening communication in *a reasonable time frame* so the other person isn't twisting in the wind.

Needing time to cool down and not to talk to another person is okay—especially if a person is concerned they are going to say something they are going to regret—and knowing that you need some time to cool down shows a healthy degree of self-awareness. Needing time to cool down could be expressed in a way such as, "I'm really upset right now and need some time to gather my thoughts. I'll call you tomorrow;" or, "Can we talk more about this tonight/tomorrow/this weekend when I see you?" or, "I'm done fighting about this—we aren't getting anywhere. I love you, but I need to go for a walk right now. Can we talk about this when I get home?"

This way, the conversation is put on pause. The other person isn't left to twist in the wind because a time frame is given, and there is the reassurance that the issue will be brought back up and resolved. In a relationship with a narcissist, many issues are never resolved. The partner is left to twist themselves into an emotional pretzel trying to "forgive," "forget," or otherwise "move past" all the hurt that their partner has caused in an effort to keep the relationship going. And because these issues aren't fully resolved they tend to keep coming up—either the partner brings them up whenever they fight, or they continue to try to keep stuffing their emotions down—and these emotions are coming out in physical ways, such as weight gain or loss, drinking/drug use, depression, anxiety, "stomach issues" such as diarrhea or constipation, chronic inflammation, etc. If you are having any of these issues, it's worth examining the relationships with the people in your inner circle. It's amazing the havoc that unprocessed emotions can cause on both emotional and physical levels—and it's also equally amazing as to how quickly people can start to heal from these things once they either leave that environment or start to effectively understand and process their feelings. (This all might sound really hippy woo-woo, but it's true.)

"My ex gave me the silent treatment twice, both times were because I disagreed with him. The first time it happened, he claimed he didn't mean to and that he was just cooling off—and he agreed not to do it again. I told him that it was okay if he needed time to cool down, but to please let me know when he did want to reopen communication so I wasn't twisting in the wind. The second time he gave the silent treatment, again, it was for something small—I disagreed with him over something political. He told me he needed several weeks before he'd wanted to talk again. I gave him the time, which in hindsight I shouldn't have, because even though he was still giving me a time frame, he was still trying to punish me for disagreeing with him. I'd

dated abusive men before, and I really thought he was different because he seemed to want to work towards a solution, but he was actually the worst, because there was never a true solution; it was all only another level to his game. It took me several years to see the truth, but once I did, I broke up with him. I've found that while a relationship does take work, it should take the work of trying to be treated with respect. That should be obvious and already there."

— *Danielle*

"Though my ex (who I now believe was a psychopath) did not do much in the way of direct overt abuse (his main crime was living a double life and keeping it completely secret from me), he did employ the silent treatment on occasion. But here is one stark difference to me between the silent treatment and cooling off: whenever he would decide the time of being silent was over and he would return, the REASON for the silent treatment was NEVER discussed or alluded to. We were simply to pick up where we left off, and there was NO DISCUSSION EVER about what caused him to do it, or what could be done to prevent it happening again. In a way, I had to learn how to live as if the silent treatment had never even happened at all. So this lack of discussion to me is an indicator that it IS silent treatment and it IS punishment. If you cannot even discuss upon their return why they left, or why they stopped talking and walked out in the first place, and you have to pretend like nothing ever happened, then it's punishment, not cooling off."

— *Luci*

No Contact vs. Silent Treatment

No Contact

Going "no contact" is a *defensive strategy* in which a person cuts off all contact with a person who has crazy-making, toxic, or abusive behavior. Going "no contact" with someone who is agitating, provoking, pot stirring, deceitful, manipulative, or abusive is a normal and healthy response to problematic behavior. You don't owe anyone an explanation for going "no contact" with problematic people in your life, especially the abusive person. This is your life—it's not a democracy. Other people—especially ones who don't have to live with the consequences—don't get to vote on what you do and don't do.

Many people who have a narcissist in their life are either told by well-intended (but misguided) people or by the narcissist that *they* are being mean or abusive by cutting off contact with them. This is not the case. You don't need to be someone else's verbal, emotional, or physical punching bag. It is normal and healthy to have deal-breaker behavior for what we allow into our lives. Taking actual steps to actually "break the deal" is the action part of having a deal breaker. It's what enforcing a boundary looks like in motion. And yes, it can be really hard at first. And yes, there will be no shortage of people out there who will give you generally well-intentioned bad advice to reopen contact because this person had a bad childhood, or is a parent, or is a family member, or that you should be more compassionate, or that they must be truly sorry because they now have found God or therapy or rehab. It can be really hard (and incredibly angering) to feel that you continually have to defend your boundaries when you are the one who is the target of abusive behavior, and are only trying to defend yourself and/or your family. It can help to anticipate (and rehearse different scenarios) as to what others will say and to come up with a planned response so you aren't caught off guard emotionally and then get angry, lash out, or fall into a depression when the topic comes up.

An example might be something like:

Family member: "Mom wants to visit you for the holidays, and she wants to stay for a month."

You: "Huh, that's interesting. ...So what are you doing for the holidays?" And then just switch the conversation to something else. Or if they push the issue, you could say something like, "I've decided I need to distance myself from her. She's been abusive to me my whole life, and I'm done being treated like that. Plus, it's not okay for her to treat my kids like that either." Or you could simply say, "I'd rather not talk about this" and stop the conversation in its tracks.

Family member: "She's your mother! You need to forgive her; she's not getting any younger, you know. One day you will be sorry you treated her like this.

You: "Believe me, no one is sadder than me about not being able to have a relationship with my own mother. But I have to cut contact because she's abusive towards me. I've put up with being treated like that my whole life, and I'm done. I'm not going to continue to let her cause damage to me or my family…. If she were a man, I'd have divorced him by now. If she were a boss, I would have quit. If she were a friend, I'd no longer talk to her. Just because she's my mother doesn't mean that she can be abusive towards me. Do you understand how twisted that is? That my own mother is abusive—the one person who should treat me with love and respect grinds me down and is abusive, and I'm the one being told that my behavior is out of line. It's not. This is me having healthy boundaries for myself, and me looking out for what's best for my marriage and my children. People need to treat me and my family with respect, or they are not welcome here. I know you don't like my decision, but I'm asking that you respect it and not bring up any of this again."

But keep in mind, you don't have to defend yourself either, and a simple, "I'm not open to discussing this" will suffice.

The Silent Treatment

The silent treatment is a form of verbal abuse and is a "grooming" behavior that is designed to "groom" (teach) a person how to behave. It is generally done by emotional manipulators if they are confronted about their problematic behavior, or challenged in any way (even ways that were unintended or only happened in their mind). The silent treatment is used to punish a person into submission, and is lifted after the abusive person decided their target has been sufficiently punished. Whereas no contact isn't a punishment, it's self-protection, it isn't intended to be lifted—it's intended to be permanent. (Although many targets end up breaking no contact because they feel "addicted" to their abuser or guilty or mean for setting a boundary.)

Low Contact

Low contact is where a person decides that they can't or don't want to limit contact with a problematic person, and so they have limited contact with them. Low contact is what many former spouses of abusive people do when they have children together, or if a person has an abusive or problematic family member that they feel obligated to stay in contact with. Low contact is where a person still has some degree of a relationship with a problematic person, but the level of their relationship depends on what *you* are comfortable with or the bare minimum that is necessary (as is often the case when children are involved).

Deciding what your boundaries are all starts with getting to know yourself, and knowing what's workable for you. I've found that a good way to start with this is to reverse engineer it. Meaning, ask yourself, "What do I need to do in order to keep myself safe and sane in this situation?" And then work your way backwards from that point. So, for example, if you realize that spending a week with family over the holidays is always stressful and ends in fighting, then something needs to change.

Perhaps you realize that about five hours with certain family members is your limit before tension ensues and the yelling starts; then make five hours your limit. If you are flying to see family, you could stay somewhere else and then visit them until you are ready to leave. Then you can go back to your hotel, or friend's house, or other family member's house, or what have you.

There is no reason to stay with family for a week if everyone is fighting and miserable the whole time, and you wind up frustrated to tears, stressed out, or sick. Maybe you decide to take a family vacation to some neutral place where everyone has their own space, and can do their own thing. If a situation is not working for you, then come up with some ideas on what would work and try that instead—and then continue to adjust accordingly.

Change is *always* somewhat difficult and intimidating—even if it's for the best. So when people start drawing boundaries (changing things)—especially in families—things rarely go over well at first, especially if the family dynamic is dysfunctional and full of people who don't have boundaries and they are all used to walking on eggshells around all the elephants that are packed into the room. A great way to tell the degree of dysfunction in your family is based on how you feel. Do you go home sick, or does going home make you sick? If it's the latter, then it's time to examine your boundaries and standards, and to re-evaluate your approach if necessary. So for example, let's say instead of your abusive mother staying with you and your family for one month over Christmas, you decide that is too long, and that it'd be better if she stayed for three days. Then you try that out. If that doesn't work, perhaps you decide to fly out to visit her for a week and stay in a hotel, so you can get a break when you need one. If that doesn't work, then perhaps you move to giving a phone call only, and if that doesn't work, then perhaps a card in the mail, and if that still doesn't work then maybe you go no contact. What you decide to do is up to you, and only you have the right answer for what that is.

Speaking Out vs. Smear Campaign

Speaking Out

Speaking out after being abused is something that many targets/victims of abuse often feel the need to do after the relationship is over. In part, it's because the fog of manipulation and confusion is lifting, and they are both incredibly angry and want to speak *the truth*, and in part it may be to warn others. To those who have never been abused by a narcissist, it might sound like they are acting in ways that are bitter, jaded, or "overly dramatic." Or perhaps others may feel that they are unfairly attacking the abusive person's reputation and character. However, when a person speaks out about what happened to them, they are often doing so as a way for them to reclaim their power and control over what happened to them. Finding their voice, and speaking up and out about how they were treated, plays a big part in that. It is incredibly invalidating, minimizing, infuriating, and revictimizing to be told by others to stop talking about what happened, or that they need to move on.

Healing from trauma takes time, and many people who have been through narcissistic abuse have lived in a fog of guilt, manipulation, fear, shame, doubt, confusion, and crazy making for a long time. Oftentimes they were made to feel as if they were the problem, and when they realize what's really been going on, all that hurt and anger gets stirred up within them, and they often want to shout their truth from the rooftops. Part of healing means finding your voice and speaking your truth—and everyone does that in different ways and for different lengths of time. To have others try to control what they say and do is micromanaging, stifling, and feels very controlling and reminiscent of the abusive relationship they were in before.

Not to mention that many people who go through an abusive relationship feel "crazy" by the end of it, and struggle with C-PTSD—which makes them feel even crazier. Part of healing from this involves rehashing what happened, because in order for the brain to fully process emotions, it needs to understand what happened and where those emotions are coming from. A traumatic event affects a person's memory and leaves them feeling (and remembering) the situation in a fragmented way. Recovering from trauma involves putting together all of the pieces and incorporating what happened to them into a workable narrative that they can incorporate that into their life—instead of feeling that this is a bomb that went off and dividing their life into this event and then everything else.

Smear Campaign

A smear campaign is an unfair and untrue attack on the target's reputation or character by making *false* accusations (that are often believed by others). Emotional manipulators are notorious for launching smear campaigns after the ending of a relationship (regardless of who ends it). In part, it's their way of maintaining their public image, and it's also a way that their level of denial and their lack of self-awareness about their behavior shows itself, by letting others know (and reassuring themselves) that they are not the problem. A smear campaign often involves half-truths to full-out lies, and usually the abuser paints themselves as the victim.

For example, the abuser might claim that his ex-wife is manipulative and won't let him see "his" kids, and that is nothing more than a greedy gold-digging "whore" who sleeps around. What he's left out is that he was incredibly abusive to both her and the kids, and that the kids are terrified to see him. Her "gold digging" is wanting child support, and her being a "whore" is her starting to date someone new.

So please know that while there may be two sides to every story, not every side is equally valid or even honest.

"I thought being in an abusive relationship was hard. I thought leaving an abusive relationship was hard. None of that was as bad as the ongoing smear campaign my ex has launched against me. He's telling people that I was the one who cheated, lied, manipulated, and abused him—and many people believe him! His abuse just doesn't stop, and what's worse, I think he believes many of his own lies and is getting our children to believe them too."

"When I began speaking out about what happened to me, many people didn't want to hear it. They kept telling me to 'get over it' or that I should be happy he's no longer in my life. What they don't seem to realize is that I was abused and terrorized by this man for decades, and during all of that I lost my voice and I nearly lost my mind. Now that I am free, I share my story in hopes of warning and educating others. I find it infuriating when people try to tell me what I "should" be doing, and how I "should" heal. They aren't me and they haven't been through what I've been through, and no, I'm not going to stop talking about what happened to me."

— Betty

Abuse vs. Reactive Abuse

Abuse

Abusive behavior is to treat a person with cruelty—usually (but it doesn't have to be) on an ongoing basis. Abusive behavior is behavior that is disempowering, defining, demeaning, devaluing, degrading, destructive, dangerous, or deadly towards another person.

At the core of all abusive behavior is a person's need to gain and keep power and control over their target and over the situation and is done in at least one of these seven ways: physically, verbally, emotionally, psychologically, financially, sexually, or spiritually.

Reactive Abuse

Reactive abuse is also any type of abusive behavior that is disempowering, defining, demeaning, devaluing, degrading, destructive, dangerous, or deadly towards another person. However, the difference between reactive abuse and abuse is that reactive abuse is a reaction a person has after being abused. It's the proverbial straw that breaks the camel's back and is where the target gets pushed (either verbally, emotionally, psychologically, or physically) to where they "snap" and react back in an abusive way.

The root of reactive abuse is an attempt for the target to reclaim some of their power and control over themselves and over their situation, and sometimes being assertive or leaving isn't an option. This can be due to any number of reasons including: fear that being assertive will make the abuse worse, trauma bonds/Stockholm Syndrome, fear that their partner will leave, intimidation, or out of cultural, religious, financial, or other social pressure.

Reactive abuse can be done in ways that are either passive aggressive or aggressive, such as cheating in response to being cheated on (in an attempt to "settle the score") or stealing money, lying, or lashing out and yelling/name calling, or becoming physically violent.

When targets of abuse start to become abusive themselves, they often experience a tremendous amount of confusion and concern regarding their behavior, wondering if they are just as hurtful and harmful as their partner, or fear that they have now become a narcissist or an abuser. While both forms of abusive behavior are highly problematic in their own way, the target who has become reactively abusive generally doesn't stay abusive once they are away from their crazy- making, provoking, and otherwise abusive partner. Even though abuse of any kind is problematic, the upside of a target getting to the point where they are becoming reactively abusive is oftentimes their emotional rock bottom. This is their wake up call to where they realize they can't stay in a relationship like this, as being around this other person is causing such a radical negative change in their behavior.

"I think one of the reasons I stayed so long was because I felt guilty for becoming abusive. He would push my buttons or not give me a clear answer about other women or about money that would go missing, and it got to the point where I'd fly into a rage and start screaming at him. I'd never felt that kind of anger and rage before, and I thought that leaving him because he was abusive was hypocritical of me, since I had become abusive too. When I heard the term 'reactive abuse' I realized that's what was going on, and I also realized that I needed to leave because our relationship was toxic, and I didn't like the person I was becoming."

— *Cindy*

The Cycle of a Narcissistic Relationship vs. The Cycle of a Normal Relationship

The Cycle of a Narcissistic Relationship

The cycle of a narcissistic relationship tends to run the course of: idealize, devalue, discard. But a more fleshed out view of this cycle tends to run the course of: idealize, devalue, discard, replace, smear campaign, hoover.

A narcissistically abusive relationship is often one that is full of intense and extreme highs and lows, where the good times are really good, but the bad times are really bad.

Idealize. The idealize stage is often full of intensity, false flattery, mirroring, love bombing, and rushing intimacy, all of which creates a whirlwind situation where the target feels like they've met their soul mate. But what's really going on is that they are getting caught in a web of manipulation and deceit that the narcissist is weaving. To a person who is not familiar with narcissistic abuse, the idealize stage not only doesn't come across as problematic, it comes across as, well, ideal. This is because the narcissist is morphing into being their perfect partner, which normal people don't do. This is why they feel like a soul mate or like the perfect partner.

Over time, the idealize stage gradually begins to morph into the devalue stage, which often starts out with small, strange blips of confusing behavior that aren't in alignment with who you thought they were. These blips might be small things that they say that seem disturbing, "confusing," or strange, flashes of anger, rage, or silent treatment if you ask them a question about something that they are doing that seems strange or "off," dress a certain way, or express an opinion that differs from theirs.

Devalue. The devalue stage often progresses, and involves any or all forms of abusive behavior which includes verbal, emotional, psychological, financial, sexual, spiritual, and/or physical. This abusive behavior comes across in ways that are either overt (more obvious) or covert (less obvious/hidden) or both, and often includes lying (often to a point that would be considered well outside the realm of normal behavior—such as lying when the truth would serve them better), cheating, stealing (i.e. opening up hidden bank accounts, loans, credit cards, using household money to fund a double life), and/or manipulating (pretending to want to work on things but living a double life). The devalue stage can be done to the person's face, behind their back, or both. None of this is "normal" behavior, *and any one of these things* is highly problematic and worthy of being a deal breaker.

Discard. The discard stage involves the target being dumped out of the clear blue without sincere empathy or remorse as to the pain—such as coming home one day and filing for divorce with no notice or seemingly even any issues, and insisting that you and the children move out. Or suddenly breaking up with the target in a detached, indifferent, and immature way. The discard stage is not only cold and calloused, but it is usually done in a cruel way to inflict maximum pain on the target, such as breaking up with them after they've been diagnosed with cancer, right after you've signed a lease together, bought a home, or adopted a pet or child, or right before a major holiday, vacation, or birthday. The reason for this seems to be that the narcissist feeds off of the extreme pain from their target—as it makes them feel smug and superior.

Replace. You might find that you were replaced in record-breaking time. You might be shocked if you find out that not only do they have a new partner, but they seem so happy and in love, like your relationship with them didn't matter, or didn't even happen. The odds are that they didn't find this new person after your relationship ended, but that this person had been in their "pipeline" for quite awhile. Narcissists tend to keep a ready supply of people on hand that they use, abuse, exploit, and neglect so that they can get their needs met. And while it may look like they are going to live happily ever after, it's all an illusion, and this new person is most likely going to experience a similar cycle that you did. *What you are really seeing is the idealize stage for the next person which is also part of the devalue and discard stage for you.*

Triangulation. Triangulation is where the narcissist tends to create a triangle involving one or more people, usually with themselves in the middle. They begin pitting other people against each other and then sit back and watch as all of the drama unfolds. This is commonly done between their old partner and their new partner, in which the narcissist has "stirred the pot" and made each one believe that the other one is the problem, to where they are fighting with each other over the narcissistic person. If you find yourself fighting over a person who has lied, cheated, stolen, or abused you, and that person returns to you—you might feel like you've won, but you haven't. You've lost, and the narcissist has won, because they've managed to get their way (and to get out of having consequences for their bad behavior), convince you that you've won, and hurt the other person all at the same time.

Smear Campaign. It's bad enough to have a relationship come to an abrupt end, but then to find out they are telling everyone all these lies about you can be shocking, confusing, and feel almost emotionally unbearable—especially if they are running around telling people (usually those who know you) that you were the abusive and manipulative one. To add to the level of confusion and crazy making, they may be telling people that you did everything that they actually did to you!

A smear campaign involves smearing another person's character, and with narcissists it's very common for them to spin things around to make themselves the victim of the situation, conveniently leaving out everything that they did—when this is not the truth of the situation. And again, because they can come across as so intense and sincere with their claims of being abused *by you*, many other people tend to believe them. They may say that you were the one who was emotionally or physically abusive, when it was them.

And oftentimes many of the stories that they spin have just enough of a kernel of truth in them that they can be seen as believable. So for example, they may say how cruel and mean you are because you won't let them see the children, but they leave out that you have a restraining order against them for being physically abusive to both you and the children. ....And of course, if they can provoke you into being reactively abusive, then this only further cements their twisted narrative that you are the problem, and that *they* are the victim of *you*.

Flying monkeys. A flying monkey is a person who has been manipulated by a narcissist to do their bidding (thinking that they are doing the right thing), which usually involves attacking their former target or pushing their former target back into the manipulationship. The flying monkeys can be unrelenting, and can (and often do) attack a person online and in person, making their life a living hell. This is one of the many reasons when people get out of an abusive relationship they are often forced to cut contact with many other people in their life, or even move to escape the ongoing abuse and torment.

Hoovering. This is where the narcissist attempts to reopen communication with the goal of "sucking" a person back into a relationship or back into the pipeline to be used again at some point down the road. A hoover can come across in a wide variety of ways, and targets usually respond if they feel guilty for not responding, obligated to respond, or painfully alone and miss the good times they had with the narcissist. Frankly, I view any form of communication by an abusive or exploitative person as an act of aggression and a potential hoover, no matter how seemingly innocent it is. And I think you'll find that the more you can distance yourself from that person, the better off you'll be.

The Cycle of a Normal Relationship

The cycle of a normal relationship runs something close to: infatuation, realization, breakup or recommit.

It's normal to be infatuated with someone right away and to only be focused on the good, especially during the beginning of a relationship. Much like a job interview, everyone is on their best behavior at first, and then over time, the rosy blush of infatuation wears off, and the reality of the person starts to be seen. Traits that were once cute, or even seen as wonderful can now become annoying or even problematic. It's during the realization phase that a real relationship is formed, and that both people either try to work as a team, or realize that they really don't have enough in common to try and work as a team; so they break up.

The infatuation stage. The infatuation phase is often full of lust and some degree of idealization. Both people may want to talk to each other for hours on end, and may rush into having sex or sharing a lot about their lives.

The difference between the infatuation stage of a normal relationship and the idealize stage of a narcissistic relationship is that the infatuation stage may move fast but it doesn't come across as immature (saying I love you when they really don't know you, or otherwise wanting to combine lives right away), and there isn't an intense soul-mate connection that is established within a few hours, days, or weeks.

Now I'm not saying that all people who profess their love right away are emotional manipulators. But what I am saying is that it is problematic and immature when a person claims to love another person without really knowing them, and it is problematic to get caught up in a whirlwind, because whirlwind romances more often than not turn into tornados, and it's hard to see the damage that is being done until the dust settles. If a relationship is real, then there is no rush. It will still be there a month from now. The reward of going slow far outweighs the risk of rushing in and making major decisions when you aren't seeing things clearly, and only have the information they are providing you with (which may or may not be true).

The realization phase. This phase happens a few months into the relationship, when both people start to get more comfortable with being themselves. Both partners begin to really examine if this other person is a good fit for them and their life.

The break-up or double-down phase. Once each person is thinking more clearly, they are able to make a decision as to how to proceed. Do they need to break up, or are things worth "doubling down" and really committing to the relationship?

A "normal" (healthy) relationship does not include abuse of any kind, and it does not include treating the other person (or their boundaries) with a lack of dignity or respect.

"I spent a lot of time trying to figure out how much abuse in a relationship was normal. Then someone told me that abuse in a

relationship was like having poop in your soup. They said you wouldn't eat soup with any amount of poop in it, and abuse in a relationship is very much the same thing. Being in a relationship with any amount of abuse in it, is still toxic. That really clicked for me! No amount of abuse is okay. Ever."

Going Through So Much Together vs. Being Put Through So Much by Them

Going Though So Much Together

Going through so much together involves riding out the highs and lows of *life* together.

The highs and lows of life often include learning to work together as a couple, starting and ending careers, navigating good and bad economies, learning to communicate effectively, learning to parent together as a team, raising children, etc. In other words, it's the ups and downs of *life* and learning to work as a team that are the challenge, and involve setting aside what's in the individual's best interest, and focusing instead on what's in the best interest of *the team*. Going through so much together is a lot like taking up kayaking with another person and learning how to paddle in sync with them and navigating the rapids, rocks, debris, and other challenges that come up.

Being Put Through So Much by Them

Being put through so much means riding out the highs and lows of *someone else's* selfish and destructive behavior.

What many people are put through often includes addiction, adultery, chronic lying, manipulating, deceiving, and abuse of all kinds. Being put through so much by another person is a lot like taking up kayaking with another person and *thinking* that you are learning to paddle in sync with them—only to find out they are drilling holes in the boat when you aren't looking, but then blaming you, someone else, or pretending to want to stop when you catch them.

"I stayed for so long because I guess I kept thinking we'd finally turn that corner and that he'd stop drinking, cheating, lying, and so on. I think there was a fear on my end, like we'd already been through so much together; that if I left now, he'd find someone else and live this amazing life with them. That someone else would then benefit from all my hard work, pain, and suffering that I'd put into this relationship. I was telling a friend this and she pointed out that "we" hadn't been through anything together. That he'd been busy living his life, and doing whatever he wanted to do, but that I was the one who being put through hell by holding on. When I realized she was right, that's when I knew I needed to let go. A relationship takes work, but it also takes two people who actually want to make it work. I can't make him get sober or make him faithful; he has to sincerely want to change, and he never did. He just wanted me to "forgive" him and put up with it all."

— *Tina*

"I love the kayak analogy! Except I have to tell you in my case with my family members, I felt like I was doing all of the paddling, and meanwhile they were using me for target practice while I was so very busy paddling. And of course when I asked for them to stop shooting at me, they'd tell me that I had screwed up paddling so badly that they'd"had" to shoot me, just to get me to straighten up and paddle right! And it took me decades before I stopped to wonder why they weren't paddling and why I was doing all the work."

— *Luci*

Acting the Part vs. Actually Changing

Acting the Part

Acting the part involves an emotional manipulator being on their best behavior or being what their target needs in order to stay in the relationship.

Acting the part often involves an emotional manipulator talking about going to therapy, rehab, church, or even showing great insight into their problematic or abusive behavior—which often leads their partner to think that they are finally getting through to them and that this time things really will be different. They may becoming helpful around the house, starting to be responsible with money, and taking up a seemingly strong interest in recommitting to the relationship to make things work.

Acting the part is similar to speeding and then seeing a police officer on the side of the road. Most people (even if they aren't speeding) instantly put on their best driving behavior. They usually slow down and are hyper aware of the speed limit, they use their turn signals, make sure they have their seat belt on, etc. But after a period of time, that fear goes away and so does their level of concern, and they slip back into their old driving behavior. Emotional manipulators work very much the same way. They can really do a great job of acting the part—for awhile, until they get comfortable again and the threat of their partner leaving is over. Unfortunately, what tends to happen is that they not only settle back into their old ways, they learn to cover their tracks much better.

Actually Changing

Actually changing involves no longer having the same problematic behavior.

Actually changing means being fully and totally open and honest about all problematic behavior, having open and honest conversations about their problematic behavior and how their partner feels, being willing to live a life of total transparency, as well as being eagerly willing to take sincere, ongoing, and massive actions to fix the damage done by their problematic behavior. Change can only be measured by consistent behavior over time (a minimum of 18 months) to see if a person has really changed.

What tends to happen with narcissistic partners who lie, cheat, steal, manipulate, or who have an addiction, is that they learn what they need to say and do in order to keep their target sucked in so they can go on doing what they are going to do—and the whole time they get better at hiding their behavior by opening up hidden credit cards, extra email accounts, having multiple phones or phone numbers, fake social media accounts, etc.

In my opinion, it's a mistake to try to rebuild trust let alone a relationship with a person who acts single and/or selfish when you aren't looking—because odds are what you know is only the tip of the iceberg. And when you find out that someone lacks a moral compass, it's a good idea to see that clearly and not think that they'll ever change. Because holding onto hope that they'll someday be something they are not is setting yourself up for a lifetime of hurt and heartache with this person.

"After I caught my ex cheating, he became the perfect husband. We went through couples' counseling for ten sessions' he gave me all the passwords for his phone and his computer, and he was incredibly attentive and helpful with the kids. Even though he seemed to change so fast, I felt like I didn't want to question it, because, after all, he was acting like the perfect husband and seemed sincerely remorseful for what he'd done. A coworker was the one who told me to check online dating sites, and sure enough, he had profiles on a few. The more I dug, the more I realized that he had fake email accounts, fake Facebook profiles; you name it. All the information he gave me were

to the accounts he knew were "clean." He hadn't changed at all, he'd just gotten better at hiding what he was up to and acting the part of changing."

— *Jaime*

Insincere Remorse vs. Sincere Remorse

Insincere Remorse

Insincere remorse involves saying or doing whatever a person needs to say in order to get what they want. Insincere remorse is often what's given by emotional manipulators, and often includes either giving an apology that the abuser doesn't really mean, crying crocodile tears, or giving excuses as to why they acted the way they did (but continuing to withhold the full truth—or otherwise not being fully accountable for their actions).

Insincere remorse comes across in a wide variety of ways, perhaps the most common being either intense and sweeping gestures (such as grand professions that things will change, begging, pleading, or the abuser crying to the point of sobbing like a child, sending a large bouquet of flowers to the target's work, acknowledgment of wrong doing to friends, family, or on Facebook, or a seemingly thoughtful surprise romantic evening), or cold and calloused indifference with crumbs of acknowledgment given for what they did.

Insincere remorse, when done in these ways is often followed by the abuser's insistence that their target immediately forgive or trust them, and if they don't, then the target is blamed for holding a grudge or for being manipulative, controlling, or abusive.

In addition, for the more highly-skilled emotional manipulators out there, insincere remorse can be done in ways which look like they are being fully accountable, have appropriate remorse, and that the relationship has truly turned a corner. They may say and do all the right things. They may actually go to therapy, check into rehab, close their Facebook account (if they have been caught sexting or flirting with other people), offer to answer any and all questions their partner has, or even offer up their phone for their target to check if they want. What I've seen happen (and have personally experienced) is that these acts of sincere remorse are, in fact, nothing more than another level to their emotional con game. I've had people share experiences with their partner having multiple phones, or having their partner actually meet the person they cheated with—while manipulating each of their targets to think the other one was the problem. Emotional manipulators are damn good at what they do, and normal, decent people cannot even begin to fathom all of the ways and levels that they will go to in order to manipulate. For these reasons, having deal-breaker behavior is vitally important, as what's come to light about their behavior is only ever the tip of the iceberg.

Sincere Remorse

Sincere remorse involves a person having full accountability (and transparency) regarding their actions, not blaming others, not giving half-baked apologies where the target or someone or something else is blamed, and them taking massive, consistent action to repair the damage done by their behavior.

A person who is sincerely remorseful also understands that their behavior was damaging and that trust will need to be rebuilt, and that will take time. They do not insist that their partner "get over" being hurt or immediately trust them again. And while they might not like all the questions their partner has regarding their breach of trust, they understand that their partner needs answers in order for them to start rebuilding trust. A large part of rebuilding trust also comes from taking massive action towards repairing the relationship.

Remember, the only sincere apology is changed action. If a person continues to have the same hurtful behavior, then they aren't sorry, and you are being manipulated.

"Whatever I would catch him doing, he'd either deny it, flat out blame me, or give me some half-assed acknowledgment of what he did, and then he'd blame me. Getting the truth out of him was like pulling teeth, and even then, he'd never fully own what he did. It was always someone else's fault. It was like being married to an ill-behaved child."
   — Cindy

"He would always say all the right things whenever he got caught cheating, lying, racking up debt, or whatever. I'd believe all his promises of change, and then sure enough a few months or a few years later he was back doing the same things again. I couldn't figure out why he could never change for long. It took over ten years for me to realize that he was totally fine with lying, cheating, stealing, and didn't want to stop. I guess I thought that he would want to have a drama-free life and settle down, and have a family, because I thought that's why people got married. It didn't even dawn on me that people would get married with no plans of ever being faithful. I think that's what really bothered me, was that he led me to believe that we would be faithful and honest with each other, and he never had any intentions of being that way. It took me awhile to understand why he even wanted to be married, when he apparently was acting single whenever I wasn't around. He wanted the best of both worlds is what it was. What's crazy is that he's upset that I divorced him, like I was immoral or selfish for doing so!"

— *Virginia*

Being In Love vs. Feeling Addicted to Them

Being in Love

Being in love with a person means having a relationship with a person that is based on mutual trust, support, dignity and respect, and includes open, honest, sincere, and solutions-oriented communication. It's a dynamic where both people feel empowered and secure in being themselves and growing and exploring who they are and who they want to be. Being in love with a person feels comfortable, safe, and secure. A loving relationship is one that is both nurturing and nourishing, where both people are getting their needs met in an empowering and supportive way. A loving relationship doesn't make a person feel anxious, nervous, insecure, jealous, unhinged, needy, or distrusting of their partner, and it doesn't include abuse.

Feeling Addicted to Them

Being addicted to love is an addictive and *intense* type of feeling that either stems from deep-rooted codependency and abandonment issues and/or is created from the highs and lows of a narcissistic relationship, so that the other person feels like they "crave" this other person (like they would any other addictive substance), and that this other person is all they think about. The highs and lows of an abusive relationship are a type of "intermittent reinforcement."

Intermittent reinforcement is a term that comes from the psychologist, B.F. Skinner, and his studies on operant conditioning and behavior. His original study was done with rats; they would push a lever and food would drop into their cage. The rats quickly learned that in order to get their food needs met, they needed to push the lever. Then he changed up the experiment to where food would only drop some of the time when the rats pushed the lever.

In terms of an abusive relationship, the relationship tends to start out with the target behaving in a certain way in order to get their needs met, but then over time, the abusive partner's behavior become erratic, and the target quickly finds themselves trying all different ways to find the right lever with their partner so that they'll be treated with kindness or care. This is more commonly referred to as walking on eggshells. And sometimes walking on eggshells, and avoiding certain topics, or acting in a certain way works, and the abuser is kind, considerate, and loving, and sometimes it doesn't work—or leads to abuse.

This type of erratic behavior can be crazy making, as it can seem like this time things have turned a corner, and that their partner has changed. This stage has a name, and it's called the "honeymoon or idealize" phase in the cycle of abuse. This phase is a big part of the reason as to why targets cling to hope that things will be different. The intermittent reinforcement of the bad times peppered with good times leads to trauma bonds, which plays a big part in Stockholm Syndrome that many targets develop for their abuser.

In addition, feelings of love addiction can also be fueled if the person has made the narcissist their whole world, meaning, they are relying on the narcissist to meet all of their physical, emotional, and financial needs. This desperate clinging can also be coming from a (subconscious or conscious) place of insecurity and fear of how they will survive, or fear of being alone or what will happen to them if this person leaves for good.

Because if and when their abuser does leave, they aren't just left alone, they are generally left trying to cope with tremendous amounts of shame, embarrassment, confusion, guilt, remorse, insecurity, and deep feelings of inadequacy, wondering what was so wrong with them that their partner treated them this way. This is especially true if their partner has moved on quickly with a new partner that they seem to treat so well (not realizing that what they are seeing with this new partner is the new partner's idealize stage of a narcissistic relationship, as well as a continuation of their devalue stage). Please remember that with emotional manipulators, nothing is as it seems. They manipulate not only emotions, but people's impression of them.

Feelings of love addiction do pass with time, and like with kicking any other addiction, the best way for this to happen is to get a plan to handle the cravings—even realizing that there will most likely be cravings is a big first step. Getting clear in your mind why this person is toxic for you, joining a support group, potentially finding a therapist who *truly* understands abusive relationships, and then getting busy on filling up the void and meeting your needs in a healthy way (hobbies, and spending time with supportive friends and family—or making some new friends or developing new hobbies) goes a long way. As soon as you are able to "crowd out" these cravings with positive and enjoyable things, you will find in time that you will miss them less and less, and one day you will shake your head in disbelief as to how you could have ever confused being treated abusively with love. (And when this does happen, try to be compassionate with yourself for not seeing their manipulations for what they were. Normal, decent people don't even have their radar set to scan for these kinds of people or these kinds of manipulations.)

"I felt addicted to him the first few weeks we began talking. I was very quick to make him my whole world and didn't mind doing so. What we had felt so amazing, like it was out of a movie. When the abuse started up, I was so eager to keep the peace because I didn't want him to leave. I would have done anything to make that relationship work, and he knew that. We'd have an amazing weekend and then a few days later he'd fall off the planet, and I'd be a mess wondering what I did wrong and fearing that I'd never hear from him again. He'd make comments about how attractive other women were and then get upset if I got hurt by that. I was continually walking on eggshells with him and always felt jealous, insecure, and like I craved his approval and his attention and validation. I realize now that none of how I was treated or how I felt was love. Love makes a person feel comfortable, confident, safe, and relaxed. I felt the exact opposite in that relationship. I loved him like an addict loves heroin. That's not love, it's addiction."

— Linda

Hoovering vs. Harmless Communication

Hoovering

"Hoovering" is a term named after the Hoover vacuum, and is used to describe any attempt made by a narcissistic person that is designed to reopen communication with their target. The intention of a hoover is usually either to "suck" the target fully back into the "manipulationship," to provoke a response from the target (which is a form of supply, as it makes them feel smug and superior to upset their target), or to suck the target back into their supply pipeline so that they can be used in the future.

Hoovering attempts can be small and seemingly innocent (such as an abuser texting their target, "hi" or "Happy Birthday.") Or it can be more intense, including offering to be friends, or false apologies full of false awareness that might come across as something like, "I know I've caused a lot of pain, and I'm sorry. You deserve better than me. I hope you find what you are looking for." A hoover can also be love bombing, future faking, pity ploys, confusing, such as texting a person a bunch of jibberish or pretending to have sent the message to the wrong person; accusatory, accusing the former target of cheating on them or being an abusive or neglectful parent, saying all the right things, begging, pleading, texting and emailing multiple times, promising change, (such as offering to go to therapy or rehab) or messages that are designed to provoke or instill fear, such as "I'm going to kill myself tonight, I hope you are happy;" or, "My mother has cancer, and I need to talk." Hoovering is what sucks a person back into the relationship or, at a minimum, back into the supply line, in case the narcissistic person wants to use them again.

Harmless Communication

It is really difficult to have harmless communication with an abusive person. If going no contact won't work for you because you have children with them, then a good way to limit the damage that they are doing is to have all communication go through a third party court-appointed mediator or website service. Of course, prepare yourself emotionally for the abusive person to be upset by this, because it means their game can't continue. They will often exclaim that you are being difficult or trying to rack up costs by getting a third party involved. Don't fall for this, and don't make decisions based on whether they are okay with things—*they will never be okay with your having boundaries or denying them of what they want.* You don't need to be their emotional punching bag. Many targets often struggle with telling the difference between a hoover by a narcissist and a problematic ex just trying to reopen communication.

Let me be clear; toxic is toxic, and either situation is problematic and not worthy of your time or energy. You don't owe a toxic person one more second of your time, you do, however, owe it to yourself to have peace in your life. You do not owe anything to a person who continues to cause you hurt or heartache. It's okay to cut ties and never look back. It doesn't matter if they are a friend, a former spouse, a coworker, or a family member. And it doesn't matter if no one else agrees with your decision to cut ties with them. It's not being mean, and it's not lacking compassion—it's self-protection, and other people don't get to set your boundaries for what you want in your life, only you do.

"It took me awhile to stop feeling bad for not responding to him when he'd send me texts asking me how I was doing, or just saying 'hi.' I realized that even seemingly innocent texts like that always led to either us talking again, which led to more abuse, or him not talking to me again, and then staying on my mind for weeks and me feeling like crap. I've since blocked him across the board and am so glad I did!"
— *Susan*

Possibility vs. Probability

Possibility

Emotional manipulators are often pathological liars. They will often lie when the truth would work better for them. Trying to sort out the truth from a lie is an exercise in crazy making, and frankly, there is no point—because a pathological liar can never be trusted. So it doesn't matter if they were truthful about one thing; if they'd lied about a dozen other things, you'd be wise to see them as the manipulative people that they are. After all, lots of things are possible, but that doesn't mean they are probable. After all, there is a possibility the Loch Ness Monster exists too, but this doesn't mean this is a probability.

Probability

A probability is more of a statistical chance that something is true more so than it not being true. If a person has a pattern of lying, then there is a probability that they are continuing to lie about whatever they've done that you've confronted them about. Emotional manipulators will often cling to the few truths in the story that they have told in an attempt to be trusted again, but like with everything else, the few truths they tell are often wrapped in a lie and what you know is probably just the tip of the iceberg.

"I kept all the wrong people in my life and kept giving people multiple chances to hurt me or screw me over because I didn't have solid proof as to what they were up to. This was especially the case when I began dating again. I came across lots of guys with red flags—they'd stand me up, or show signs of having anger issues, or start being creepy, flirting, or making inappropriate advances right away, but I would gloss over all these red flags because they would offer up excuses that were somewhat believable. And my friends kept pushing me to give them another chance, saying that I saw red flags in everyone and that I didn't want to miss out on a great guy because I was making too big of a deal about nothing. What helped me was to think about what

the healthiest person I know would do in the same situation. I realized that they wouldn't give these guys another chance, and so why would I? Was I really that lonely that I was going to accept being stood up, or being around some guy who was creepy and just wanted to use me for sex? I decided that while I wasn't going to ever know what someone's intentions were, that I needed to do what I felt was right and quit giving all the wrong people the benefit of the doubt."

— *Shannon*

Sincerity vs. Intensity

Sincerity

When a person is being sincere, they are being genuine. There is no hidden agenda, and they are being on the level with their words and actions.

A person who is sincere realizes that trust is earned, that love is built over time, that forgiveness doesn't mean forgetting, or who has hypocritical behavior, especially demanding trust when they've had a long-standing pattern of breaking it or getting annoyed with their partner's hurt feelings over their abusive behavior. A person who is sincere in their actions has respect for another person's boundaries and feelings. They do not try to push that person into letting them back into their life, and they don't expect for things to go back to the way they were— because *they have the emotional maturity to realize that things can't ever go back to the way they were.* Once trust is broken, the relationship is broken and both people will be spending the remainder of their time together picking up the pieces and trying to glue them back together again. It's like breaking a glass vase and then gluing it back together again. It's still a vase, but it's not the same as it was before—and now it needs to be handled and maintained differently than before. Trust isn't rebuilt in a week, month, year, or even a decade. It's an ongoing process, and feelings of distrust and hurt will *always* be there to some extent.

Intensity

Emotional manipulators are often very intense in their behavior—this is especially true if they are in the love bombing/idealization phase at the start of a relationship, or if they are in the love- bombing/hoovering stage where they are trying to suck their target back into their "pipeline of supply" to use.

If they have been caught for problematic behavior, or if their partner has left or is threatening to leave, then this intensity tends to increase. To the outside world, (as well as to the target) they may confuse this intensity with sincerity, as their behavior tends to go to great and romantic lengths, such as sending large bouquets of flowers to work, planning a romantic vacation, hopping on a plane and flying across the country so they can apologize in person, sending dozens of texts professing their love and devotion and begging for another chance, throwing a surprise birthday party or vacation for their target, going to therapy and crying and promising that they'll change…if only you'll give them another chance.

For those who are new to the topic of narcissistic abuse, or manipulative behavior in general, you may find yourself struggling with trying to figure out how to tell if this "problematic" person in your life is being sincere, or if they are being intense. And perhaps the best way to understand this, is to realize that if a person has a pattern of lying or manipulative or "squirrelly" behavior, it's a good idea to assume that they are continuing to lie, manipulate, and act squirrelly. Normal, decent people don't have a pattern of this kind of behavior, and to try and figure out when a liar is being truthful is an exercise in crazy making.

"He always spoke with such certainty about us and our future. He seemed so sincere, and wouldn't let up until I broke down and would give him another chance. I thought his persistence meant that he really cared. I now see that it was all about control and winning a game that I didn't realize I was playing."
— *Michelle*

Sympathy vs. Stockholm Syndrome

Sympathy

Sympathy is when a person has feelings of compassion and concern for what someone else is going through. Because we can relate/imagine ourselves in the situation, the emotions and experiences that are shared during an emotional time often lead to two people becoming closer because of this experience. Having sympathy for others based around their vulnerabilities is how many healthy bonds are formed and strengthened.

However, the sympathy of good and decent people is also often preyed upon by emotional manipulators because it is such an effective way to hook and then reel people in. Good and decent people often think that other people in the world are like them, and so they tend to take people at face value. And if someone is reaching out to them or has some sort of sad story as an excuse to justify their behavior, many people will gloss over the problematic behavior because they feel sorry for this person. If a person feels pity when the situation more appropriately calls for fear or anger, this can lead to them having skewed thinking and actions that put them in danger to where instead of distancing themselves from problematic people, they get physically or emotionally closer. *Emotional manipulators know this, and they are relying on it,* and their level of manipulation can be taken to jaw-dropping levels when this happens. An extreme example of this would be with the serial killer Ted Bundy who used his charm, good looks, a pity ploy and a staged event in order to lure his victims in. He would appear helpless and harmless by pretending to have a broken arm and unable to get his groceries into his car. Upon seeing him struggle, his target would approach him, and offer him help...and that's when he'd attack.

Some emotional manipulators will comfort another in their time of need, only to prey upon how vulnerable they are. Some will claim to be addicts, alcoholics, had a bad childhood, had an abusive ex, or they play stupid and pretend to not know what flirting, cheating, stealing, or appropriate boundaries or behavior is—and that they need *you* to teach them. If you ever find yourself trying to teach an adult the fundamentals of adult behavior, there is a problem, and you are being manipulated. If you are letting your guard down around a person who has a pattern of hurtful and harmful behavior because you feel guilty, sad, concerned, obligated, please know that you are being manipulated. They don't need you to rescue them, they know exactly what they are doing.

Stockholm Syndrome

Stockholm syndrome is when a person has feelings of *misplaced* pity or sorrow for a destructive or dangerous person based on the traumatic situation that the controlling person is putting them through. It's considered to be a psychological defense mechanism where good and decent people look for signs that this person is somehow good and decent, so their brain can keep calm by holding onto crumbs of hope that this situation can work out, and that they can survive it. The emotions and experiences that are shared during an emotional time like this come from both misplaced sympathy that stems from "reverse projection" where we are projecting all of our good qualities onto them, instead of seeing them and their actions for what they are. In addition, these situations are often a roller coaster of extreme highs and lows which confuse a person's brain and lead them to link up a series of misplaced cause and effect, and in turn alter their behavior in an attempt to control their environment so that they can "survive" it. All of these highs and lows, misplaced sympathy, and "reverse projection" form unhealthy bonding known as "trauma bonds" and make up what's known as Stockholm syndrome.

Stockholm syndrome is a term that was coined after a bank robbery in the 1970's where it was first noticed that there were seemingly illogical and irrational emotional bonds that had developed between bank robbers and their hostages—to the point where the hostages defended their captors and described them as "lovely" and "nice" during and after their hostage situation. While the police were trying to rescue them, the hostages became angry and distrustful *of the police*—despite the fact that their captors had threatened to kill one of the hostages and had another sit with a noose around her neck for several days. Researchers concluded that the hostages had developed illogical and irrational bonds with their captors as a psychological defense mechanism in order to prevent emotionally collapsing. If they could convince themselves that their captors weren't "that bad" or were somehow normal, decent people, then it would give them hope that they could survive the situation.

The dynamics of a hostage situation, including Stockholm syndrome, are very similar to those of an abusive relationship. The partner of an abusive person often feels a desperate or addictive irrational clinging to their partner or to their relationship, and incredibly defensive if anyone criticizes their partner or their relationship.

In part, this is because abusive people are rarely overtly abusive 100% of the time, and the good times can confuse the partner into thinking that the relationship can be saved, or that it's not *that* bad. It doesn't take a lot of really good times to give the target of an abusive person hope to cling to. In the Stockholm bank robbery incident, all it took for one hostage to develop warm feelings for their captor was their captor telling them that they were going to kill them—*but* that they'd let them get drunk before they did. The hostage clung onto this crumb of kindness as proof that their captor was not only not "that bad," but that they were a considerate and caring person!

In addition, if a person is married to an abusive person, they often have a high emotional (and physical and financial) investment in having the relationship work out.

Because this relationship fills multiple basic human needs, they not only don't want to walk away, they need to believe that they can "survive" the situation by changing their actions. So they work towards being more agreeable and trying to anticipate their partner's needs (aka walking on eggshells), not discussing their partner's problematic behavior—or discussing a small part of it, but not to the level where true communication is present—clinging to crumbs of hope that things will change, and avoiding people and advice that try to get them to see the situation more clearly, or to help them to get out.

This is the perfect storm, because here you have a person who is highly manipulative and usually a chronic liar who says whatever they need to say in order to get what they want, and a target who is a normal, decent, trusting person who takes them at face value *and* who needs to believe that everything will be okay and that this relationship can work. The emotional manipulator *wants* the relationship to work out—not because they are in love with their partner, but because they are using them for their own selfish wants and needs—perhaps for sex, housing, money, social status, and/or public image; you name it. The target *needs* for this relationship to work out because they are dependent upon this person and this relationship for their physical, emotional, or financial survival, as many targets have made this other person their whole life and place a high value on commitment at all costs.

When a person has such a high level of commitment regardless of how they are treated, they will often be desperate to "fix" their partner or their relationship, and because of this they will believe pretty much anything— because they *need* to if they are going to stay. This is where the phrase, "Who are you going to believe, me or your lying eyes?" comes into play. Because that's exactly what starts happening. As the manipulative partner continues to have deceitful and problematic behavior, if they get questioned or caught, they will continue to manipulate and distort the truth and their partner's perception of events in order to keep their emotional con game going. This is known as gaslighting, and is psychological abuse. Psychological abuse is perhaps the most damaging type of abuse because when a person's perception of reality is altered, it can take them a long time to trust their own perceptions and judgment again.

Some symptoms of Stockholm syndrome (as well as the dynamics in an abusive/codependent relationship) are: positive feelings towards the controller and negative feelings towards those trying to help, continuing "supportive" behavior by the captive in an attempt to help the abuser (which may include lying to friends, family, refusing to file charges or take them to court because they "love" them, etc.), and a lack of desire to be rescued. The target of abuse is stuck between a rock and a hard place. They don't want to leave, but they don't want to be abused...they just want their abuser (who has no sincere accountability or desire to change) to change back into the charming, likable person that they first met—not realizing that person was only an illusion to suck them in to begin with.

Stockholm syndrome doesn't just develop within abusive relationships between adults. It can develop at any age, and with any type of abusive person. The resulting trauma bonds that are forged between an abuser and their target can (and often do) occur between a rape victim and their rapist, an abused child and their abusive parent, a pimp and a prostitute, or a cult leader and a cult member. The people who get tangled up in these situations are not stupid or crazy: they are subconsciously trying to meet some very basic human needs that we all have. And generally, when a person denies the truth of the situation to themselves, it's because the truth is too much for them to bear. And if they have an emotional investment in the situation working out, then the level of their denial tends to match the level of their emotional investment, as the more problematic a situation becomes the more a person has to justify to themselves that what they are experiencing either isn't happening, or if it is happening, it isn't that bad, or if it is bad, then they somehow deserved it. This is also why it often takes those who are in an abusive relationship leaving seven times before they leave for good...or in cases of physical violence, before they are killed.

The unhealthy trauma bonds that form Stockholm syndrome can be forged with any narcissistic person at any stage in a person's life—and for those who grow up in dysfunctional homes, these bonds often start when they are children. This is because all children have the hardwired biological need to bond with their primary caregiver/parent. This need stems out of a basic need to survive, as a child has very little power and control over their environment and so must depend on their parent in order to get their needs met. In an emotionally healthy home, a parent would appropriately and effectively bond with their child and gladly help them to not only get their basic needs met but would also help them get their more "advanced" needs met of nurturing their uniqueness so that they can feel safe in exploring and discovering who they are.

One of two main defense mechanisms that is used is that of "ingratiation" or "befriending" the captor in order to get on their good side so that they can get their needs met. A child may realize that the best (or only) way to get attention or to get some crumbs for their needs being met is to be doting, people pleasing, overly mature for their age, to offer excessive caretaking, and to continually go above and beyond for their parent.

When this happens, their own sense of self/self-identity doesn't form properly, as they are not allowed or encouraged to explore their own individuality or to have their own thoughts, feelings (especially anger or sadness at how they are being treated), and opinions (that there is a problem with how they are being treated). They are only there to meet the needs of the parent, or otherwise take care of the parent (whether this is stated or implied).

Any protests made by the child of how they are being treated would be continually invalidated or minimized, and in cases where there is a parent (or parents) who are narcissistically abusive, their protests would most likely increase or exacerbate the abuse. So in order to keep the peace, the child learns to stuff their anger, sadness, or any other feelings (or expressions of individuality) that show that there is more to them than that of the emotional or physical caretaker of the parent. In a home with a narcissistic parent, there is no acknowledgment of anyone else's thoughts, feelings, or individuality besides the narcissistic family member. And what happens at a young age, is because the child needs to believe that their parent cares about them, they will mistake any act of kindness, no matter how small, as proof that they are loved and that they do matter. (An example would be a parent who is not in their child's life for five years, then sends a birthday card and the child is elated, or a parent who has a pattern of making promises they don't keep such as promising their child that they'll be there for their school play, but then they cancel. The child is devastated, but then they see their parent in the audience, and now the child is excited and feels loved. These are the highs and lows of trauma bonds as experienced by children in dysfunctional homes.)

Because our need for survival is our most basic (and often our strongest), a child's bond with their primary caregiver/parent is incredibly deep, and it often takes an *intense* amount of abuse and neglect for that bond to be broken. Oftentimes, no matter how abusive or neglectful a child's home life is, it's very common for a child to continue to hold out hope that given enough love, understanding, patience, time, therapy, or rehab, their parent could change and that they could eventually get the love and connection that they've been seeking all along, just like the trauma bonds between two adults in an abusive relationship.

As with most trauma bonding, the cognitive dissonance that a child (or spouse) has is very strong, as hope dies last.

If the only way a child knows how to effectively navigate their relationships is to put up with being mistreated and to replace their anger with being more compassionate and understanding, then this thinking will (and has) set them up for poor/no boundaries, not having a clear idea of what deal breakers are (to them everything is workable), a hard time with effectively being in tune with their emotions, expressing anger or sadness, or being able to speak their mind.

As an adult they will most likely find themselves in a series of one-sided friendships and relationships where they lack healthy boundaries, have careers where they can usually put those people-pleasing skills to work (such as caregiving/nursing, social work, or being a therapist). They often don't have a clear sense of deal-breaker behavior, because they were never taught or allowed to walk away from harmful or hurtful situations; they were only taught to endure them.

They most likely confuse intensity with sincerity, love bombing with love, rushing intimacy with true intimacy, and controlling with caring. Then, when the low times hit or were uncovered (lying/deceiving, cheating, siphoning funds, abusing, etc.) the partner usually doubled up their commitment to their partner in an attempt to "save" the relationship.

So they give second (and twenty-second chances) in hopes that they can earn the love of their partner (who is also most likely narcissistic), in order to keep their partner faithful, honest, sober, or otherwise not abusive.

This endless endurance of abuse and mistreatment (captivity) was sold to them by an emotional manipulator as what commitment, family, marriage, religion, and forgiveness are all about. And because they don't know any different, they often sell these same messages to their children...and the cycle continues.

This may sound extreme, but I fully believe that any dynamic with a narcissistic person *is* a hostage situation. Because this is what narcissists do: *they hold their targets emotionally hostage.*

There is no equal give and take—it is a one-sided dynamic where the narcissistic partner takes and everyone else is expected to give—give them money, second (and twenty-second) chances, loyalty, understanding, compassion, caring, respect, and honesty. Narcissists are also huge hypocrites. They will become offended and outraged if they are treated any less than how they expect to be treated, but they see no reason why they should treat their partner the same way. It's like the saying goes, "a narcissist will demand that you make them your everything, while they make you their nothing."

"He would hit me. I would get angry or scared. He'd blame me for doing something that made him hit me. I put up with this for many years. Only once did I ever call the cops, and when they arrested him, I felt terrible—like I'd just ruined his life. It took me a long time in therapy to realize that I had sympathy towards the wrong person."

— *Rachelle*

Healthy Bonding vs. Trauma Bonding

Healthy Bonding

Healthy bonding is when bonds between two people are formed based on dignity and respect, as well as open, honest, sincere, solutions-oriented communication. Healthy bonds tend to start forming between two people when there is either empathy or similarities present, as we all tend to be drawn to people who are either like us, or that we can relate to in some way. However, if both people are tolerant of differences and seek to understand one another's point of view, then healthy bonds can be forged over any topic or situation if the foundation of dignity and respect is present. Healthy bonds grow deeper, stronger, and more empowering, fulfilling, and nourishing with time.

Trauma Bonding

Trauma bonding is an unhealthy bond between an emotional manipulator and their target, and they are formed by the highs and lows that make up an abusive relationship. They occur as the result of ongoing intermittent reinforcement of reward and punishment and are forged due to emotional wounding and a psychological defense so that person can try to convince themselves that they can stay safe and sane in an environment that is neither safe nor sane. Trauma bonds are a one-sided bond and are not based on dignity, respect, and instead are based on misplaced empathy and similarities. The target assigns the qualities of empathy and morality to the trauma-causing person (who is not demonstrating either of these qualities). There is no ongoing open, honest, sincere, or solutions-oriented communication, and the emotional manipulator is not sincerely motivated to work as a team but instead is motivated to work out of his own best interests—which is often at the expense of others around him (especially those who are trauma bonded to him).

Trauma bonds are best seen by those who are not emotionally invested in the situation, because to those who are not in the situation, they can generally see the situation as dangerous and destructive, and so the target's defense of their abuser seems illogical, bizarre, frustrating, exhausting, and destructive (which it is). An interesting point to realize is that those who are trauma bonded to someone often feel that their "connection" to this person is also illogical, bizarre, frustrating, exhausting, and destructive and get upset with themselves for continuing to go back or for feeling so "pulled" in by this person. Trauma bonds also grow deeper and stronger with time; however, they become more disempowering, destructive, diminishing, and dangerous over time.

"When I was with my ex, I continually felt uncertain, insecure, and always on edge—waiting for the other shoe to drop. I found myself walking on eggshells and trying so hard to prove my love to him with the hopes he'd eventually treat me right. I confused feeling this intensely towards him with

love. It wasn't. It was a trauma bond. I am now married to a wonderful man who is one of my best friends. Our bond is based on treating each other with dignity and respect, as well as our mutual enjoyment of each other's company. We both really like each other for who we are, and if either of us has an issue, we know we can talk about it. The way I feel in this relationship is so nice; it's like I can breathe, and relax, and be myself. I don't know how I ever put up with anything less."

— *Nikki*

Normal vs. Healthy

Normal

What's considered normal is often different degrees of dysfunction.

Healthy

The foundation of a healthy dynamic includes mutual trust and support, as well as being treated with dignity and respect, and having open, honest, sincere, and solutions-oriented communication. But keep in mind; this is only the foundation. What's healthy for you is something that only you can determine and that comes from getting to know yourself well enough that you realize what is empowering and nourishing for you.

"When I began dating after several years of being out of an abusive marriage, I had a hard time sorting out what was normal and what

was problematic. I made the mistake of looking around at my friend's marriages or relationships and using them as a guide to what was normal. It took my dating several men who did similar things to what friends' husbands did (such as drinking a lot, yelling, or cussing) for me to realize while that might be normal for them, it wasn't what I wanted in my life. I had to turn inward and figure out for myself what I wanted and didn't want in my life and use that as the measuring stick for what I was looking for, and not to look at what everyone else was doing."

— *Patricia*

Caring vs. Controlling

Caring

Caring about someone means that you are concerned about them, what's in their best interest, and empower and encourage them to become their personal best.

Controlling

Controlling someone has nothing to do with caring about another person—it stems from the controlling person's need to dominate and their need to be in control over every aspect of their lives—including their partner.

In an abusive relationship, controlling behavior may come across to the target and to others as concern for the target and what's in their best interest—but it's not. To many targets, a controlling partner can seem like a concerned parent—which can seem comforting, especially if a person either grew up without a parent in their life or if they had a domineering parent in their life.

Control is about domination, and it's about getting and keeping power over the other person. Some examples of controlling behavior that can come across as caring (especially when the target first starts dating an abusive person) are:

- Continually texting a person while they are out with friends or family and insisting that the target gets back to them right away.
- Showing up uninvited or unannounced to the target's work, home, or when they are out with friends.
- Demanding to know where the target is and when they'll be back.
- Insisting their partner dress a certain way, and shaming them if they don't.
- Planting seeds of insecurity about their appearance or intelligence.
- Planting seeds of jealousy, and eluding to how many other people are trying to date them with the ultimate goal of the target working harder to "earn" or "win" their loyalty, love, affection, attention, or time.

- Telling the target that if they loved them that they would act a certain way, such as change their appearance.
- Accusing the target of sleeping with coworkers or with other people if they are doing things without the abuser.
- Monitoring how much money they spend/putting them on an allowance.
- Demanding that the target not spend time with certain friends of family that they are (or were) close to.
- Using "intense" statements such as, "No one else can have you;" "You are mine;" "You are my whole world;" "All I need is you;" "I would kill for you;" "I would kill you if you ever left me;" or, "I'd kill myself if you ever left."

Abusive people will rarely have sincere accountability or remorse for their actions, because they feel justified in what they are doing. Because of this, they always have an excuse for everything, especially their controlling and abusive behavior. So they might say that they don't want their target to talk to certain friends, because those friends are a bad influence on their target (which generally means these certain people see the abusive/manipulative behavior for what it is and are encouraging the person to leave). Or they may yell, belittle, or hit their target, but then claim that the target made them do it.

Controlling behavior tends to come across as feelings of being smothered, micromanaged, and exhausted, as if you have to continually walk on eggshells, or as though everything you do is wrong. Over time walking on eggshells can lead to a whole host of other issues including anxiety, depression, low (or no) self-esteem, loss of identity, loss of independent thought or decision making, substance abuse, fatigue, pain, inflammation, digestion issues, weight gain or loss, and a whole host of other physical ailments.

I want to stop for a moment and address a very important point: because an abusive person always thinks they are right, it's not uncommon for them to use every tool out there to get their target to comply. They may use friends, family, coworkers, the police, therapists, and self-help, or relationship books to push the target into being what they want them to be. With self-help or relationship books, they may highlight passages or insist that they each read the book, and use examples like I gave above against the target. This is a very dangerous form of gaslighting, and regardless of whether this gaslighting is intentional or unintentional, it really shows the depth of their problematic thinking—and that they are very far away from changing. So don't confuse activity (therapy, reading self-help books, going to relationship retreats, etc.) with productivity (true change).

The abuser will generally have an issue with any boundary the target tries to set, and may insist that the target is being controlling, manipulative, and abusive if they have an issue with their behavior or with how they are being treated. Here is the same example, and how it can be manipulated by the abuser (and confusing to the target).

Sarah is not okay with John messaging women on Facebook or meeting up with women that he's slept with or dated in the past. He often hides his phone when he's on it, and sleeps with it under his pillow. She mentions her concerns to him, and he claims that these women are all friends and that Sarah is jealous and controlling. John then suggests that they go to couple's therapy, as well as read some relationship books together. He manipulates the therapist into thinking that he is a good guy who just happens to have female friends, and that he loves Sarah, but hates her trust issues. Sarah tries to explain her reasons for her concern, but feels that her examples comes across as her being petty and immature, and she begins to wonder if perhaps she really is the one with the problem. Their therapist recommends that they read some relationship books together, and they do. During this time, John skews what is in the books to meet his agenda, which is to make Sarah the problem. Sarah feels like she can't argue with what's written on the page, and because she wants the relationship to work, she reluctantly agrees to stop bringing up issues she has with John's squirrelly behavior.

The point I'm trying to make with this is that *context matters*. Having friends of the opposite sex isn't necessarily the problem, but texting strangers and hanging out alone with an ex (especially if there seems to be feelings still there) is a problem. Sarah isn't being controlling by having a problem with John hiding his phone and meeting up with women she doesn't know about or that he has a sexual past with. John is being wildly inappropriate by expecting her to not have an issue with this, especially when all of his behavior (hiding his phone, etc.) points to the fact that he actually does have something to hide. A normal person with platonic friends does hide what they are doing. They are okay going out in groups, and introduces their partner to their friends.

Please don't do what so many of us have and think that you need to stay in a relationship with a person who has perpetually confusing behavior, thinking that you need concrete proof that they are in fact abusive or cheating. Any relationship that is controlling, crazymaking, or perpetually critical or crazymaking is not worth being in, because you are being manipulated. A relationship built on mental anguish, deceit, and dominance isn't a relationship. This is not love. This is a trauma bond. And feeling like you are losing your mind or trying to convince yourself that you need to trust an person who has continually proven to you that they can't be trusted is a big sign you are in an emotionally and psychologically abusive relationship.

"When we first began dating, he would insist that I text him when I woke up in the morning, when I went to lunch, when I got off work,

and when I got home. He always wanted to know who I was out with and what I was wearing. I'd never had attention like this before, and I thought he was so caring. My friends thought he was controlling, and I thought they were just jealous, so I stopped talking to them about my relationship, and over time we grew apart. Over time, he had more and more demands. He wanted me to stop going to college, because he felt it was a waste of money and began telling me I was stupid. He wanted me to change how I dressed because he thought I looked too sexy. My life was all about walking on eggshells trying to please him, but it was never enough. I walked around feeling anxious and avoiding bringing up anything that I knew he'd disagree with. My anxiety was so bad that I was on medication for it and for depression. No one (including me) connected that maybe I was anxious and depressed because I was in an abusive marriage. It was an exhausting way to live, and now that I'm no longer with him, it's hard to believe that I lived like that for as long as I did."

— Maureen

"I met Scott through a friend, and after a few text messages he began calling me "babe" and "hun." Part of me liked the attention and felt flattered that he was calling me pet names. It made me feel close to him. He began dropping hints that he needed to talk to me throughout the day, and before he went to bed. At first it was kinda romantic, but I had a bunch of internal alarms going off the whole time. He had told me that his ex-girlfriend had filed fake domestic violence and stalking charges against him, and that he had issues with trusting women. I didn't want to be another woman who hurt him, so I brushed aside all of my concerns and tried to convince myself that all his attention was romantic and that I must have issues. The more

time went on, the more demanding and insistent he became. I finally broke up with him because I couldn't handle how needy and demanding he was. Frankly, I wouldn't be surprised if his exes charges against him were legitimate."

— *Savannah*

Intimacy vs. Intensity

Intimacy

Intimacy is a feeling of *appropriate* closeness and togetherness with another person. True intimacy happens *over time,* during which both people are open, honest, and sincere in their interactions with each other. True intimacy grows over time and is forged through getting to know another person for who they really are in each moment—not who you think they are, or who you hope they'll eventually be. When intimacy is developed based on a person misrepresenting themselves, or when we fall in love with who they hope they can become, this isn't intimacy, *this is falling in love with an illusion.*

Intensity

Intensity and emotional manipulators often go hand-in-hand. Both the highs and lows are severe (the good times being really good and the bad times being really bad) or there are very few good times and lots of intense bad times. When the good times are really good, they are often full of future faking, love bombing, intense mirroring, amazing conversations that last for hours, rushing intimacy, and them overall being the perfect partner with a deep "soul mate" connection. Things feel SO perfect, almost like a fairy tale or that they've won the relationship lottery.

When the bad times are bad, they are full of lying, cheating/ongoing affairs, stealing/"mishandling" joint finances, yelling, name calling, controlling and irrational demands, double lives, intimidating or violent behavior. Both the make-ups and break-ups are intense. And this intensity during the make-ups that include love bombing, future faking, and promises (or even actions) towards change are often (understandably) confused for sincerity because the emotional manipulator seems so sincere—like this time they really will change. Because most normal people mean what they say and say what they mean, it's hard for them to wrap their mind around the idea that other people don't do this—especially if there is so much on the line (like their marriage or their relationship with their children) or if there is seemingly no reason to lie or manipulate. Emotional manipulators use emotions because they either want or need to in order to get what they want, because they feel somehow entitled to, or if they are sadistic, because it's fun.

"I was attracted to how intense and certain he was—about everything, including wanting to date me. Right off the bat he was in full pursuit of me and told me everything a woman would want to

hear. I was very quick to trust him and to sleep with him, thinking that we had this great connection. After we slept together, he stopped texting like he normally did, and I realized that he never wanted a relationship, he was just looking for sex. I felt so foolish and used."
— *April*

Treating Others How We'd Like to be Treated vs. Treating Others According to How They are Behaving

Treating Others How We'd Like to be Treated

Emotional manipulators often manipulate not only their target's emotions, but the emotions of those around their target. They can (and do) manipulate everyone into thinking that they are the victim, and that their target is the problem. This level of manipulation takes a dangerous and new low if a target is religious, as spiritual texts are often twisted into becoming extensions of power and control for the abusive person. The "golden rule" of treating others how we would want to be treated is often skewed to push the target into staying in an abusive situation, because if we treat others how we'd like to be treated, then odds are this would mean that we want to be treated fairly, and with dignity, compassion, in a way that is respectful, and that we'd want to be given another chance if we've done something hurtful to someone else. The part about being given another chance is often continually twisted by both the abuser and the target. If given a person another chance puts you or your children in harm's way, then this isn't the golden rule. This is a manipulation.

Treating Others According to How They are Behaving

Treating others how we'd like to be treated doesn't mean that we need to (or should) let go of having healthy boundaries or deal-breaker behavior for those who hurt us. It doesn't mean that we need to allow a person open access to our lives when they've had hurtful or harmful behavior either towards us or that impacts us—or even impacts others. What it does mean is that we treat people based on a fair and *reasonable* way if we had done the same things they did. <u>And it's never reasonable to continue to put yourself or your children in harm's way.</u>

"Oh the "Golden Rule." My father would continually use this against me, claiming that I was a hypocrite, didn't know the value of family, and didn't honor God because I wasn't treating him like I'd want to be treated. What he really meant was that he wanted me to continually turn the other cheek and let him keep getting away with hurting me. The reality was that I would never treat people like how he treated me, and if I did, I would realize that there are consequences."
— Kevin

"My new understanding of the golden rule is, 'Do unto yourself as you would do unto others.' Meaning, treat yourself as good as you treat others. For years, I had treated everyone much better than I treated myself, because I thought to treat myself good (or even to take

my wants, needs, or feelings into consideration) meant that I was somehow greedy or selfish. I now realize that I matter, and that I am worthy of treating myself with dignity and respect, and that my wants, needs, and feelings matter. If I'm treating others in a way that puts me at harm, then there is something wrong, and I know now that I need to not do this."

— *Luci*

Nobody is Perfect vs. Tolerating Abusive Behavior

Nobody is Perfect

Many partners of abusive people justify the abuse to themselves with the rationalization that "nobody is perfect." And while this is true, nobody is perfect, it doesn't mean that being used, abused, exploited, or neglected is somehow okay. It's a reasonable expectation for you to be treated with dignity and respect and to not be abused, lied to, cheated on, or dragged through hell by a person who is supposed to be on the same team as you.

Tolerating Abusive Behavior

Abusive behavior isn't a mistake, and it's not an anger issue. It's intentional behavior that's driven by power and control, and worse, the abusive person often (if not always) feels justified in their abusive treatment of those around them.

Tolerating abusive behavior because the abuser is a friend, coworker, spouse, or family member is to be held emotionally (and generally financially and physically) hostage every single day. This means you have to walk on eggshells and continually try to read the abuser's mind and anticipate their mood. If a person has behavior that includes them being abusive, having active addictions, or committing adultery, then this is a big problem. It is a mistake to use the defense of "nobody is perfect" with any of these things, and to think that this relationship is workable. In order for a relationship to work, there needs to be two emotionally available, committed, and present people. If one person isn't ready, willing, or able to be emotionally invested in a relationship, then no relationship is possible. ...And don't confuse the relationship continuing with the relationship working. Lots of people have stayed in one-sided relationships full of abuse, addiction, and adultery for decades. This isn't something to celebrate, or to use as a model of an ideal relationship.

"Whenever I would confront my ex about something (usually another woman I'd catch him texting, or if I tried to explain how he hurt my feelings), he'd spin things around, blame me, and then accuse me of thinking I was perfect. What started out as a conversation would quickly escalate to an argument with the focus on me and everything I did wrong. I can't believe how twisted and turned around my thinking was when I was with him. He really had me thinking all his abuse and cheating was my fault, and then he'd try to make me

feel guilty and like I was the problem whenever I tried to hold him accountable."

— Tiffany

"My parents were married for thirty-four years when my father died. My father was an alcoholic and a rage-oholic. I used to think this level of commitment at all costs was what a 'real' relationship was all about, and I thought my mother was a saint for putting up with him. I also used to justify his abuse because he had an abusive childhood. I now realize that there is no excuse for abuse, and that my mother wasn't a saint for putting up with him, she was scared of being alone and lived in fear of what he'd do to her and to himself if she left. I didn't realize that they had an abusive or dysfunctional relationship until I got out of my own abusive relationship, and began going to therapy. That's when I learned about boundaries, standards, and deal breakers...and that I didn't have any. I realized that I was using my parent's relationship as a template for my own, and if I wanted to break the cycle, then I needed to get a new template. I slowly began to realize that my parents didn't have a relationship. They had an unspoken understanding. Basically, that my dad was going to do whatever he felt like, and that my mom was going to put up with it— even if that meant him destroying her emotionally. What breaks my heart is that she thought this was love."

— Laura

Being Judgmental vs. Being Discerning

Being Judgmental

Being judgmental is often viewed in a negative way when one person has an attitude of moral superiority over someone else/others by declaring themselves right or good and the other person as wrong or bad. Many targets continue to keep problematic people in their life because they feel harsh by drawing a line in the sand for what they won't tolerate. You don't necessarily have to judge other people; you can leave that up to the court system or your understanding of God, but it is, however, important that you are being the judge of what is right or wrong, or acceptable and unacceptable *for you and for your life*. It's very important that we all have a clear idea of what's acceptable and unacceptable in our lives— especially when it comes to how we are treated by those in our inner circle.

Narcissists will often protest that their target is being judgmental of them when the target brings up any issue they have with their behavior or tries to set a boundary. They will often throw out the "you're being judgmental" card in an effort to manipulate their target using guilt or obligation—*especially* if their target is religious. An emotional manipulator will not be okay with you having boundaries, so it's important that you realize that they will throw out every trick in the book to manipulate you in order for them to continue getting their way—and these manipulations tend to escalate until their target caves in and gives them what they want.

For the record, having standards for how you are treated, and cutting destructive people out of your life isn't being judgmental—it's important and necessary if you want to have peace in your life.

Being Discerning

Being discerning means to know ourselves well enough to discern what is workable, and what we consider deal-breaker behavior for how we are treated, or for other situations in general. Having a level of discernment for what we will and won't tolerate is important, so that we can assess situations accurately and respond accordingly. Discernment isn't about morally judging others—it's about making healthy and empowering decisions for ourselves, regardless of what others think we "should" do.

"I kept many of the wrong people in my life for way too long, because I felt judgmental for having boundaries and trying to cut them out. My ex and my father were the two abusive people in my life, and they would both tell me that God was the only one who could judge them. I was continually pushed into forgiving them and keeping them in my life by people in our church as well as other family members. I now realize that I have the right to be discerning and to choose who is in my life, and I no longer keep abusive or manipulative people in my life. That might sound harsh to some people, but I want peace in my life from here on out."
        — *Carla*

Unhealthy Narcissism vs. Healthy Narcissism

Unhealthy Narcissism

Unhealthy narcissism is what most people mean when they are talking about narcissism in general, whether they are referring to a person who is narcissistic or to an extreme, "Narcissistic Personality Disorder." When most people use the term "narcissistic" or "narcissist" they are usually referring to a person who is self-centered to a problematic degree. While that is part of the problematic behavior that makes up narcissistic behavior, it's not just that the person is full of themselves; it's that because they are so full of themselves they have no room for anyone else. In other words, they are so focused on their wants and needs that they are not emotionally available to nurture or empower those in their inner circle. They are all about themselves all of the time—at the expense of others.

I think it's helpful to view narcissism in terms of a person's self-orientation, or of them understanding themselves and their place in the world. Our self-orientation is on a spectrum ranging from healthy narcissism, which would be where healthy self-esteem falls. This mindset is where a person believes that they are worthy of having goals and have faith in their abilities to achieve them, while understanding that they will be continually learning and growing along the way. This is an "I can do it" or "Why not me?" type mentality. Where this mindset starts to become problematic is when it starts to become more of an "It's all about me" or, "It's all about me at the expense of you" type mentality. Having a relationship with someone who is so self-absorbed, selfish, and entitled will not work, because they have no emotional understanding or capacity to work as a team.

Context is key in understanding this spectrum of narcissism, as there is a time and place for some degrees for all of these types of behaviors. If a person is playing sports or is competitive in business, they will most likely take on the attitude of "me vs. you," and that's okay (to a reasonable degree) within that context. However, the attitude of "me vs. you" is a problem if they view themselves in unnecessary competition with their spouse or children or others that are on their same team. But if a spouse is abusive, then it's important for the other spouse to realize that while they may be married and "should" be on the same team, that once abuse enters into the dynamic they are not on the same team and they need to take defensive action (leave if they can, get an attorney, develop an escape plan, etc.)

When targets of abuse start developing boundaries, they often feel selfish, and as though they are being mean to others, by putting themselves first. Having boundaries with someone isn't being mean or controlling. It's making ourselves a priority, and realizing that our wants and needs are important too, and that we weren't put on this Earth to be mistreated or to serve them. Keep in mind that while we weren't meant to be mistreated, other people - especially those who are used to you always saying yes or giving in - will exclaim that you are mean or selfish for not letting them to continue to mistreat you. So prepare yourself emotionally for this.

It encompasses several different components, but mainly it is when a person is so motivated by their own desires that (at a minimum) they emotionally or physically starve out or suck energy from those around them, because their wants and needs come first—and they do so by using, abusing, exploiting, or neglecting others. The vast majority of people who are caught up in addiction would be considered to have narcissistic behavior, because feeding that addiction tends to be at the forefront of their mind, even if it means destroying their marriage or family to get it fed.

Healthy Narcissism

Healthy narcissism is a psychological term that describes a person having the self-confidence and self-esteem to believe that they can set and achieve their goals—even if (or perhaps, especially if) others don't understand or support their vision. A person with healthy narcissism believes in themselves and their ability to figure things out and to move forward. They don't have an attitude of superiority or unnecessary competition. Healthy narcissism is the attitude of "Why not me?" And it's the belief that a person is worthy of setting goals and obtaining them, without feeling that that they need to tear everyone else down around them in order for that to happen.

"The concept of healthy narcissism was a game changer for me. I had heard of narcissism before, and I thought any type of big plans or goals or putting myself first was a bad thing. I didn't want to be a narcissist like my mother, and so I continually put myself last as a way to prevent that from happening. I didn't realize that my putting everyone else first was also a problem, and I didn't realize that it was normal and healthy to have goals, as my mother was always cutting me down and telling me why I'd never succeed. I'm now working on building healthy self-esteem and self-worth."

— *Heather*

Self-love vs. Selfishness

Self-love

Self-love is when a person treats themselves with dignity, respect, and value, which includes having healthy boundaries with others, making their time, safety, and sanity a priority, and realizing that their wants and needs do matter. Self-love is best seen by how a person treats themselves, how they treat others, and how they allow others to treat them.

Selfishness

Selfishness (unhealthy narcissism) is the attitude of a person getting their needs and wants met at the expense of others, which often includes them using, abusing, exploiting, or neglecting those in their inner circle. Selfishness is an attitude that a person should be able to do what they want, when they want, as much as they want, and be allowed to get away with it, all because it makes them happy—regardless of who it hurts.

Let me be clear:

Setting boundaries with problematic or abusive people is not being selfish; it is self-protection, which is a form of self-love.

Cutting off contact with problematic or abusive people is not being selfish; it is self-protection, which is a form of self-love.

Refusing to reopen contact or to "help" an abusive person because they "need" you or because their children or animals "need" you isn't selfish; it is self-protection, which is a form of self-love.

Fighting for full custody because the other parent is hurting the children isn't selfish; it's trying to protect you children and is an act of love for your child.

Limiting or cutting off contact with a family member who has abused your children isn't selfish; it's being protective and loving towards your child.

"I always thought the idea of self-love was narcissistic and thought continually putting others ahead of myself was the right thing to do and what love looked like in motion. I thought that was healthy, and it wasn't. I didn't realize that I was neglecting myself, putting all the wrong people first, and then resenting them because I was always there for them. This whole experience has been very eye-opening, and I'm now on the path to finding more balance in my life and making myself a priority."

— *Amy*

The Right Therapist vs. The Wrong Therapist

The Right Therapist

I am not a believer in the blanket advice that therapy is a cure all (in general) and especially not for people who have been in a narcissistically abusive relationship. Rather, I believe that the *right* therapy from the *right* therapist (or life coach) can be incredibly helpful, but unfortunately finding that can sometimes feel like trying to find a needle in a haystack.

Just like in any other profession, not all therapy or therapists are created equal. And also like in any other area of life, there is an ocean of difference between theory and application—between studying something and actually living it. Frankly, I'm not sure how much about the dynamics of abuse are even studied or taught—which is absolutely mind-boggling to me.

If a therapist does not understand:

- The difference between an abusive relationship and a "normal" relationship
- That abuse is about power and control
- That abuse is not about gender or strength
- The different types of abuse
- How power and control are manipulated and used against a person
- The differences between an individual issue and a relationship issue
- The differences between commitment and codependency/trauma bonds

Then they are giving out nothing more than well-intended bad advice.

An abusive relationship has more in common with a hostage situation or a cult than a relationship, and to not be familiar with the dynamics of manipulation and trauma bonds is to not be familiar (or helpful) *at all* with what's going on.

What I have seen a lot of (and have experienced) is well-intended therapists who have their own unexamined biases and codependency (or sometimes even narcissism) issues, and who are not familiar with the dynamics of abuse to the degree they need to be in order to actually be effective.

What I have seen from a lot of therapists who aren't familiar with abuse is that they don't want their clients to talk about this abusive or controlling person and instead they want them to focus on themselves. And I can understand that; I really can. After all, we only have control over ourselves.

However, there is a time and place in healing for the focus to shift from what happened to understanding our part in things. A big part of understanding and healing from narcissistic abuse comes from pulling apart the damage done, and examining things piece-by-piece in an effort to make sense of what in the hell happened. Because this isn't a relationship, it's a manipulationship, and when a person's been manipulated, they often don't realize it until the very end. When they do realize it, it's incredibly painful and troubling to wonder how you didn't see what was going on for so long. They need to get that validation and clarity before they can effectively move forward into the next stage of healing. It's a lot like being in a cult. The trauma and confusion of all that doesn't end when the person leaves the cult—they have to untangle the dynamics of how they got sucked into one, why they stayed, reexamine their belief system, sort out how they were being manipulated, and learn to trust again. It's a lot to go through, and this takes time.

What a person needs the most when they are fresh out of a narcissistically abusive relationship (or any trauma, for that matter) is to feel validated, safe, believed, listened to, and empowered to continue finding their voice in all this. So it's very normal that when a person gets out of these kinds of situations that they will want to research into narcissism, and manipulation, and rehash (ruminate) about this topic—and this can go on for months or even years. Again, this is because they weren't in a "bad relationship;" they've been held emotionally hostage, and there's often a lot of PTSD that goes along with that. It's not helpful to try and stop them from researching or rehashing things, and it is also not helpful to encourage them to date again. What's helpful is to listen to them, and to give them the time they need to put together the pieces of this puzzle that they are finding. When this starts to happen, then, and only then, can they begin to process this trauma into a cohesive and understandable series of events that makes sense.

Because this "researching" phase can last for quite a while, and because people do have so many questions about what happened, I think it's incredibly helpful for people to be around others who have gone through the same thing. I am a strong believer that the best combination out there to get people the clarity, validation, and understanding they need, is to have both a support group as well as a good therapist (or life coach) who is familiar with narcissistic abuse, where a person can then take their aha moments from the support group and explore them in individual therapy.

Now, don't get me wrong; the right therapist can be worth their weight in gold, but the wrong therapist can cost a person lots of time, money, and emotional hurt and heartache—not to mention potentially revictimizing them and doing even more harm. I don't think that many people—including many therapists—fully realize just how much harm they can do...especially with well-intended bad advice.

The right therapist is one who:

- Understands the difference between a relationship and an abusive relationship.
- Has in-depth, working knowledge and experience with emotional and psychological abuse.
- You feel reasonably comfortable opening up to (you probably won't at first—and that's okay—open up at the pace you feel comfortable with).
- After a rapport is built, you feel safe doing a "deep dive" on certain highly-emotional and deeply-personal topics.

- Understands that it is normal and healthy to have deal-breaker behavior and that going "no contact" with someone—even if they are family—is sometimes what a person needs in order to heal.
- Doesn't have their identity, ego, or religion wrapped up in "fixing" you or your "relationship."
- You feel believes you and is on your side.
- Understands the difference between a communication issue and a personality disorder.
- Encourages you to explore other resources.
- Recognizes the value in a support group/additional resources.

The Wrong Therapist

The wrong therapist is one who:

- Isn't familiar with abuse—or that you are having to educate on what an abusive relationship is.
- Isn't familiar with the seven different types of abuse (or only recognizes physical abuse as being problematic).
- Thinks that both people had an equal part in this relationship (or that there is some sort of excuse for the abuse, such as the abuser's childhood, or communication issues, etc.).

- Is unable to tell the difference between a "normal" relationship and an abusive relationship.
- You aren't comfortable opening up to.
- Gets annoyed or frustrated that you aren't "moving on."
- You feel doesn't believe you or that you don't feel is on your side.
- Minimizes, invalidates, or discounts verbal, emotional, or psychological abuse.
- Corrects your use of terminology (telling you that what you experienced wasn't abuse, or that being verbally, emotionally, or psychologically abused is somehow normal).
- Tells you that no one is perfect and pushes you to reconcile after you've experienced something that you feel is deal-breaker behavior.
- Thinks that family is forever and that family members should always keep in contact no matter what.
- Thinks that everything can be fixed given enough time, understanding, love, religion, or rehab.
- Is in any way abusive or abrasive.
- Minimizes, invalidates, or "discounts" what you went through.
- Does not understand trauma or C-PTSD and how it affects a person mentally, emotionally, psychologically and/or physically.

- You become attracted to, or who you feel is attracted to you.

"I thought all therapists were about the same, and picked one because she took my insurance. I stayed seeing her for close to a year, and felt revictimized the whole time. Hindsight being what it is, it was very clear that she wasn't familiar with abuse, but I just assumed she'd be able to help because she was a therapist. At the time, I didn't even realize I had been abused, I just knew something was very wrong with me, and that I felt like I was going crazy. It wasn't until I got into a support group, that I realized my mother was psychologically and emotionally abusive. I knew then that I was wasting my time and money with that therapist and needed to find a new one. It took a few phone calls to some other therapists, and asking them if they were familiar about abuse and what abuse was to them, and how they felt about me not talking to my abusive mother, before I was able to find one that could help. I'm so glad I found one that gets it now, and who has been able to help guide me to more solid emotional ground. It's really made a difference."

— *Lisa*

Choosing the Right Partner vs. Choosing a Partner Who is the Opposite of Your Ex

Choosing the Right Partner

Choosing the *right* partner involves knowing ourselves to the point where we know what we want and what we don't want, and loving ourselves enough to think we are worthy of good people and things in our life, as well as that we are worth walking away from people and things that cause us hurt and harm. Loving ourselves also includes realizing that we don't need to stick around to make sure questionable behavior is indeed problematic, and that they really are lying, cheating, stealing, or otherwise abusing us, and instead realizing that if it's questionable, or if we aren't comfortable with how we are being treated, then we value ourselves enough to walk away. The right partner is one who treats us with dignity and respect, is trustworthy, doesn't have continually "squirrelly" or hurtful behavior, and has open, honest, sincere, and solutions-oriented communication.

Choosing the right partner and getting into the right relationship starts with getting into the right relationship with ourselves.

Choosing a Partner Who Is the Opposite of your Ex

Choosing a partner who is the opposite of their ex is what many people tend to do. On the surface this makes sense. So for example, if your ex was arrogant, selfish, and verbally abusive, it's very common (and understandable) for a person to never want to be tangled up with someone like that again. So they might find themselves attracted to (relationship-wise, or even friendship-wise) someone who is the complete opposite—however, the complete opposite of an overt narcissist tends to be a love bombing, sweet-talking, fast-moving, charming, covert narcissist.

If a person doesn't realize that love bombing, moving fast, future faking and superficial charm are red flags, or if they have unexamined or unresolved vulnerabilities within themselves, such as being lonely or scared, low self-esteem, a blurred sense of what healthy boundaries are—including thinking that everything is workable and not having a clear line for deal-breaker behavior until things get really, really, bad—then they are *unknowingly* primed to get tangled up with a covert abuser.

And when the reality of this relationship comes crashing down, this person will most likely feel that they are cursed, or that there are no good people out there, or they get caught up in another spiral of shame or self-doubt wondering what on earth is wrong with them, how this could have happened again…and are terrified to date or even get to know new people.

Interestingly enough, dating or befriending the opposite kind of person works the other way around as well. A lot of people who have been involved with a charming, covert abuser have found themselves attracted to someone who has more outright problematic behavior. Perhaps they do this because, on a subconscious level, they might feel a certain sense of security in knowing that at least they know what this partner's issues are and what they can expect from them, versus a covert abuser whose behavior alternates between Dr. Jekyll and Mr. Hyde at any moment, or who may go for long periods of time acting like a decent or even great partner—up until their double life kind of behavior (siphoning funds, cheating, etc.) comes to light.

"My last relationship was with a very controlling, arrogant, jealous, mean man who continually put me down. So when I came across "Sam" I fell hard for him. Sam was everything my ex wasn't. He was seemingly kind, compassionate, attentive, and supportive. Things moved fast, and I felt like I'd met my soul mate. We were married within the year. And then I discovered he was cheating and that he had lied about a lot of major things. I fully believe he married me because I had money, and he wanted me to support him, and when I didn't, that's when things began to go south with us. I realize now that he was just as abusive as my ex, but in a different way. I vowed to never date anyone like my ex again, and I really thought I'd be able to steer clear of a snake like him, and so when I came across Prince Charming, I thought this was what love was supposed to be. I never thought in a million years that if a man comes along like Prince Charming, that this is also a big red flag!"

— *Sandra*

Needing Someone in Your Life vs. Wanting Someone in Your Life

Needing Someone in Your Life

When we chronically *need* someone in our life—especially if that person is damaging to us, this is a sign of a deeper issue, and one that is important for us to explore and resolve. This level of neediness is very common in an abusive relationship, and it's formed through intermittent reinforcement and trauma bonds. However, if we tend to have a pattern of making someone else our whole world, thinking that they "complete" us, then this is what codependency (also often referred to as "love addiction") looks like in action. Many people who have this type of thinking tend to go from relationship to relationship, being fearful of (or hating) being "alone" or single, settling for crumbs of affection, attention, or loyalty and trying to convince themselves that a toxic relationship or friendship is somehow "good enough."

While it is completely normal to want or need love and validation, it is abnormal to feel that sick intensity and obsession that is associated with love addiction, or to seek it from people who are abusive. Being in love with someone and being addicted to "love" or to them are two very things, and it's important that we are able to tell them apart.

So yes, companionship, relationships, and friendships are an enjoyable and rewarding part of life, but only if they are with people who actually treat us with dignity and respect. Anything less, and we feel drained, exhausted, perpetually "confused," anxious, depressed, nervous, distrusting, and overall unhappy. The great irony in this is that if we are holding onto relationships that don't nourish us because we think crumbs are better than nothing, we will continually find ourselves with a string of failed relationships and friendships, because these dynamics were forged from a place of fear and scarcity and not from a place of self-love and abundance.

If you are finding yourself continually trying to justify your worth to someone else, or walking on eggshells in order to "earn" their love or loyalty, then there's a problem. If you feel jealous, nervous, insecure, anxious, distrusting of them and in a scramble to keep them around no matter what they do, then this is a problem. If you feel like you are in competition with other people for their affection and attention, then this is a problem. If you have to sacrifice your dignity or respect in order to keep this relationship together, then this is a problem. You are worth more than crumbs.

Wanting Someone in Your Life

Wanting someone in your life means that you are approaching relationships and friendships from an attitude of abundance and self-love. You have a life full of friends and hobbies, and you aren't looking for a relationship to make you feel loved or to fill a deep void.

Loving yourself means having healthy boundaries, making your self-care a priority, and treating yourself (and expecting to be treated), with dignity, respect, and value…and to be okay with walking away (or distancing yourself) from others who treat you with anything less.

"It took me awhile to realize that I had a hard time being single. I was boy crazy since I can remember and continually bounced from one relationship to the next. I didn't realize it then, but I needed to be in a relationship in order to feel love, because I didn't know how to love myself. Now I have friends and hobbies, and when I date, it's not out of desperation or a need for someone else to validate me. It's because I enjoy that person, and I appreciate having them in my life. If they were to leave, sure I'd be upset, but they are no longer my whole world, and my life would go on."

— *Eva*

"You do have to absolutely believe you deserve to be loved and validated, just because you exist, then you deserve to be loved and validated. If you are finding yourself in a desperate scramble to try and cling tighter, try harder, work harder, trying to earn their love or to be treated with respect, and continually "confused" as to why you can't trust them—when in reality they are not safe people to trust, then you are in a one-sided relationship. If you are not being loved and validated, then you have to learn how to let go, leave, and look elsewhere."

— *Luci*

Gut Instinct vs. Hypervigilance

Gut Instinct

Our gut instinct speaks to us through our emotions, which we often refer to as "red flags." These red flags serve as an early warning sign of potential danger, and, unfortunately, are warning signs that many of us ignore. When we ignore a red flag, it's generally for one of five different reasons:

- Red flags aren't seen, they are felt, and because we don't see anything obviously wrong, we feel the need to stick around until we have more proof and are actually proven right—that this person or situation is indeed problematic.
- We don't want to be seen as over-reacting if we take action without an overwhelming amount of concrete evidence that points to there being actual danger.
- We don't want to be embarrassed, or seen as rude, weird, "difficult," or over-reacting by others if we don't have proof that something is wrong.
- We aren't taught to give red flags the significance that they deserve; instead we are taught that they are more of a "vibe" or feeling and to not make decisions based on feelings.
- We have an emotional investment in staying in the red-flag situation.

In addition, the more you become aware of what manipulative or abusive behavior looks like, your feelings about what you are experiencing will move from being hard-to-place red flags to outright deal breakers. This might make you feel a mix of being both empowered, because you saw the bullet and dodged it, as well as feel a little crazy if no one else sees the problem for what it is. Learning to tune into your emotions is critical and will help you to better avoid problematic people and situations in the future; therefore, I'm going to cover each of the previously-mentioned points in a bit more depth with the hopes of getting you to give those red flags the weight that they deserve.

In order to better understand our gut instincts, so we can take them seriously, it can be helpful to understand how the human brain processes information.

Our brain takes in a tremendous amount of information all the time, and our brain's primary job is to make meaning out of all that information. In addition, it's important to realize that while we have what looks like one brain, it's really three brains that have evolved over time to form one brain. We have a reptile or primitive brain, an emotional brain (limbic system), and a logic and reasoning (pre-frontal cortex) part of our brain. Where most of us go wrong is in thinking that we only (and only need to) use our logic and reasoning part of our brain to make all of our decisions. This is not the case. In fact, our brains process information from the bottom up, and not the top down. Meaning, all that information first passes through the reptile brain, which sorts the information based on what we either need to do (fight or flight) or what we could do (feed, breed, rest, or digest).

Once meaning is assigned to this new information, it passes up to our second brain, our limbic system. This part of our brain is the largest part and connects the base of our brain stem to the vagus nerve, which runs from our brain stem to our rectum and touches pretty much every major organ in between. So when we have a "visceral" reaction to something, meaning we become nauseated, get a stomach ache, urinate in fear, become repelled, or feel our heart start to race, it's because our limbic system is preparing us to act on that fight or flight mechanism that was kicked off by the reptile brain. Our logic and thinking brain is the final filter, and only a small portion of the information that was originally taken in by the brain reaches this level.

If we think of our body in terms of being a vehicle, then the reptile brain is both the gas and the brake pedal, the limbic system is the GPS system, and the logic and reasoning brain is the steering wheel. If any one of these components is missing, a person will not be able to navigate through life effectively.

In order for it to do this, it initially filters the information based on some pretty basic questions, the first major question being, "Will this kill me?" If our fight or flight filter isn't triggered, then our brain filters information based on whether or not we could breed, feed, friend with this information, and if not, then our brain may register that it's time for us to rest or digest. Keep in mind that all of this is being done at a subconscious level.

The last point with our gut instinct is that if you listen to it, and take action early enough to avoid the problem, *you will actually avoid the problem*. Meaning, you will rarely have the validation of concrete proof that you did in fact avoid the problem, because you avoided it early enough.

"I am an engineer, and I never gave a lot of credit to my gut instinct. I always felt that if I didn't have solid proof that somebody was cheating, lying, or stealing, then I needed to stay in a relationship until I knew for sure. Now, I realize that we have gut instincts for a reason, and I take them seriously. I no longer hang in until the bitter end to have my gut instinct be proven right. If it feels off to me, it's because odds are something is off. And the world is too big and too full of people who don't have squirrelly behavior for me to spend time on those who do."

— Betsy

Hypervigilance

Hypervigilance is the feeling of being continually on edge. It is part of our fight or flight defense and is a healthy and normal response to problematic behavior. When it becomes unhealthy or problematic is when we can't turn it off and remain in a state of cat-like readiness, ready to run at any time. It is normal to feel on alert and on guard around people who are acting in "squirrelly" or suspicious ways. This is where trusting your judgment comes into play, because you may reach out for validation from others who may or may not be able to see the problematic behavior that you are seeing—not because it isn't necessarily there, but perhaps because their idea of what is problematic is much more overt and tangible. It takes time and practice to trust your judgment, but once you do you will feel incredibly empowered.

After you get out of a narcissistically abusive relationship—especially one where there was a lot of "covert" abuse such as emotional and psychological (especially gaslighting and projection)—you may seriously begin to wonder if you are crazy or in the process of becoming crazy. You may feel really on edge and distrusting of people and situations that never made you distrusting before. And you may find yourself continually questioning what normal behavior is and what is a normal way to feel. While all of these feelings are a normal part of C-PTSD, or C-PTSD type symptoms that occur after an emotional trauma, they are also a very normal part of increasing your awareness and realizing that there is a whole other layer of danger (and dangerous people) out in the world that you previously weren't aware could ever be a threat.

Feeling Hypervigilant vs. Seeing Problematic Behavior for What It Is

Feeling Hypervigilant

Feeling hypervigilant often feels like a perpetual state of fight or flight (which feels like being in a state of cat-like readiness for seemingly no good reason). Feeling hypervigilant and having your defenses up after you've been through the emotional rock tumbler that is a narcissistically abusive relationship is normal. It's normal to be on edge and to start seeing problematic or abusive behavior almost every time you turn around. This is in part because you might be hypervigilant due to the emotional trauma, but it's also in large part because you are starting to see problematic or abusive behavior or situations for what they are—for perhaps the first time.

Seeing Problematic Behavior for What It Is

Seeing problematic behavior for what it is can really be its own level of crazy making and can feel like you have entered the Mad Hatter's tea party, and no one seems to see problematic behavior for what it is. Everyone seems to participate in all of this madness, and they might be looking at you like you are the one with the problem for thinking that anything is wrong. This is because the vast majority of people out there are not aware of what exactly manipulative abusive behavior is, let alone the initial stages of how it happens—and this includes not just friends and family, but it can (and often does) include police, therapists, social workers, attorneys, and judges.

And odds are that when you wake up to what problematic behavior is, you will want to try to tell everyone about what you've learned about abuse and abusive behavior because you want to get validation. You also want them to be aware of the danger so they can avoid it too. I will tell you from experience that most other people won't understand what you are trying to say, especially if they haven't experienced anything remotely like it. And trying to get them to wake up to it is a lot like putting lipstick on a pig; it will frustrate you and it will annoy them.

At first you may feel really unsettled by just how many people don't seem to see that there is a problem, and this may make you wonder if perhaps you really are making a big deal out of things, or if you are being too judgmental, harsh, bitter or jaded from your past experiences. As time progresses, and you realize that the red flags you were seeing really were there, you might feel like you have a superpower, like some sort of hidden insight into human behavior. But again, the reality is that most people don't live in reality; they live in a heavily-rationalized reality, based on either what they think is reasonable (even if reality doesn't match up and their being reasonable puts them in harm's way) or what they want reality to be. You will become more comfortable in time with your judgment the more you use it, and it is okay to err on the side of caution. You don't need to explain yourself to anyone.

"After I got out of an abusive marriage, I was very anxious and on edge and terrified of being hurt again. When I started dating again, I kept seeing red flags in people and all my friends kept saying that I was making a big deal out of nothing. After a few brief relationships with men that also turned out to be abusive, controlling, jealous, or

cheating, I finally decided that I wasn't making too big of a deal out of those red flags and that I needed to trust my gut, even if no one else agreed with me."

— *Josephine*

"I have learned to keep my mouth shut, and if I can't, then I discuss it with my therapist or a forum. People seem to have to wake up to this stuff on their own. And if you try to discuss it with someone who is not at least somewhat awake and aware they just think you are a little bit crazy. Also, in most cases, the people I was trying to alert were actually disordered themselves, so of course they did not want to hear about it or discuss it. They were very interested in getting me to: drop it, stop talking about, and above all, to go back to sleep. The people who actually get angry about it are usually disordered or dysfunctional themselves, and it is always in their best interest for you to shut up, and stop talking about these things, because it means the risk of their own exposure has just gotten exponentially greater. Most normal people don't get upset with others setting a boundary, and, worse case, they might just think you are little bit off your rocker. But setting a boundary with an abusive person? Oh boy, watch out!"

— *Luci*

Forgetting vs. Forgiving

Forgetting

Most of what you see and do today, you will forget by tomorrow. In addition, most of the annoyances you encounter will be forgiven and forgotten. This is normal and healthy, as our brains tend to only fixate on to things that represent significance of some kind — either a reward, or a threat, or a trigger for other meanings or curiosities, such as a contradiction. In functional, healthy relationships, most mistakes and annoyances are forgiven and forgotten because they are quickly resolved, there is mutual acknowledgment that ensures any given problem is not a threat in and of itself — and the offending person will adapt behavior for the relationship. However, when there is an abusive person in the mix, the concept of forgiveness gets so distorted and skewed to where it's just another tactic used to keep the target stuck in the web of dysfunction.

The concept of "forgetting" is a popular concept especially among dysfunctional families and relationships— especially when there is abuse involved, and it is how abusive behavior goes about being tolerated, perpetuated, and passed on through the generations. Forgetting often gets twisted into being a part of forgiveness, which in turn is twisted to mean reconciliation and allowance of abuse. This thinking is incredibly dysfunctional by itself, but when it's mixed in with a skewed sense of morality or with religion, it becomes downright destructive, dangerous, and even deadly.

And worse, the more abusive behavior becomes wrapped in a twisted sense of morality, the harder it is for a person to break free from it, because their moral compass is being set to steer towards allowing problematic behavior instead of to run from it—and the whole time thinking that in doing so makes them the bigger or better person, or somehow more spiritual.

Just because a person is family does not make it okay for them to abuse other members of the family, nor does it mean that the family members need to put up with it—although in dysfunctional families, boundaries (let alone healthy boundaries) are often not present. People are used to allowing a lot of destructive behavior, enabling it to continue, minimizing or justifying it when it does happen, pushing the victim(s) to keep contact, blaming the target when it does happen again, or acting like nothing problematic happened and then blaming the target for being too sensitive.

In short, life inside of a dysfunctional family, relationship, or dynamic of any kind is all about being forced to walk on eggshells and avoiding the elephants in the room. When a person starts to get a healthier sense of what problematic behavior is, and the self-esteem and self-worth to realize that they don't need to be someone else's emotional, verbal, or physical punching bag, and starts to develop some healthy boundaries in order to keep themselves safe and sane, many others will not be okay with this. Oftentimes, distancing ourselves from an abusive person is only the beginning—it's holding to our boundaries and potentially distancing ourselves from others that don't respect them (especially enabling family members) that can be really difficult.

Another type of forgetting that tends to happen, has to do with trauma. If you've had a traumatic event happen, you will most likely find yourself going through a cycle of forgetting many of the traumatic things that have happened, and then remembering them later—and then wondering how on Earth you could have forgotten them to begin with. This is very normal, and it's often referred to as "abuse amnesia." Any type of trauma can cause this fragmentation in a person thinking. They don't need to have been several beaten, or even hit at all. If you are with a partner who chronically cheats, lies, steals, or who has any other type of shocking or jarring behavior, you may feel like a bomb went off in your life, and, at first, feel like you are "shell-shocked" and walk around feeling numb and fixated on this event. And then in time, you may find an old journal, or something might trigger an old thought or feeling, and you may find yourself surprised that you could have forgotten that. All of that is very normal, and is, in part, how the brain processes trauma. With time and healing, all of the pieces will come together and your recollection of events won't feel so fragmented.

And of course, the conversation on forgiveness isn't complete without discussing the phrase "forgive and forget." When a person goes through something traumatic, while they may not remember the most painful parts of that trauma because it's too much for them to handle, they will never forget every aspect of that event. Instead, with time, and generally with support, they become more emotionally equipped to endure it. If someone has wronged us, it is really important that we don't fall into the thought hole of thinking that we need to forget what they did, because oftentimes forgetting is a slippery slope that fuels denial and cognitive dissonance and leads to reconciliation which often leads to being abused again. We need to always remember that this person is dangerous and destructive so that we can (and do) stay away from them...especially if we are still holding on to the fantasy that they won't hurt us again down the road.

Forgiving

The word and concept of forgiveness has been so twisted, misused, and tied to so many contradictory connotations, that I don't even like using the word. In addition, telling a target of abuse that they "need to" or "should" forgive their abuser (especially when they are fresh out of the situation) can often be (and is) revictimizing and minimizing.

Forgiveness is a personal journey. It's insensitive, invalidating to be told what we should do— let alone to tell a person who is fresh out of a traumatic situation that they need to immediately jump to forgiveness. It's appropriate and healthy to have a wide range of emotions, anger being one of those emotions, after being abused or exploited, and it's also appropriate and healthy for a person to explore and work through these emotions as they surface, and at their own pace.

So here's how I approach this topic when people ask me about it. If they say, "You need to forgive your ex," my response would either be something along the lines of, "I appreciate your concern, but I'm not open to discussing this," or "If by forgive, you mean release anger towards myself for not realizing what was happening, or for thinking that it was okay that I was treated that way, then yes I am working on that," or, "I'm working on releasing the anger I have against them now that I realize they have a destructive personality and that their treatment of me wasn't a reflection of me but of them." This way we are clear about what forgiveness means, and giving an answer like that usually tends to stop those in their tracks who are giving their unsolicited opinion on what we should do. Keep in mind that you don't need to discuss or defend what happened to you to anyone. You aren't obligated to stand there and argue your boundaries or your feelings.

While forgiving someone means to release the anger you have towards them for their wrongdoings, it isn't complete until we forgive ourselves for staying. It's only a one-sided type of forgiveness to release our anger towards them, if we are left carrying guilt, shame, and regret for how we were mistreated—especially after the fog of manipulation clears and we start to see their actions and our responses to their actions a lot more clearly.

Forgiving a person doesn't mean forgetting, allowing, or reconciling. You can "forgive" someone and decide that you don't want them back in your life ever again. When we go about forgiving someone, it can be helpful to realize that the anger we have is justified, and that it's part of healing. If someone hurts us, and we aren't angry about it, then we are either numb from the pain, we are suppressing the pain, or we are so disconnected from our feelings, or that we have such low self-esteem and have been mistreated for so long that we don't feel worthy of being angry. If we do feel angry, it can be hard to let that anger go, because it can feel like a safety blanket and the one thing that's protecting us from going back to an abusive person. Please know that you can release your anger and still not go back, but in order to do this, it's important that you remember why you need to keep your distance from them.

Releasing the anger we have towards them isn't a one-time decision (although just realizing that we want to work towards releasing anger is a huge first step!) Releasing anger towards them and towards yourself (if you have any) takes time. You will most likely notice changes in your behavior and thinking as anger is often deep-rooted and comes out as emotional triggers. As these emotional triggers surface, it can help to try and observe both the trigger and your reaction to it.

It's also important to realize that all of your emotions are working in your best interest—even the unpleasant ones. These unpleasant emotions are there to act as a signal to either warn you to stop doing something, to stay away from certain people or situations, or serve as a signal to alert you to unresolved issues. It might also help to reframe your understanding of anger and realize that it is the bodyguard to your hurt. If you can start acknowledging and addressing the hurt, the anger will often start to subside.

This is going to sound harsh, but I want to be clear: *it is not being forgiving to allow a person who is dangerous and destructive (especially if they aren't sincerely remorseful) to remain an active part of your life; that is being foolish, and will only set you up for further hurt and heartache.*

If you want or need to keep contact with an abusive person for whatever reason (they are a parent and you feel guilty or obligated to keep in contact with them, or they are an ex and you have a child with them) you can still set some boundaries to limit their destruction in your life.

"My family was always pushing me to reopen contact with my father who had molested me when I was a child, and for decades I would tell myself and others that I'd forgiven him just to keep the peace in the family. I fell for the whole, "Well, but the kids should know their

grandfather" line my family kept giving me. The truth was, I didn't know how to navigate healthy boundaries with him, and so I caved in and let him be a part of our lives because I felt like that's what I was supposed to do. I've since realized that he was (and I'm sure still is) a predator, and I was being foolish for having him in my life and in the lives of my children, and putting them at risk—not to mention feeling revictimized every time I saw him. Once I realized this, I cut off contact. It disgusts me to think how toxic my family really is and how they used so much guilt, shame, and obligation to keep me in contact with my father. Do I forgive him? No. Because he never asked for it, and he doesn't deserve it. I still have a lot of anger that I have to work through, and I know it's important that I do so it doesn't destroy my life, but it's a process. Even if I were to forgive him, I'd never have anything to do with him. That would just be dangerous. Do I forgive myself for not realizing how toxic he and my family are? Yes, and this is something that I work on every day."

— Diane

Forgiveness is necessary for a relationship to work, however, if someone does something wrong, and there is no acknowledgment present, or instead there is only denial or minimization, the resulting invalidation can hurt as much or more than the bad behavior itself. It's adding insult to injury. You can forgive and forget a single instance of a bad behavior if it is properly acknowledged — but if a pattern forms, then the apologies begin to sound hollow, and you question the person's intent or ability to change behavior. Intent doesn't matter much, because whether a person is unable, or unwilling, to curb harmful behavior, the result is the same.

Forgiving and forgetting can be healthy, but only if there is sincere remorse present, following by appropriate action to repair the damage done...and most importantly, that they have stopped doing whatever it is that they are doing!

If they don't have accountability, remorse, and if the issue keeps happening, and we keep forgiving them when all they offer up is more empty words, then this isn't forgiveness, it's us being in denial. This is very common in abusive relationships. Especially if the person giving the blind forgiveness is denying the pattern because they want to hang on to the relationship.

One of the most difficult things to deal with in a relationship with an abusive person, is they may partially admit doing wrong, but attempt to minimize it with excuses, demand that you forgive or forget the incident because they forgive you for your wrongs — but they will deny the pattern. Or they may acknowledge the problem, and say everything you need to hear in order to get you to stick around. This is why looking at actions over a consistent period of time and not focusing on their words is so important."

— *George*

"My take on forgiveness is a biblical one, which is that it is ALWAYS a two-part process. In the Bible we are taught that the process begins when one person who has done the wrong feels remorse, and expresses that remorse, and then desires to make restitution, and also commits to stop the behavior and to not repeat it. The wronged one then has opportunity to give the one who did the wrong forgiveness.

In my opinion, you will never get the opportunity for this with the disordered. Not sincerely, and not in any lasting and meaningful way.

So yes you can and must forgive yourself, you need to feel remorse, and make restitution to yourself, and commit to not repeat it, and forgive yourself. But all you can ever do with them after working through the stages of grief is get to a point of acceptance of who and what they are. That is the BEST you can ever hope for. You will rarely if ever get a chance to offer them forgiveness because they will never feel remorse, nor will they ever desire to make restitution, nor can they commit to stop the behavior and not repeat it. They literally cannot do it. It's not within the realm of their emotional and psychological wiring capability. But with great effort you can get to acceptance. But you cannot forgive anyone who is not sorry, and who does not desire to make restitution, and who won't commit to do better. It's simply ludicrous to even talk about it. It's a two-part process. And it's not going to happen in this lifetime."

— *Luci*

Leaving vs. Leaving Safely

Leaving

Leaving an abusive partner is rarely an easy or safe thing to do, and yet this is the most common advice that is given to partners of abusive people. Abusive behavior is driven by the desire to get and keep power and control over their target(s) and over the situation. If the target decides to leave, then the abusive person usually doesn't take it well, as they are losing power and control over their target and over the situation. This can (and often does) lead them to become very unpredictable, which can lead to a potentially dangerous or deadly situation. A person is in the most danger when they go to leave, and for the first six months to a year after they do leave, for this reason.

Even if the abusive person does not have a history of physical violence or aggression, they can still become violent. These situations can become especially dangerous if the person trying to leave is used to being threatened, intimidated, or getting into a physical fight with their partner—because to them this is just how things are, and this is normal. While it may be their normal, that doesn't make this current situation any less dangerous.

Leaving Safely

Leaving safely involves awareness of the kind of behavior they have, some degree of anticipating what they might do (or are capable of), and ideally preparing if there is time. If there is no time, then don't worry about preparation, just leave—the rest can be figured out later. Developing a safety plan or exit strategy is often a key piece in leaving, because leaving an abusive relationship has a lot more in common with a person leaving a hostage situation than it does with a person leaving a relationship.

A safety plan is a personalized plan that involves brainstorming and planning for everything for a target to get to safety, if they need to leave immediately.

Here are some potential elements of a safety plan:

1. Develop a "safe word". A safe word is a word that you agree with a friend or family member ahead of time that lets them know you can't talk and are in danger. Make this word something that is unique, but nothing that would raise a red flag to anyone else. Something like "kitten" or "coffee." Agree on a word that you could work into a sentence like, "Did you see that cute kitten video I sent you?" or "I've had a long day and could really go for a cup of coffee." The goal here is to alert the other person that something is wrong, but in such a way that the abuser wouldn't realize that you are speaking in code if they are overhearing you or monitoring your texts or calls. The person who knows your safe word needs to know that you might not be able to answer any more questions, and that if you hang up they need to call 911 and use a GPS locator on your phone to find your location (if possible.)

2. Get copies (or ideally take originals) of all important papers. These would be copies of your birth certificate, social security card, driver's license, auto insurance, auto registration, divorce papers, citizenship papers, immunization records, and anything else important.

3. Make extra *sets* of keys. Make extra sets of keys for your house and vehicles. Give a set to a friend and keep a set somewhere hidden on the different vehicles or outside in case you need to get out fast, or in case the abuser takes your keys.

4. Pack a "go" bag. Pack a bag of several sets of clothing and some shoes for the kids and yourself. Keep these bags someplace safe, perhaps at a friend's house. Do not keep these bags where the abuser might find them. You do not want to alert him or her that you are leaving.

5. Keep extras of medications. If you or the kids are on medication, keep extras in your "go" bag. Make sure to also pack any medical supplies that might be needed, such as insulin syringes, blood testers, blood testing strips, asthma inhalers, etc. Make sure you check them periodically to make sure they aren't expired.

6. Have a safe location. If you leave, you don't want the abuser to know where you are going. Safe houses and shelters are good, as are motels and hotels that are out of the way.

7. Change the passwords to your email, phone, and any online accounts. If your abuser knows your passwords for any accounts, err on the side of caution and assume that you are being monitored. Change all the passwords for every account, and it's a good idea to use a different password for each, as well as a password that your abuser doesn't know. If you are finding that your abuser still seems to know what you are doing or saying, it's a good idea to take your computer and phone into Best Buy or a technology store and see if they can check for any hidden tracking software as well as clean your computer to be on the safe side.

8. Make sure to turn off the "Find my iPhone" or GPS feature on your phone. Your abuser can track you this way. If you aren't sure how to do this, do a google search on this topic to learn more. This GPS feature can also be on for Facebook and other social media, so make sure if you are posting on social media, that it's not giving a location update to where you are. It's also a good idea to set your social media accounts (especially Facebook) to "private" so you can review the posts you are being tagged in, or to create fake social media accounts (with a fake name and without pictures you've used before) so you aren't being stalked by your abuser or by their friends, family, or coworkers.

9. Know what info is out there about you on the internet. If they seem to keep finding you, it could be that they are doing a google image search on what you've used on Facebook or some other site. If you want to see what information is out there on the internet about you, google your name, as well as any screen names you've used in the past. It's also a good idea to do a google image search for any pictures that you've used in the past (or to click on the google images search after you've searched your name).

10. Don't hesitate to call the police. You may be struggling with whether or not to call the police as maybe it might mean he gets fired from his job, or maybe you don't think the abuse is "that bad" yet. If you are feeling like you are in danger, call the police. Abusers can either be physically dangerous or they can hint at being physically dangerous. "If you left me/cheated on me, I'd kill you." Or, "It'd be a *real* shame if something happened to you." Or, "I took my vows seriously and will be with you until death do us part." Take all threats (either real or perceived) seriously.

11. Find alternative placement for your pets. If you are staying because of your pets (lots of victims do), line up alternative placement with a friend or family member. Some shelters can also help you find temporary housing for your pets. I know that you want to protect your pets, but please remember if you don't protect yourself, you may not be around to protect them.

12. Only give out your location to people you trust. If you are leaving, or thinking of leaving, it's really important that you only tell people you can trust. It's also a good idea to let them know that your former partner can be very manipulative, and regardless of what they say (generally, that they need to get ahold of you because of some major issue with the kids, for example) that they should not give them any information—instead, they can take down their info and offer to pass it along if they happen to see you. (I'd also encourage you to have friends and family read more on the hoovering and flying monkey sections of this book, so they can also prepare for it.)

13. Get a PO Box for at least the first year. If you are concerned about them finding you, which would be an appropriate and reasonable concern if you are having to develop a safety plan, I would highly recommend keeping a PO Box for a minimum of one year and using it as your primary address for everything—your children's school, your pharmacy, your bank, credit card companies, etc. There is no reason anyone needs to know your physical address. If a place requires a physical address for shipping, you can still use a PO Box number, you just may need to write it differently. For example, if you PO Box address is:

Jane Doe
PO Box 123
Atlanta, GA 30301

You could also write it as:

Jane Doe
5555 Main Street #123 (The 5555 Main Street being the address of the post office)
Atlanta, CA 30301

14. Remember, this is not your fault. Many men and women find themselves in physically abusive relationships. It's not easy to leave. People who haven't been in one generally don't understand. Find supportive friends, family or groups on Facebook for domestic violence. You are not alone; many people do care, and you deserve more.

Hoping For the Best vs. Erring on the Side of Caution

Hoping for the Best

Hoping for the best is what optimism looks like in action. However, staying hopeful that a situation will change when nothing points to it actually changing (or when things are getting worse) isn't being optimistic, it's being in denial, and that level of denial can be not only destructive and dangerous; it can be deadly.

Erring on the Side of Caution

Erring on the side of caution is what being realistic and seeing the situation clearly looks like in action. When we do this, then we are able to work with facts based on a person's prior behavior so we can anticipate what they might do in the future.

Let me clarify this point a bit. If a person has been dangerous in the past, it's a good idea to err on the side of caution and to assume that they will be dangerous in the future. If a person has had a pattern of concerning behavior in the past that hasn't resulted in dangerous behavior, please know that it's usually a matter of time before it does. So for example, just because a person has received threatening text messages in the past, and nothing has happened, doesn't mean that nothing will happen in the future. In fact, it's usually the exact opposite. This kind of behavior is the early warning sign that some sort of violent behavior will occur in the future. So please don't let your guard down or think that you are somehow safe just because they haven't done anything yet.

It's not uncommon for other people (including friends, family, therapists, police, attorneys, etc.) who do not know how highly manipulative, unhinged, or dangerous this person potentially is, to think, or even tell you that you might be overreacting. And while that's incredibly infuriating and frustrating, please realize that sometime no matter how much proof you have, they still may not see that this person is dangerous and destructive. Keep a paper trail (emails, voice mails, video, etc.) of what's going on so you can try to prove your side, especially if it comes down to getting a restraining order or taking this person to court. Also realize that it's important for you to do what you need to do in order to keep yourself safe and sane— even if others think you are making too big of a deal out of things.

I want to caution you for a moment here, because often times if a person has been around destructive or dangerous behavior or situations for any length of time—and especially if they've been able to survive the situation so far—then their internal alarm system may not be going off when it should. So when it comes to erring on the side of caution, ask yourself what advice you'd give to a good friend, your child, or a younger sibling if they were in a similar situation, or ask yourself what the most emotionally healthy person would do if they were in your situation. If your plan for handling a dangerous or destructive person in your own life doesn't match up to what you'd encourage someone else to do, then this is a sign something is off. If you would encourage a loved one to get out of harm's way, then it's a good idea to take that same advice for yourself. Don't wait until the harm actually happens to take action to keep yourself safe.

"Everyone kept telling me to just leave him, but it wasn't that easy. He was really scary when he didn't get his way, and I knew he'd flip out and do God-knows-what to me. I didn't have time to put together a whole safety plan, but I did some of the basics, and when I left, I never looked back. I moved to a new state, changed my number, changed my social media accounts, and got a PO Box. I feel like I can finally breathe. I didn't realize how stressed out I really was until I left. I don't know how I lived like that for so long."
— Cheryl

Confusion vs. Clarity

Confusion

Problematic situations and behavior both have one thing in common: the first warning sign is always confusion. When any of us start experiencing problematic behavior, we often question what we are experiencing. This is normal, because what we are experiencing isn't normal, and our brain is trying to make sense out of something that is nonsensical to us. This confusion leaves us at a cognitive-dissonance crossroads, where we do a double take, or start second- guessing ourselves, wondering if it's us or if it's them. *This confusion compounds when we experience problematic behavior that we hope isn't problematic.*

After an abusive relationship (especially an emotionally and/or psychologically abusive one), it's normal to continue to feel intense anger/rage, anxiety, depression, hyper vigilance, distrust/paranoia, and the desire to isolate. Any dynamic with a "crazy maker" will make a person feel "crazy," and these feelings of doubting your perceptions of reality can last for months or even years after the crazy maker is gone. This is a normal response to gaslighting (aka psychological abuse).

The best way I can describe this period of time from between when the relationship with the crazy maker ends and your trust in your perceptions of reality and judgment returns is a "lag time."

When a person gets out of an abusive relationship—especially one that is full of covert abuse, such as gaslighting—they often struggle with understanding why they feel so numb or angry or terrified. This is especially true if there's nothing they can concretely point to and say, "This—this right here is how they abused me. They called me these names, or physically did these things to me." And because they can't point to what exactly happened, or why a seemingly small thing, such as a text message from this crazy maker simply saying "hi" or "Happy Birthday" makes them totally come unglued, they often feel that this reaction is an overreaction, especially when they start getting funny looks from other people when they try to explain why a simple text message makes them feel like an anxious, depressed mess.

Please know that you feel that way for a very valid reason, because an abusive relationship is a confusion relationship, and that confusion doesn't end when the relationship ends—it continues on. And for those who haven't been through something like this, they can't even come close to beginning to understand it. While this confusion can feel exhausting, it's also part of an awakening that's happening within you. You are now starting to see problematic or abusive behavior for what it is, and you may notice that it wasn't just this one abusive person who acts this way—you may come to see the behavior of certain "friends," coworkers, neighbors, people at church, and things you see on TV as problematic; whereas, you didn't see this before. Others may tell you that you are overreacting, paranoid, or too judgmental of others, but odds are, you aren't. You are just seeing the behavior of others (and within yourself) clearly for perhaps the first time.

If this is where you are emotionally, please don't fret. You are so not alone in this, and I fully believe that you can heal from this. When I say that you can heal from this, please understand that you can't go back to being who you were. Healing never works like that—not on a physical and not on an emotional level. And you aren't broken. You are emotionally bruised but not broken. And life from here on out will be different, because you see things more clearly, but it can be confusing and crazy making if you are the only one who is awake to this. (This is why I encourage people to join a support group, so you can be around others who are awake to this as well.) And while things are different, that doesn't mean seeing the world through a new set of eyes is necessarily bad—it's just, well, different. If anything, with time you will start to become more confident in your new-found abilities of perception, and you will start to rely on others for validation that something is off. You will learn that no relationship is worth your safety or sanity and that you have no time for "confusing" or crazy making people, and you will get more comfortable figuring out what your deal breakers and boundaries are and unapologetically implementing them.

I strongly encourage you to not do what so many of us have done during this time, and that is to try to jump back into dating. The worst time to try and date is when you are lonely, can't tell the difference between problematic behavior and healthy behavior, and don't trust your judgment. The odds of you getting tangled up with another emotional manipulator are really high. That level of vulnerability brings out the problematic people like you wouldn't believe. And it's important that you are grounded in who you are, and have a life you love, before you look to bring someone else into it. So I encourage you to spend this time right now focusing on your self-care and healing. Because true healing isn't just not feeling blown apart anymore, it's knowing who you are, having a life you love, having healthy boundaries, and trusting your judgment—and all of these things take time and practice.

There is no hurry to get into a relationship. There really isn't. The right person will still be there when the time is right. *What's most important right now is finding yourself again— and then learning to love what you find.*

Because when you truly love yourself, everything else— your boundaries, standards, relationships, etc.—all fall into place. This takes some time, but believe me, it is so worth it. And frankly, discovering who you really are and loving what you find is the big gift in all this. This may sound really wild, but I wouldn't trade what I went through for anything. It's easy to see the gift in all this when enough healing has passed—I would have probably attacked a person had they told me that when I was fresh out of my situation. So if you feel like chucking this book into the garbage or writing me hate mail after me saying that, well, know that's very normal too.

Clarity

The flip side to confusion is clarity. Clarity is what we experience when we have certainty about what is going on in our environment along with our place in it. Some others words that describe how clarity generally feels is "relaxed," "excited," "safe," "secure," and "peaceful."

Getting clarity starts with getting in tune with your emotions and realizing that all of your emotions, especially the unpleasant ones, are there to help guide you. Yoga, therapy with a good therapist who is familiar with narcissistic abuse, support groups, journaling, or meditation can all really help with this.

One exercise that has really helped me to start getting in touch with my emotions has been to rank things on an emotional scale from 0 to10, with 0 being ice cold, 5 being neutral or luke-warm and 10 being a state of absolute joy. Let me stop for a moment and point out that a lot of people who have either been in a narcissistically abusive relationship, aren't in tune with their gut instinct, or are who are starved out emotionally in some way tend to feel really good around emotional manipulators…at first. These dynamics can feel like a 10 on the emotional scale, but what I've found is that they only feel this good if we gloss over the red flags they come with. Joseph Campbell once said, "Follow your bliss," and while that's a good course to set, it's a mistake to follow our bliss if we are sacrificing our peace. In other words, it's important that we learn to follow our peace before we follow our bliss. Because if we follow our bliss, but that leads us to feeling confused, like something is too good to be true, or like something is "off," then we are most likely being manipulated through charm, flattery, and love bombing.

Okay, so back to understanding your emotional scale. It helps to start off with objects—ideally objects that you feel strongly one way or another about, and then to assign them a number based on how you are perceiving/feeling about them right now. Then go a level deeper and try to figure out why. The number that you assign to an item or to a relationship will grow and change as you do. (That's where things really start to get interesting.) So what might be a "10" for you today might not be a "10" for you six months from now. Think about some clothing, or even friendships or relationships you've had in your life. Probably at the time you had them they were pretty high up on your scale—but now you might look back and think they'd be really low on your scale. This isn't to say that those people or those items were necessarily bad or wrong (although maybe they were); it simply means that you've grown and changed and are more in alignment with your authentic self.

So for example, an item around me right now is an ink pen. I'm not talking about anything fancy—just an ink pen that you might get at an office supply store. My initial feeling about it is that I'd say it's around a 9 or a 10 for me. My "why" is because I really love writing with ink pens. I like how inky they are and how easily the pen moves across the paper.

As a contrast, I could also say that writing with a ballpoint pen is around a "0" for me. I really don't like it. Writing with one even kind of stresses me out. I know that sounds weird. And when you go through this exercise, odds are you will come to your own "quirky" realizations about yourself too. And that's okay—it's actually really fun once you release any judgment you have about what your inner self has to say about things and focus on how you feel.

Another example is a handful of really nice button-down shirts hanging in my closet. I realized that I really don't like button-down shirts on me. In fact, I hate them. They aren't flattering on my body type whatsoever, and I'm always tugging and pulling on them when I wear one. I had bought these shirts many years ago based on how I thought I should present myself and who I should be, instead of who I am, I didn't even realize it!

I encourage you to go through your closet, rank items, and ask "why." The insight you'll get it is really amazing. Once you get comfortable assigning numbers to things that you don't have a huge emotional investment in, then take things to the next level and apply this emotional scale to the food you find in the fridge and your hobbies.

Then transfer this scale over to your friendships and relationships (either current ones or past ones). ...Actually, let me stop for a second and just say that I'm so excited for you right now, because this next part is really, really interesting. Okay, so now transfer this scale of 0 to 10 over to your feelings and how you feel around certain items or people. And again, release any judgment that you might feel bubbling to the surface that feels that this exercise is judging people. This isn't about judging people or things. It's not about trying to convince ourselves to be grateful for what we have. *It's about tuning into what your inner self has to say.*

Get in tune with how you feel emotionally about certain situations, people, and things, and I think you'll find that much of your confidence with judgment is restored.

Ask yourself how you feel around people who do seem to have your best interest in mind. Odds are you feel calm, cool, collected, and capable. You don't question yourself, and you don't continually wonder if they are trying to bait or provoke you into an argument or if they are trying to stir the pot, or if they are being insensitive or rude, or if you are the one with the problem. Most likely you don't spend much, if any, time wondering about these things when you are with them, because these things aren't happening.

(This the concept of a "constant" that I was first introduced to in the book *Psychopath Free* by Jackson MacKenzie, which is a fantastic book, and a must read.) A constant is someone or something that you feel consistently comfortable around. My constant is my brother, as he's a good guy with consistently good behavior, and I don't find myself second-guessing his behavior or his motivations.

Whenever I find myself coming across questionable behavior from a guy that I'm dating or from a "friend," I take a step back and ask myself if my brother would treat a woman or friend like this, or what he'd say about it. Giving myself some emotional distance by imagining what he'd say or do in this situation often gives me the extra validation and clarity I'm looking for.

Even with a constant, and even with validation and clarity, it's still not easy to walk away from a problematic person or situation with whom we feel we have an intense connection. It takes time and practice with learning to trust your judgment again, and it's okay to go slow. If the relationship is solid, then it will still be there no matter how slow you go.

"At first I was so focused on trying to sort out whether a person was a narcissist or if they were just a normal person who lies and manipulates. Now my focus is on how I feel around people. I no longer tolerate confusing or crazy-making relationships or friendships. If anything starts feeling "off" or if I start questioning or doubting myself wondering if I can trust them or if I'm making a big deal out of nothing, I distance myself from that person. I don't feel unsettled and unnerved around normal people with good intentions. It's so nice knowing I don't have to hang onto "squirrelly" friendships or relationships and wait until they really screw me over before I leave. That was such a powerful realization for me."
— *Jasmine*

"I am sadly am discovering one of my "friends" that I hosted a girl's weekend for this past summer is ringing my alarm bells pretty frequently, and usually when nobody else is around or paying attention. And it's pretty distressing. I STILL don't know what to do about it. Since this group is a package deal, and I really don't have many friends, then if I lose her? Then I also lose two other women I care deeply for and about. I have literally spent HOURS agonizing about how I am going to respond to her in the future.

Because my normal modus operandi is to just go mute, and to stand there stunned, and not say anything. So I am trying really hard to get some sort of a "flippant" response prepared, and to be armed and ready for when this happens again. And to accept she's never going to stop doing this. So if I want to remain a part of this group? I'm going to have to learn how to put on some emotional armor, and learn how to rebuff her.

It makes me feel really sad sometimes to have to do this? But I now know I do have to do something if leaving the group is not an option for me. I can't just stand there and suffer. I don't know WHY this is so incredibly hard for me to learn to do, but it is really, really difficult to learn how to react differently.

But I know my silence encourages "these people" to continue, and it will happen more and not less. I can literally FEEL her poking around, looking for an "in", looking for a button to push that will make me say Ouch. And it's an incredibly saddening experience to watch someone do this, act this way. It makes me feel very sad that I have to learn how to protect myself from someone I once thought was my friend."

— *Luci*

Letting It Go vs. Moving Forward

Letting It Go

When people say to let "it" go, they usually mean to not let an abusive relationship or traumatic event continue to control so much of that person's life, or to define them, and this advice, much like the rest of the well-intended hurtful things that people say, usually comes from a place of either love and concern from seeing their loved one stay emotionally "stuck" in this situation.

The problem with telling someone to "let it go" or "get over it" is that doing so is not that simple, and to tell someone who is in tremendous emotional pain to "let it go" often comes across as very minimizing and revictimizing. No one wants to be stuck in pain, and believe me, if they could "let go" they would. Telling someone to let it go of the trauma caused by an abusive relationship is about as helpful and compassionate as telling a war veteran to let go of their trauma caused by war, or a person whose spouse died to get over it.

People don't "get over" a traumatic event, but with time, compassion, and support, they can get to a place where they are better equipped to cope with their trauma. Please know that rehashing and feeling (or being) emotionally stuck is a sign of emotional trauma that needs to be processed and healed, and is to a degree, a very normal part of healing. Some estimates are that it takes around

18-24 months for this phase to calm down enough to where a person's brain is able to "shift gears" and really begin to start integrating what happened to them and making it from *the* destruction/traumatic event *of* their life to *a* traumatic event *in* their life.

Moving Forward

Moving forward is not a straight line, and it is also not an event; it's a process. Moving forward is done on a day-to-day, moment-to-moment basis. Moving forward involves experiencing a wide range of painful emotions and can include questioning everything and everyone. While this is a profoundly intense process, it can also be profoundly transformative, and allow for the discovery and healing of old wounds that a person may have never known were even there, or perhaps thought that they had already worked through.

I want to leave you with one last concept that was very encouraging and empowering for me, and that I hope will be for you too. The concept is called "PTG" and that stands for Post Traumatic Growth. Post Traumatic Growth is the growth that can only come from trauma, as with great pain can also come great transformation. Life after abuse can leave a person feeling incredibly angry and overwhelmed by all the damage and destruction that has happened and at a loss as to where to begin picking up the pieces. Please know that the up side to having your whole world blown apart, is that you can now go about consciously choosing the pieces with which you want to rebuild. You get to choose who and want you want in this next chapter in your life, and you can get rid of all kinds of limiting beliefs about who you are and what you are capable of. This takes work, but it can be done, and it starts with making small, empowering decisions about who and what you let into (or keep) in your life on a regular basis.

"I heard a quote from Maya Angelou, 'I can be changed by what happens to me, but I refused to be reduced by it.' That really resonated with me. I realized that even though I felt changed, that I could still decide what that meant and that I wasn't going to let what I went through ruin my life. In fact, I used all the pain and anger I had from this and got into the best shape of my life and had a ton of personal growth that I wouldn't have had otherwise, and in many ways this experience woke up my highest and best self."

— Dorothy

Chapter 6
Conclusion: Moving into Healing

I hope that you found this book helpful, and that it has led you to question and examine some disempowering beliefs you might have been holding on to.

If this book was able to give you some of the clarity and validation that you were needing, you might now be struggling with the, "Well, what now? How do I move forward and heal?" pieces of the puzzle.

For those of you who are really struggling and feel like you are barely hanging on, I want to share with you four decisions I made a handful of years ago that have radically helped me heal, as well as radically altered the course of my life in a very positive way. I hope that they will help you too:

1. I WAS NOT going to let what happened to me end my life.
2. I WAS NOT going to let what happened to me ruin my life.

3. I WAS going to take what happened to me and use it towards my highest and greatest good.

4. I WAS going to take what happened to me and use it towards my highest and greatest good and the highest and greatest good of others.

This isn't to say that you have to start a blog about your abuse or do something similar to what I'm doing...unless you feel compelled to do that, in which case, go for it! What this does mean is for you to become the highest and best version of *yourself* and to express that in whatever way resonated the most with you. Whether that means you take up art, singing, gardening, dance, writing, chess, or cooking, start a new profession, or end some "frenemy" type dynamics. Perhaps it means getting rid of all the limiting beliefs and "shoulds" you've been carrying. Or perhaps it means doing all of the above. This next chapter in your life can be what you make it, and I sincerely hope that it involves you reconnecting to who you truly are and being that person on a regular basis. Everyone has their own unique gifts, and you do too.

So I encourage you to take all of this pain, hurt, and anger, and make it work for you. I know it may feel as though you need to wait until you are fully healed to start living again, but please know that healing tends to happen in the reverse order. It's not that we heal and then we start living again, it's that we make the decision to start living again, and that's when we start to heal. I know you may not feel you have the energy for healing, since carrying around the tremendous weight of the anger, hurt, anxiety, and depression (not to mention trying to pick up all the pieces) can be exhausting in and of itself. And if you are like many people, all that anger and rage can feel absolutely overwhelming and even scary. For these reasons, I encourage you to think of all that pent-up anger and hurt as rocket fuel that can help propel you to the next level. This is how post-traumatic growth happens, and I'm excited for you, because right now you are on the cusp of radical positive transformation in your life—even if it doesn't feel like it right now. Keep moving in the direction that gives you peace and joy in your life—this is the path that is meant for you.

If you are interested in joining a support group, please know there are many out there, and it can be a good idea to join a few to see which ones resonate the most with you. You can find mine at www.ThriveAfterAbuse.com and you can also google "narcissistic abuse" to find other groups out there.

You are not alone.
You are not crazy.
You can heal from this.

(((HUGS)))
Dana

About the Author

My name is Dana Morningstar, and my formal background is in education, domestic violence awareness and prevention, crisis intervention, trauma response, and psychiatric nursing. Over the past twenty years, I've had extensive experience working with both victims of abuse and abusers, as well as with those with a wide range of mental health challenges including a wide variety of trauma, crises, mental illness, and personality disorders. However, I started down this road of talking about narcissistic abuse by trying to understand several of my own "problematic" relationships and friendships that I've had in my life. The more that came into focus, the more I felt compelled to share my aha moments with others in hopes that perhaps some of my hard-won lessons could help them get the clarity and validation that they were looking for. I have since combined both my personal and professional experience into forming ThriveAfterAbuse.com, a website, podcast, and YouTube channel that is designed to help educate and empower those who are going through or who have been through abuse of any kind.

Narcissistic abuse is not only a very real problem, but perhaps is the largest and yet, the most seemingly unknown, misunderstood, minimized, and destructive mental and physical health crisis out there.

However, while the fall-out from abusive behavior often leads to tremendous amounts of devastation and destruction, it's with destruction that comes the possibility for transformation. And in my journey I've come across so many others who were on the same path looking for clarity and healing, as well as looking to share their experiences and insights. I receive many emails every day from people seeking support for themselves, their clients, or those they help teach or advise—including therapists, domestic violence agencies, college professors, and religious/spiritual leaders.

It truly makes my heart sing to see such massive amounts of healing, teamwork, and dedication from people and professionals from all walks of life, and from all across the world, who are committed to sharing resources, as well as their knowledge and experience, and supporting others. Every single one of us has a different piece to this puzzle, and when we come together, that's when understanding and healing truly start to happen. And while the pain of abuse can make people feel profoundly alone, I've found that when that pain is shared, important conversations are opened up and with that comes a great unifying ability that transcends gender, nationality, religion, sexual orientation, economic status, and education level—and serves to bring us closer together as people in ways that perhaps nothing else could.